WITHDRAWN

THE ROYAL HISTORICAL SOCIETY
ANNUAL BIBLIOGRAPHY OF BRITISH
AND IRISH HISTORY
Publications of 1977

ROYAL HISTORICAL SOCIETY

ANNUAL BIBLIOGRAPHY OF BRITISH AND IRISH HISTORY

Publications of 1977

General Editor: G. R. Elton

R. Barker   D.A.L. Morgan
A. Bennett   J.S. Morrill
N. Brooks   G. Mac Niocaill
R.A. Griffiths   T.I. Rae
M.W.C. Hassall   A.T.Q. Stewart
          J.A. Woods

HARVESTER PRESS LIMITED
HUMANITIES PRESS INC

For the Royal Historical Society

First published in 1978 for
The Royal Historical Society by
THE HARVESTER PRESS LIMITED
Publisher: John Spiers
2 Stanford Terrace, Hassocks,
Sussex, England
and in the USA in 1978 by
HUMANITIES PRESS INC.,
Atlantic Highlands,
N.J. 07716

© 1978 Royal Historical Society

British Library Cataloguing in Publication Data
Annual bibliography of British and Irish
    history: Publications of 1977.
        1. Great Britain — History — Bibliography
        I. Elton, Geoffrey Rudolph
        II. Royal Historical Society
        016.941   Z2016

    ISBN 0-85527-754-0

    ISSN 0308-00619-3

Humanities Press Inc
ISBN 0-391-00881-1

Printed in Great Britain by
Redwood Burn Limited,
Trowbridge and Esher

CONTENTS

PREFACE

The Bibliography is meant in the first place to serve the urgent needs of
scholars, which has meant subordinating absolutely total coverage and
refinements of arrangement to speed of production. Nevertheless, it is
comprehensive and arranged for easy use. A new source of possible
error appeared this year. The British National Bibliography now includes
cards for books announced but not yet published, and while every
effort has been made to exclude these items a few have slipped in. Information on them may be premature and incomplete.

Because the sectional headings are those approved by section editors
they are not uniform. Searchers are advised to use the subdivisions in
conjunction with the Subject Index which, apart from covering all place
and personal names, is designed to facilitate a thematic and conceptual
analysis.

Pieces contained in collective works (under Bc and sometimes in a
chronological section) are individually listed in the appropriate place
and there referred to the number the volume bears in the Bibliography.

Items covering more than two sections are listed in B; any that
extend over two sections appear as a rule in the first and are cross-
referenced at the head of the second.

The editors wish to express their gratitude to the assistance received
from the Institute of Historical Research (London), the International
Medieval Bibliography (Leeds), especially Mr R.J. Walsh, and Mr S.J.
Hills (Cambridge University Library).

Abbreviations

Arch. — Archaeological
B.   — Bulletin
HMSO — Her Majesty's Stationery Office
J.   — Journal
P.   — Proceedings
Q.   — Quarterly
R.   — Review
Soc.   — Society
T.   — Transactions
UP   — University Press

A. AUXILIARY

(a) Bibliography and Archives

1. Public Record Office. *Chancery patent rolls, 7 James I, Calendar.* London; List & Index Soc. 121; 1976.
2. Public Record Office. *Ministry of Transport, Railway Department; papers: part 3 – 1902–1919.* London; List & Index Soc. 123; 1976.
3. Public Record Office. *Exchequer, Augmentation Office: Calendar of ancient deeds, series B, part 4: Index.* London; List & Index Soc. 124; 1976.
4. Public Record Office. *Treasury Board papers, mainly 1756–1758.* London; List & Index Soc. 125; 1976.
5. Public Record Office. *Prime Minister's Office: class list.* London; List & Index Soc. 126; 1976.
6. Tumer, P.M. (ed.). *Lancashire History* [general editor, S. Horrocks]: *Historical period, Stuart.* Manchester; Joint Committee on the Lancashire Bibliography; 1976. Pp x, 122.
7. O'Brien, P.K., 'Essays in bibliography and criticism: LXXVII, Agriculture and the industrial revolution,' *Economic History R.* 2nd ser. 30 (1977), 166–81.
8. Morgan, R., 'Annual list and brief review of articles on agrarian history, 1975,' *Agricultural History R.* 25 (1977), 44–52.
9. Porter, R.; Poulton, K., 'Research in British geology 1660–1800: a survey and thematic bibliography,' *Annals of Science* 34 (1977), 33–42.
10. Public Record Office. *Calendar of Patent Rolls, 8 James I.* London; List & Index Soc. 122; 1976.
11. *The Same, 9 James I.* London; List & Index Soc. 133; 1977.
12. *The Same, 10–11 James I.* London; List & Index Soc. 134; 1977.
13. Public Record Office. *War Cabinet Memoranda, Sept. 1939–July 1945.* London; List & Index Soc. 136; 1977.
14. Public Record Office. *Calendar and Index of Ancient Deeds series BB.* London; List & Index Soc.; 1977.
15. British Library. *'Rough Register' of acquisitions of the Department of Manuscripts 1971–1975.* London; List & Index Soc.; 1977.
16. Owen, G.D. (ed.). *Calendar of Salisbury MSS, 24: Addenda 1605–1668.* London; Historical MSS Commission; 1976. Pp xvi, 401.
17. *A London bibliography of the social sciences, vol. 33: 1975* (10th supplement). London; Mansell; 1976.
18. *The central records of the Church of England: a report and survey*

1

presented to the Pilgrim and Radcliffe Trustees. London; CIO Publishing; 1976. Pp iv, 100.

19. *Cheshire Record Office and Chester Diocesan Record Office.* [Cheshire County Council, 1975].

20. National Maritime Museum. *Catalogue of the library, vol. 5: Naval history, part 1: the middle ages to 1815.* London; HMSO; 1976.

21. Cordeaux, E.H.; Merry, D.H. *A bibliography of printed works relating to the city of Oxford.* Oxford; Clarendon; 1976. Pp xiv, 377.

22. Whalley, J.I.; Richmond, A.T. *Catalogue of English non-illuminated manuscripts in the National Art Library up to December 1973* (volume and supplement). [London; Victoria and Albert Museum]; 1975. Pp iii, 130; 12.

24. Conway, E. *Labour history of Manchester and Salford: a bibliography.* [Manchester Centre for Marxist Education; 1977]. Pp 34.

25. Brown, L.M.; Christie, I.R. (ed.). *Bibliography of British history, 1789–1851.* Oxford; Clarendon; 1977. Pp xxxi, 759.

26. Ker, N.R. *Medieval manuscripts in British libraries, 2: Abbotsford-Keele.* Oxford; Clarendon; 1977. Pp xliii, 999.

27. Droker, J., 'Bibliography 1976,' *Soc. for the Study of Labour History*, 34 (1977), 86–109.

28. Smith, R.A.H., 'The Guest Papers, Add. MSS 57934–57941,' *British Library J.* 2 (1976), 29–37.

29. Auckland, R.G. *Catalogue of British 'black' propaganda to Germany, 1941–1945.* St Albans; compiler for Psywar Soc.; 1977. Pp 32.

30. Fraser, K.C. *A bibliography of the Scottish national movement (1844–1973).* Dollar; D.S. Mack; 1976. Pp 40.

31. Woolven, G.B. *Publications of the Independent Labour Party, 1893–1932.* Coventry; Soc. for the Study of Labour History; 1977. Pp xiv, 38.

32. *18th Annual Report of the Keeper of the Public Records . . . ; and the Report of the Advisory Council on Public Records.* London; HMSO; 1977. Pp ii, 32.

33. Toole Stott, R. *A bibliography of English conjuring, 1581–1876.* Derby; Harper & Sons; 1976. Pp 288.

34. LeMire, E.D., 'The Socialist League leaflets and manifestoes: an annotated checklist,' *International R. of Social History* 22 (1977), 21–9.

35. Walker, D. (ed.). *Catalogue of the newspaper collection in the India Office Library.* London; The Library; 1977. Pp ix, 19.

36. Steer, F.W. (ed.). *Arundel Castle archives, vol. 3: a catalogue.* Chichester; West Sussex County Council; 1976. Pp ix, 108.

37. Tobias, R.C. (ed.), 'Victorian bibliography for 1976,' *Victorian Studies* 20 (1977), 449–553.

38. Field, C.D., 'Bibliography of Methodist historical literature, 1975–,' *P. of the Wesley Historical Soc.* 61 (1977), 53–60.

39. Sims, J.M.; Jacobs, P.M. *Writings on British history 1955–1957.* London; Institute of Historical Research; 1977. Pp xx, 362.

40. Bromley, J. *The clockmakers' library: the catalogue of the books and manuscripts in the library of the Worshipful Company of Clockmakers.* London; Sotheby Parke Bernet Publications; 1977. Pp xii, 136.

41. British Library. *Catalogue of additions to the manuscripts 1756–1782, Add. MSS 4101–5017.* London; British Museum Publications; 1977. Pp ix, 706.

42. Cunningham, P. *Local history of education in England and Wales: a bibliography.* Leeds; Museum of the History of Education; 1976. Pp 188.

43. Brockett, A. *The Devon Union List: a collection of written material relating to the county of Devon.* Exeter; University Library, 1977. Pp iii, 571.

44. Farrant, J.H. *Sussex in the 18th and 19th centuries: a bibliography* (2nd ed.). Brighton; Centre for Continuing Education; 1977. Pp 44.

45. Allison. A.F.; Goldsmith, V.F. *Titles of English books and foreign books printed in England: an alphabetical finding-list by title of books published under the author's name, pseudonym or initials.* Vol. 2: 1641–1700. Folkestone; Dawson; 1977. Pp 318.

46. Elton, G.R. (ed.). *Annual bibliography of British and Irish history: Publications of 1976.* Hassocks; Harvester Press; 1977. Pp ix, 193.

47. Steel, D.J. *National index of parish registers.* Vol. 1: General sources of births, marriages and deaths before 1837; vol. 5: South Midlands and Welsh border counties. London; Phillimore; 1976.

48. Holmes, M.E., 'Sources for the history of food supplies and marketing in the eighteenth and nineteenth centuries in local record offices,' Bc10, 95–105.

49. 'Place-names and settlement history: a review with a select bibliography of works mostly published since 1960,' *Northern History* 13 (1977), 1–26.

50. McLaren, C.A.; Stephen, M.A., 'Reports and surveys of archives in northern Scotland,' *Northern Scotland* 2 (1976–7), 183–190.

51. Frow, E., 'Publications of the Independent Labour Party,' *B. of the Soc. for the Study of Labour History* 35 (1977), 35–41.

52. Forrest, G. *Southampton's history: a guide to the printed sources* (2nd ed.). Southampton District Library; 1977. Pp 24.

53. Knafla, L.A., 'Crime and criminal justice: a critical bibliography,' Bc7, 270–98.

54. Historical Manuscripts Commission. *Accessions to repositories and reports added to the National Register of Archives* [in 1976]. London; HMSO; 1977. Pp vii, 75.

55. South Humberside Area Record Office. *Humberside County archives: summary guide*. [Grimsby; The Office] ; 1977. Pp v, 28.
56. Creaton, H.J. (ed.). *Writings on British History 1958–1959*. London; Institute of Historical Research; 1977. Pp xxi, 229.

(b) Works of Reference

1. Historical Manuscripts Commission. *Secretary's Report to the Commissioners, 1975–1976*. London; HMSO; 1976. Pp 24.
2. *Biographical memoirs of fellows of the Royal Society*, vol. 22: 1976. London; Royal Soc.; 1976. Pp 653.
3. McDonald, R.W., 'The parish registers of Wales,' *The National Library of Wales J*. 19 (1976), 399–429.
4. Rozkuszka, W.D., 'British Cabinet Office records on the second world war,' *Albion* 8 (1976), 296–9.
5. Anderson, R.G.W.; Simpson, A.D.C. *Edinburgh and medicine: a commemorative catalogue of the exhibition held at the Royal Scottish Museum*. Edinburgh; The Museum; 1977.
6. Aked, C.K. *A complete list of English horological patents up to 1853*. Ashford; Brant Wright Ass. Ltd.; 1975. Pp 33.
7. Stenton, M. *Who's who of British members of Parliament*, vol. 1: 1832–1885. Hassocks; Harvester Press; 1976. Pp xvi, 444.
8. Blackmore, R.M. *Cumulative index to the annual catalogues of HMSO publications, 1922–1972* (2 vols.). Washington; Carrollton Press; 1976. Pp xxi, 567; xxi, 583.
9. Bellamy, J.M.; Saville, J. (ed.). *Dictionary of labour biography*, vol. 3, 4. London; Macmillan; 1976/7. Pp xix, 236; xix, 236.
10. Adams, I.H. *Agrarian landscape terms: a glossary for historical geography*. London; Institute of British Geographers; 1976. Pp xii, 314.
11. Johnson, J.; Greutzner, A. *The dictionary of British artists, 1880–1940*. Woodbridge; Antique Collectors' Club; 1976. Pp 567.
12. Sainty, J.C. *Colonial Office officials*. London; Institute of Historical Research; 1976. Pp x, 52.
13. Hume, J.R. *The industrial archaeology of Scotland, 1: The Lowlands and Borders*. London; Batsford; 1976. Pp 279.
14. Busby, R. *British music hall: an illustrated who's who from 1850 to the present day*. London; Elek; 1976. Pp 191.
15. Craig, F.W.S. *British electoral facts, 1885–1975*. London; Macmillan; 1976. Pp xv, 182.
16. Mallalieu, H.L. *The dictionary of British watercolour artists up to 1920*. Woodbridge; Antique Collectors' Club; 1976. Pp 299.
17. Hayden, A.J.; Newton, R.F. *British hymn writers and composers: a check-list giving their dates and places of birth and death*. Croydon; Hymn Soc. of Great Britain and Ireland; 1977. Pp 94.
18. Historical MSS Commissions. *Accessions 1975*. London; HMSO; 1976. Pp vii, 93.

19. Freeman, R.B. *The works of Charles Darwin: an annotated bibliographical handlist* (2nd ed.). Folkestone; Dawson; 1977. Pp 235.
20. Royal Commission on Historical Monuments (England). *The town of Stamford: an inventory of historical monuments.* London; HMSO; 1977. Pp xci, 182.
21. National Maritime Museum. *General catalogue of historical photographs, vol. 2: merchant sailing ships.* London; The Museum; 1976. Pp xii, 193.
22. University College, London. *Manuscript collections in the library: a handlist.* London; The Library; 1975. Pp 18.
23. Tallis, J.A.; Peach, E.O. *Original parish registers in record offices and libraries*, 1st supplement. Matlock; Local Population Studies; 1976. Pp 60.
24. Harrison, R. *The Warwick guide to British labour periodicals, 1790–1970.* Hassocks; Harvester Press; 1977. Pp 685.
25. Bilboul, R.R.; Kent, F.L. *Retrospective index to theses of Great Britain and Ireland, 1716–1950, vol. 1: Social sciences and humanities.* Oxford; EBC-Clio; 1976. Pp x, 393.
26. Taylor, R., 'English Baptist periodicals, 1790–1865,' *Baptist Q.* 27 (1977), 50–82.
27. Reel, J.V. *Index to biographies of Englishmen 1000–1485 found in dissertations and theses.* Westport/London; Greenwood Press; 1975. Pp xiii, 689.
28. Sainty, J.C.; Dewar, D. *Divisions in the House of Lords: an analytical list 1685 to 1857.* London; HMSO; 1976. Pp ix, 41.
29. Freshwater, P.B. (ed.). *Working papers for an historical directory of the West Midlands book trade to 1850, no. 3: 1790–1799.* Birmingham Bibliographical Soc.; 1977. Pp iv, 25.
30. Munby, A.N.L. *British book sale catalogues, 1676–1800.* London; Mansell Information Publishing; 1977. n.p.
31. Cook, C. et al. *Sources in British political history, 1900–1951, vol. 3: a guide to the private papers of Members of Parliament, A–K.* London; Macmillan; 1977. Pp xiv, 281.
32. *A catalogue of agricultural and horticultural books, 1543–1918, in Wye College library.* Ashford; The Library; [1977]. Pp ii, 100.
33. Wrigley, E.A., 'Births and baptisms: the use of Anglican baptism registers as a source of information about the number of births in England before the beginning of civil registration,' *Population Studies* 31 (1977), 281–312.
34. Lewis, M.G. *The printed maps of Radnorshire, 1578–1900.* Aberystwyth; National Library of Wales; 1977. Pp 30.
35. *Suffolk parochial libraries.* London; Mansell Information Publishing; 1977.
36. Neuburg, V.E. *Popular literature: a history and guide, from the beginning of printing to the year 1897.* Harmondsworth; Penguin; 1977. Pp 302.
37. Spufford, P.; Wilkinson, W. *Interim listing of the exchange rates*

of medieval Europe. Keele; the compiler (Dept. of History, The University); 1977. Pp xxiii, 374.

38. Whitelaw, C.E. (ed. S. Barter). *Scottish arms makers: a biographical dictionary of makers of firearms, edged weapons and armour, working in Scotland from the 15th century to 1870.* London; Arms and Armour Press; [1977]. Pp 339.

39. Farrant, S. *A guide to printed sources for the history and geography of the borough of Brighton.* Brighton Polytechnic; [1977]. Pp 33.

40. *Burke's family index.* London; Burke's Peerage; 1976. Pp xxxii, 171.

41. Cook, C. *Sources of British political history, 1900—1951; vol. 4: a guide to the private papers of members of parliament, L—Z.* London; Macmillan; 1977. Pp xiv, 272.

42. Young, G.V.C. *Subject guide and chronological table relating to the Acts of Tynwald, 1776—1975.* Douglas; Shearwater Press; 1977. Pp 210.

43. Withycombe, E.G. *The Oxford Dictionary of English Christian names* (3rd ed.). Oxford; Clarendon; 1977. Pp xlvii, 310.

44. Waters, G.M. *Dictionary of British artists working 1900—1950, vol. 2.* Eastbourne Fine Art Publications; [1976]. Pp 63.

45. Dymond, D. *Writing a church guide* (bibliography prepared by D.M. Williams). London; CIO Publishing; [1977]. Pp 20.

46. Desmond, R. *Dictionary of British and Irish botanists and horticulturalists, including plant collectors and botanical artists.* London; Taylor & Francis; 1977. Pp xxvi, 747.

47. Line, J. *Archival collections of non-book materials: a preliminary list indicating policies for preservation and access.* London; British Library; 1977. Pp ii, 60.

48. Archer, C.A.; Wilkinson, R.K., 'The Yorkshire registries of deeds,' *Urban History Yearbook* 1977, 40—7.

49. Davies, K.C.; Hull, J. *The zoological collections of the Oxford University Museum: a historical review and general account, with comprehensive donor index to the year 1975.* Oxford University Museum; 1976. Pp vii, 136.

50. Historical Manuscripts Commission. *Secretary's report to the commissioners, 1976—1977.* London; HMSO; 1977. Pp 24.

51. Storey, R.; Druker, J. *Guide to the Modern Records Centre, University of Warwick Library.* Coventry; The Library; 1977. Pp 152.

52. Druker, J.; Storey, R., 'The Modern Records Centre at Warwick and the local historian,' *Local Historian* 12 (1977), 394—400.

53. Linecar, H.W.A. *British coin designs and designers.* London; Bell; 1977. Pp xiii, 146.

54. Corps of Commissionaires. *Inventory of historical records.* London; The Corps; 1977. Pp 20.

55. Bennett, G. (ed.). *The Kent bibliography: a finding list of Kent material in the public libraries of the county and the adjoining*

London boroughs. London; Library Association; 1977. Pp ix, 452.

56. Courtauld Institute Illustration Archives. *Archive 1: Cathedrals and Monastic buildings in the British Isles*, London; Harvey Miller (for the Institute); 1976 onwards. Plans.

57. Thomson, D.; Bruce Lockhart, S. (ed.). *Concise catalogue [of the Scottish National Portrait Gallery]*. Edinburgh; Trustees of the National Galleries of Scotland; 1977. Pp 187.

58. Storey, R.; Madden, L. *Primary sources for Victorian Studies: a guide to the location and use of unpublished materials*. London; Phillimore; 1977. Pp vii, 81.

59. Delaissé, L.M.J.; Marrow, J.; Wit, J. de (ed.). *James A. de Rothschild Collection at Waddesdon Manor: illuminated manuscripts*. Fribourg; Office de Livre for National Trust; 1977. Pp 608.

(c) *Historiography*

1. *Caxtonia, or The progress of Caxton studies from the earliest times to 1976: an exhibition at the St Bride's Printing Library.* London; The Library; 1976. Pp 16.

2. Harkness, D.W. *History and the Irish* [inaugural lecture]. Belfast; Queen's University; 1976. Pp 15.

3. Owen, D.M.; Storey, R.L., 'The Canterbury and York Society,' *Archives* 12 (1976), 170–5.

4. Piggott, S. *Ruins in a landscape: essays in antiquarianism.* Edinburgh UP, 1976. Pp viii, 212.

5. Stephens, W.B. *Teaching local history*. Manchester UP; 1977. Pp x, 182.

6. Morrison, J.J., 'Strype's Stow: the 1720 edition of "A Survey of London",' *London J.* 3 (1977), 40–54.

7. Greenway, D.E., 'The use of punched cards in the dating of charters,' *B. of the Institute of Historical Research* 50 (1977), 110–12.

8. Brooks, S., 'Liddell Hart and his papers,' *War and Society* (ed. B. Bond and I. Roy; London, Croom Helm), 2 (1977), 129–40.

9. Pugh, R.B., 'The Victoria History of the Counties of England,' *Baptist Q.* 27 (1977), 110–17.

10. Guth, D.J., 'How legal history survives constitutional history's demise: the Anglo-American traditions,' *Ius Commune* (Sonderheft 7 of F. Ranieri, ed.: Rechtsgeschichte und quantitative Geschichte; Arbeitsberichte; Frankfurt/M.; 1977), 117–53.

11. Toon, P., 'The Parker Society,' *Historical Magazine of the Protestant Episcopal Church* 46 (1977), 323–32.

12. Rogers, A. *Approaches to local history* (2nd ed.). London; Longman; 1977. Pp xvii, 265.

13. Greenslade, M.W., 'The Staffordshire historians,' *North Staffordshire J. of Field Studies* 16 (1976), 23–41.

14. Gabrieli, V., 'A "ghost" in Froude's *History of England,*' *The Bodleian Library Record* 9 (1977), 308–10.
15. Elton, G.R., 'The historian's social function,' *T. of the Royal Historical Soc.* 5th series 27 (1977), 197–211.
16. Spufford, P., 'Marc Fitch and the British Record Society,' Bc3, 9–19.
17. Gilley, S., 'John Lingard and the Catholic revival,' Bc6, 313–27.
18. Elton, G.R., 'Introduction: Crime and the historian,' Bc7, 1–14.
19. Watson, R., 'Medieval manuscript fragments,' *Archives* 13 (1977), 61–73.
20. Carson, E., 'Customs records as a source of historical research,' ibid. 74–80.

B. GENERAL

(a) Long periods: national

1. Findlater, R. *The player queens.* London; Weidenfeld & Nicolson; 1976. Pp vi, 250.
2. Bond, M.F.; Beamish, D. *The gentleman usher of the black rod.* London; HMSO; 1976. Pp 22.
3. Gladwin, C. *The Paris embassy.* London; Collins; 1976. Pp 255.
4. Edwards, W.J., 'National parish register data: an evaluation of the comprehensiveness of the areal cover,' *Local Population Studies* 17 (1976), 16–24.
5. Haynes, A., 'The English in Padua 1222–1660,' *History Today,* 27 (1977), 108–16; 138.
6. Fussell, G.E., 'Countrywomen of Old England,' *Agricultural History* 50 (1976), 175–8.
7. Mingay, G.E. *The gentry: the rise and fall of a ruling class.* London; Longman; 1976. Pp xii, 216.
8. Clapp. B.W. (ed.). *England since 1760* [Documents in English economic history]. London; Bell; 1976. Pp xix, 544.
9. Cherry, J., 'Post-medieval Britain in 1975,' *Post-Medieval Archaeology* 10 (1976), 161–75.
10. Barraclough, K.C., 'The development of the cementation process for the manufacture of steel,' ibid. 65–88.
11. Bromley, J.S. (ed.). *The manning of the Royal Navy: selected public pamphlets, 1693–1873.* London; Navy Records Soc.; 1974 [i.e. 1976]. Pp 409.
12. Holford, I. *British weather disasters.* Newton Abbot; David & Charles; 1976. Pp 127.
13. Aveling, J.C.H. *The handle and the axe: the Catholic recusants in England from Reformation to emancipation.* London; Blond & Briggs, 1976. Pp 384.

14. Craton, M.; Walvin, J.; Wright, D. *Slavery, abolition and emancipation: black slaves and the British Empire: a thematic documentary*. London; Longman; 1976. Pp xiv, 347.

15. Hilling, J.B. *The historic architecture of Wales: an introduction*. Cardiff; University of Wales Press; 1976. Pp xiii, 234.

16. Coleman, D.C. *The economy of England, 1450–1750*. London; Oxford UP; 1977. Pp xi, 223.

17. Mackintosh, J.P. *The British Cabinet* (3rd ed.). London; Stevens; 1977. Pp xv, 656.

18. Taylor, S., 'The impact of pauper settlement 1691–1834,' *Past & Present* 73 (1976), 42–74.

19. Braddon, R. *All the queen's men: the Household Cavalry and the Brigade of Guards*. London; Hamilton; 1977. Pp 288.

20. Reese, M.M. *The royal office of master of the horse*. London; Threshold Books; 1976. Pp 360.

21. Paget, Sir J. *The story of the Guards*. London; Osprey Publishing; 1976. Pp 304.

22. McLeod, K. *The wives of Downing Street*. London; Collins; 1976. Pp 223.

23. Roberts, B.K. *Rural settlement in Britain*. Folkestone; Dawson; 1977. Pp 221.

24. Longrigg, R. *The English squire and his sport*. London; Joseph; 1977. Pp 302.

25. Kirk, H. *Portrait of a profession: a history of the solicitor's profession, 1100 to the present day*. London; Oyez Publishing; 1976. Pp ix, 218.

26. Wright, Sir D. *The English amongst the Persians during the Qajat period, 1781–1921*. London; Heinemann; 1977. Pp xvii, 218.

27. Tucker, K.A. (ed.). *Business history: selected readings* [essays from *Business History*]. London; Cass; 1977. Pp xvi, 442.

28. Ormond, R. *The face of monarchy: British royalty portrayed*. Oxford; Phaidon; 1977. Pp 207.

29. Donnison, J. *Midwives and medical men: a history of interprofessional rivalries and women's rights*. London; Heinemann Educational; 1977. Pp vi, 250.

30. Mingay, G.E. (ed.). *The agricultural revolution: changes in agriculture, 1650–1880*. London; A. & C. Black; 1977. Pp ix, 322.

31. Williams, D. *A history of modern Wales* (2nd ed.). London; Murray; 1977. Pp 318.

32. Bennett, G., 'Royal reviews at Spithead,' *History Today* 27 (1977), 358–66.

33. Charlton, J. *No. 10 Downing Street, SW1, City of Westminster*. London; HMSO; 1977. Pp 12.

34. Robinson, B. *The Royal Maundy*. London; Kaye & Ward; 1977. Pp 84.

35. Hibbert, C. *The court at Windsor: a domestic history* (revd. ed.). London; Allen Lane; 1977. Pp 240.

36. Aston, M.; Bond, J. *The landscape of towns.* London; Dent; 1976. Pp 255.

37. Linklater, E. and A. *The Black Watch: the history of the Royal Highland Regiment.* London; Barrie & Jenkins; 1977. Pp 240.

38. Griffin, A.R. *The British coalmining industry: retrospect and prospect.* Buxton; Moorland Publishing Co.; 1977. Pp 224.

39. Blackmore, H.L. *The armouries of the Tower of London; 1: Ordnance.* London; HMSO; 1976. Pp ix, 425.

40. Plumb, J.H. *Royal heritage: the story of Britain's royal builders and collectors.* London; British Broadcasting Corporation; 1977. Pp 360.

41. Anon., 'The Royal Bank of Scotland, 1727–1977,' *Three Banks R.* 114 (1977), 42–60.

42. Patten, J., 'Urban occupations in pre-industrial England,' *T. of the Institute of British Geographers* new ser. 2 (1977), 296–313.

43. Slater, T.R., 'Landscape parks and the form of small towns in Great Britain,' ibid. 314–31.

44. Riden, P., 'The output of the British iron industry before 1870,' *Economic History R.* 2nd ser. 30 (1977), 442–59.

45. Routley, E. *A short history of English church music.* London; Mowbrays; 1977. Pp vi, 122.

46. Dyson, J. *Business in great waters: the story of British fishermen.* London; Angus & Robertson; 1977. Pp 335.

47. *The Royal Mint: an outline history* (6th ed.). London; HMSO; 1977. Pp vii, 42.

48. McCloskey, D.N., 'English open fields as behavior towards risk,' *Research in Economic History*, vol. 1 (ed. P. Uselding; Greenwich, Conn,; Jai Press; 1976), 124–70.

49. Thompson, E.P., 'The grid of inheritance: a comment,' *Family and Inheritance: Rural Society in Western Europe, 1200–1800* (ed. J. Goody, E.P. Thompson, J. Thirsk; Cambridge UP; 1976), 328–60.

50. Cooper, J.P., 'Patterns of inheritance and settlement by great landowners from the fifteenth to the eighteenth centuries,' ibid. 192–327.

51. De Breffny, B. (ed.). *The Irish world: the history and cultural achievements of the Irish people.* London; Thames & Hudson; 1977. Pp 296.

52. Hill, C.P. *British economic and social history, 1700–1975* (4th ed.). London; Arnold; 1977. Pp xi, 322.

53. Gunstone, A.J.H. *Sylloge of coins of the British Isles, 24: Ancient British, Anglo-Saxon and Norman coins in West Country museums.* London; Oxford UP; 1977. Pp xxxvi, 99.

54. Fisher, H.E.S.; Jurica, A.R.J. (ed.). *Documents in English economic history: England from 1000 to 1760.* London; Bell; 1977. Pp xxiii, 547.

55. Yelling, J.A. *Common field and enclosure in England, 1450–1850*. London; Macmillan; 1977. Pp viii, 255.

56. Brunskill, R.W.; Clifton-Taylor, A. *English brickwork*. London; Ward Lock; 1977. Pp 160.

57. Nasir, S.J. *The Arabs and the English*. London; Longman; 1976. Pp xii, 175.

58. Forde-Johnston, J. *Castles and fortifications of Britain and Ireland*. London; Dent; 1977.

59. Cameron, K., 'The significance of English place-names,' *P. of the British Academy* 62 (1977 for 1976), 135–55.

60. Burton, A. *Industrial archaeological sites of Britain*. London; Weidenfeld & Nicolson; 1977. Pp 160.

61. Fry, P.S. *2000 years of British life: a social history of England, Wales, Scotland and Ireland*. Glasgow; Collins; 1976. Pp 256.

62. Perry, P.J.C. *The evolution of British manpower policy: from the Statute of Artificers 1563 to the Industrial Training Act 1964*. [Chichester]; the author; 1976. Pp xx, 329.

63. Shyllon, F.O. *Black people in Britain, 1555–1833*. London; Oxford UP; 1977. Pp xi, 290.

64. Scott-James; Lancaster, O. *The pleasure garden: an illustrated history of British gardening*. London; Murray; 1977. Pp 128.

65. Lobel, M.D., 'Some reflections on the topographical development of the pre-industrial town in England,' Bc3, 141–63.

66. Cullen, L.M.; Smout, T.C., 'Economic growth in Scotland and Ireland,' Bc9, 3–18.

67. Etheridge, K. *Welsh costume in the 18th and 19th century*. Swansea; C. Davies; 1977. Pp 112.

68. Goodison, N. *English barometers, 1680–1860: a history of domestic barometers and their makers and retailers* (revd. ed.). Woodbridge; Antique Collectors' Club; 1977. Pp 388.

69. Wilson, H. *A prime minister on prime ministers*. London; Weidenfeld & Nicolson; 1977. Pp 334.

70. Thomas, D. (ed.). *Wales: a new study*. Newton Abbot; David & Charles; 1977. Pp 338.

71. Birch, A.H. *Political integration and disintegration in the British Isles*. London; Allen & Unwin; 1977. Pp 183.

(b) *Long periods: local*

1. *Petersfield place names*. Petersfield Area Historical Soc.; 1976. Pp 20.

2. Protheroe, M.J. (ed.). *A history of Calday Grange grammar school, West Kirby, 1636–1776*. West Kirby; The School; 1976. Pp xiv, 162.

3. Borer, M.C. *Hampstead and Highgate: the story of two hilltop villages*. London; Allen; 1976. Pp vii, 255.

4. Lewis, L. (ed.). *Hird's Annals of Bedale*, 3 vols. Northallerton; North Yorks. County Council; 1975—6. Pp 456.

5. Sessions, W.K. and E.M. *Printing in York from the 1490s to the present day* (revd. ed.). York; Williams Sessions Ltd.; 1976. Pp viii, 105.

6. Mitchell, S.J.D. *Perse: a history of the Perse School, 1615—1976.* Cambridge; Cleander Press; 1976. Pp viii, 263.

7. Roberts, P. *The Old Vic story: a nation's theatre, 1818—1976.* London; Allen; 1976. Pp x, 203.

8. Harding, J.M. *Four centuries of Charlwood houses: medieval to 1840.* Charlwood; The Charlwood Soc.; 1976. Pp iv, 120.

9. Maclagan, I. *Rothesay Harbour: an historical survey from 1752 to 1975.* [Buteshire Natural History Soc.; 1976]. Pp 106.

10. Yates, N. *Leeds and the Oxford Movement: a study of 'High Church activity . . . in the diocese of Ripon, 1836—1934.* Leeds; Thiresby Soc.; 1975. Pp ix, 92.

11. Jones, P.E. *The butchers of London: a history of the Worshipful Company of Butchers of the City of London.* London; Secker & Warburg; 1976. Pp x, 246.

12. Morfey, W.M. *Ipswich School; an alphabetical list of Ipswichians . . . from its earliest days to . . . 1857.* [Ipswich School]; 1976. Pp 38.

13. Herbert, N.M. (ed.). *A history of the county of Gloucester*, vol. 11 [Victoria County history]. Oxford UP; 1976. Pp xix, 339.

14. Crawley, C. *Trinity Hall: the history of a Cambridge college, 1350—1975.* Cambridge; The College; 1976. Pp xvi, 289.

15. Jones, J.M. *Maps of Birmingham.* City of Birmingham Education Department; 1976. Pp 70.

16. Turbutt, G., 'Court rolls and other papers of the manor of Stretton,' *Derbyshire Arch. J.* 95 (1976 for 1975), 12—36.

17. Wilson, M.D. *The paupers of Leigh: their persecution and poor relief, 1660—1860.* Leigh History Soc.; 1976. Pp 32.

18. Grant, A., 'The cooper in Liverpool,' *Industrial Archaeology R.* 1 (1976), 28—36.

19. Lewis, F. *Essex and sugar: historic and other connections.* London; Phillimore; 1976. Pp xi, 132.

20. Yates, E.M. *Buriton and its people.* Petersfield Area Historical Soc.; 1976. Pp 47.

21. Moore, J.S. (ed.). *The goods and chattels of our forefathers: Frampton Cotterell and district probate inventories, 1539—1804.* London; Phillimore; 1976. Pp xx, 364.

22. Keynes, M.E. *A house by the river: Newnham Grange to Darwin College* [Cambridge]. Cambridge; Darwin College; 1976. Pp xvii, 259.

23. Ball, M. *The Worshipful Company of Brewers: a short history.* London; Hutchinson; 1977. Pp 143.

24. Brent, C.E. *A short economic and social history of Brighton,*

Lewes and the downland region between the Adur and the Ouse, 1500–1900. Lewes; East Sussex County Council; [1976]. Pp iv, 27.

25. Winn, C.G. *The Pouletts of Hinton St George.* London; Research Publishing Co.; 1976. Pp 202.

26. Athill, R. (ed.). *Mendip: a new study.* Newton Abbot; David & Charles, 1976. Pp 287.

27. Hopkinson, M.F. *Old county maps of Bedfordshire.* Luton Museum; 1976. Pp 50.

28. Wren, W.J. *Ports of the eastern counties: the development of harbours on the coast of the eastern counties from Boston in Lincolnshire to Rochford in Essex.* Lavenham; Dalton; 1976. Pp 207.

29. Cooper, R. *The book of Chesterfield: a portrait of the town.* Chesham; Barracuda Books; 1977. Pp 148.

30. Jarvis, R.J., 'The metamorphosis of the port of London,' *London J.* 3 (1977), 55–72.

31. *Dorchester-on-Thames grammar school.* Dorchester Archaeology and Local History Group; [1976]. Pp ix, 35.

32. Leach, R.H., 'Romano-British and medieval settlement at Wearne, Huish Episcopi,' *Somerset Archaeology and Natural History* 120 (1976), 45–50.

33. Richards, G., 'Notes on the rural deanery of Dyffryn Clwyd to 1859,' *National Library of Wales J.* 20 (1977), 46–84.

34. Trump, H.J. *Westcountry harbour: the port of Teignmouth, 1690–1975.* Teignmouth; Brunswick Press Ltd; 1976. Pp 204.

35. Pollard, S.; Holmes, C. (ed.). *Essays in the economic and social history of South Yorkshire.* [Barnsley]; South Yorkshire County Council; 1976. Pp 308.

36. Clarke, J.N. *Education in a market town: Horncastle, 1329–1970.* London; Phillimore; 1976. Pp xv, 183.

37. Busby, R.J. *The book of Welwyn: the story of the five villages and the Garden City.* Chesham; Barracuda Books; 1976. Pp 144.

38. Pike, L.E. *The book of Amersham: the story of a Chiltern town.* Chesham; Barracuda Books; 1976. Pp 144.

39. Compton, H.J. *The Oxford canal.* Newton Abbot; David & Charles; 1976. Pp 171.

40. Pugh, R.B. *The site of Southwood Park.* London; Hornsey Historical Soc.; [1977]. Pp 13.

41. Allison, K.J. *The East Riding of Yorkshire landscape.* London; Hodder & Stoughton; 1976. Pp 272.

42. Bird, V. *A short history of Warwickshire and Birmingham.* London; Batsford; 1977. Pp 176.

43. Pevsner, N. *Hertfordshire* (2nd ed.). Harmondsworth; Penguin Books; 1977. Pp 460.

44. Webb, M.J. *The history of the Chapel Royal, Brighton, 1793–1943.* [Barnet; the author]; 1977. Pp 40.

45. Heath, C. *The book of Ware: a portrait of the town*. Chesham; Barracuda Books; 1977. Pp 148.

46. Le Fevre, M., 'Education in Weybridge and Walton-on-Thames 1732—1944,' *Surrey Arch. Collections* 71 (1977), 233—54.

47. Mackay, J.A. *The Pobjoy encyclopaedia of Isle of Man coins and tokens*. Sutton; Pobjoy Mint Ltd; 1977. Pp 73.

48. Mercer, D., 'The Deepdene, Dorking: rise and decline through six centuries,' *Surrey Arch. Collections* 71 (1977), 111—38.

49. Bennett, —, 'The watermills of Kent, east of the Medway,' *Industrial Archaeology R.* 1 (1977), 205—35.

50. Daiches, D. *Glasgow*. London; Deutsch; 1977.

51. White, J.T. *The south-east, down and Weald: Kent, Surrey and Sussex*. London; Eyre Methuen; 1977. Pp 256.

52. Cox, B.G. *The book of Evesham: the story of the town's past*. Chesham; Barracuda Books; 1977. Pp 148.

53. Jones, W.A.B. *Hadleigh through the ages: a Viking royal town, medieval wool centre, chartered borough and archbishop's peculiar*. Ipswich; East Anglian Magazine Ltd; 1977. Pp 136.

54. Walker, T.E.C., 'Cobham incumbents and curates,' *Surrey Arch. Collections* 71 (1977), 199—24.

55. Ahier, P.; Ashworth, W.S. *A short parochial and commercial history of Jersey*. [St Helier] ; Ashton and Denton Publishing Co.; [1977]. Pp 145.

56. Chitty, J. *Paper in Devon*. Exeter; the author; 1976. Pp 72.

57. Smith, D.J. *Whitton School and Dame Anna Child's Charity, Radnorshire, 1703—1973*. Powys County Council Education Dept.; [1977]. Pp 48.

58. Waters, I. *The port of Chepstow*. Chepstow; The Chepstow Society; 1977. Pp 43.

59. Greater London Industrial Archaeology Society. *A hop merchant's warehouse, 24 Mellor Street, London SE1*. London; The Society; 1977. Pp 4.

60. Hinton, D.A. *Oxford buildings from medieval to modern* (revd. ed.). Oxford; Ashmolean Museum; 1977. Pp 73.

61. Whaley, P. *Dorset through history*. Melksham; Venton; 1977. Pp 144.

62. Griffiths, R.A. *Clyne Castle, Swansea: a history of the building and its owners*. University College of Swansea; 1977. Pp 61.

63. Graham, F. *The castles of Northumberland*. Newcastle/Tyne; the author; 1976. Pp 360.

64. Barnes, J.S. *A history of Caston, Norfolk, part 3*. Orpington; the author; 1977. Pp x, 133.

65. Munford, A.P. *South Yorkshire newspapers, 1764—1976*. Barnsley; South Yorks. County Council; 1976. Pp 19.

66. Roberts, B.K. *The green villages of County Durham: a study in historical geography*. Durham County Council; 1977. Pp iv, 56.

67. Barty-King, H. *The Baltic Exchange: the history of a unique market.* London; Hutchinson; 1977. Pp xx, 431.

68. Wilson, D. *A short history of Suffolk.* London; Batsford; 1977. Pp 176.

69. Sandon, E. *Suffolk houses: a study of domestic architecture.* Woodbridge; Baron Publishing; 1977. Pp 344.

70. Nuttall, G.F. *New College, London, and its library* (two lectures). London; Dr Williams's Trust; 1977. Pp 61.

71. Mills, A.D. *The place-names of Dorset, part 1.* Nottingham; English Place-Name Society; 1977. Pp xxxvii, 384.

72. Beckensall, S. *Northumberland field names.* Newcastle/Tyne; F. Graham; [1977]. Pp 72.

73. Noall, C. *The book of St Ives: a portrait of the town.* Chesham; Barracuda Books; 1977. Pp 148.

74. Owen, J.A. *The history of the Dowlais iron works, 1759–1970.* Newport; Starling Press; 1977. Pp 161.

75. Roose-Evans, J. *London theatre: from the Globe to the National.* Oxford; Phaidon; 1977. Pp 160.

76. Dunn, C. *The book of Huntingdon: a portrait of the town.* Chesham; Barracuda Books; 1977. Pp 148.

77. Torry, G. *Chelmsford through the ages.* Ipswich; East Anglian Magazine Ltd; 1977. Pp 120.

78. Hardy, E.B., 'Association life in Kent and Sussex 1770–1950 [Baptists],' *Baptist Q.* 27 (1977), 173–87.

79. Hughes, G.T.; Morgan, P.; Thomas, G. (ed.). *Gregynog.* Cardiff; University of Wales Press; 1977. Pp 146.

80. Tindall, G. *The fields beneath: the history of one London village* [Kentish Town]. London; Temple Smith; 1977. Pp 255.

81. Chapman, F. *The book of Tonbridge: the story of the town's past.* Chesham; Barracuda Books; 1976. Pp 148.

82. Hadley, G. *Citizens and founders: a history of the Worshipful Company of Founders, London, 1365–1975.* London; Phillimore; 1976. Pp xi, 199.

83. Raistrick, A. *Two centuries of industrial welfare: the London (Quaker) Lead Company* (revd. 2nd ed.). Buxton; Moorland Publishing Co; 1977. Pp 168.

84. Metcalf, P. *The halls of the Fishmongers' Company: an architectural history of a riverside site.* London; Phillimore; 1977. Pp xii, 214.

85. Eedle, M. de G. *A history of Bagshot and Windlesham.* London; Phillimore; 1977. Pp x, 262.

86. Spaul, J.E.H. *Andover: a historical portrait.* Andover Local Archives Committee; 1977. Pp 160.

87. Monier-Williams, R. *The tallow chandlers of London. Vol. 4: Ebb and flow.* London; Kaye & Ward; 1977. Pp 364.

88. Sheppard, F., 'The Grosvenor estate, 1677–1977,' *History Today* 27 (1977), 726–33.

15

89. Rowse, A.L., 'Truro as Cornish capital,' ibid. 539—42.
90. Turnock, D., 'The changing geography of smallholdings in northern Scotland,' *Northern Scotland* 2 (1976—7), 163—82.
91. Minchinton, W.E. *Windmills of Devon.* Exeter Industrial Archaeology Group; 1977. Pp 56.
92. Pounds, N.J.G., 'Food production and distribution in preindus-
trial Cornwall,' Bc10, 107—22.
93. Dulake, L. *Doctors, practices and hospitals through 300 years: a
history of general and hospital practice at Reigate and Redhill,
including Earlswood and Merstham.* [Reigate] ; the author; 1976.
Pp iv, 155.
94. Aldsworth, F.; Freke, D. *Historic towns in Sussex: an archaeological survey.* London; Sussex Arch. Field Unit; 1976. Pp 66.
95. Barnsby, G. *A history of housing in Wolverhampton, 1750 to
1975.* Wolverhampton; Integrated Publishing Services; [1976].
Pp 72.
96. Church, D. *Cuxton, a Kentish village.* Sheerness; A.J. Cassell Ltd;
1976. Pp ix, 177.
97. Handler, C.E. (ed.). *Guy's Hospital, 250 years.* London; Guy's
Hospital Gazette; 1976. Pp vi, 232.
98. Haslam, J.; Edwards, A. *Wiltshire towns: the archaeological
potential.* Devizes; Wilts. Arch. and Natural History Soc.;
[1976]. Pp 111.
99. Hoffmann, A. *Bocking deanery: the story of an Essex peculiar.*
London; Phillimore; 1976. Pp 136.
100. Mitchell, R. *Brighouse: birth and death of a borough.* Driffield;
Ridings Publishing Co; 1976. Pp x, 194.
101. Russell, P.M.G. *A history of the Exeter hospitals, 1170—1948.*
Exeter Postgraduate Medical Institute; 1976. Pp vii, 171.
102. Matthews, W.G., 'The Free Writing School, Sheffield, and its
masters,' *T. of the Hunter Arch. Soc.* 10 (1977), 280—5.
103. Lancaster, J.Y.; Wattleworth, D.R. *The iron and steel industry of
West Cumberland: an historical survey.* [Workington] ; British
Steel Corporation; 1977. Pp xii, 198.
104. Pretty, D.A. *Two centuries of Anglesey schools, 1700—1902.*
Llangefni; Anglesey Antiquarian Soc.; 1977. Pp 383.
105. Allsopp, B.; Clark, U. *Historic architecture of Northumberland
and Newcastle upon Tyne.* Stocksfield; Oriel Press; 1977. Pp 124.
106. Linnell, R. *The Curtain playhouse.* [London] ; Curtain Theatre;
1977. Pp 64.
107. Hugill, R. *Castles and peles of Cumberland and Westmorland: a
guide to the strongholds of the western English borderland.*
Newcastle/Tyne; F. Graham; 1977. Pp vii, 198.
108. Munby, L.M. *The Hertfordshire landscape.* London; Hodder &
Stoughton; 1977. Pp 267.
109. Gray, G.B.D., 'The South Yorkshire coalfield,' Bc1, 31—44.
110. Hassell, W.O., 'View from the Holkham windows,' Bc3, 305—19.

111. McKinley, R.A., 'The distribution of surnames derived from the names of some Yorkshire towns,' Bc3, 165—75.
112. Reece, R., 'From Corinion to Cirencester — models and misconceptions,' Bc8, 61—79.
113. Pounds, N.J.G., 'The population of Cornwall before the first census,' Bc10, 11—30.
114. Griffiths, M., 'The association between mortality and poverty in Exeter from the seventeenth century to the present,' Bc10, 31—47.
115. Carter, I., 'Social differentiation in the Aberdeenshire peasantry,' *J. of Peasant Studies* 5 (1977), 48—65.
116. Marmoy, C.F.A. *The French Protestant Hospital: extracts from the archive of 'La Providence' relating to inmates and applications for admission, 1718—1957, and to recipients of and applicants for the Coqueau charity, 1745—1901.* London; Huguenot Soc.; 1977. 2 vols: ca. 1200 pp.
117. Sheppard, F.H.W. (ed.). *Survey of London, vol. 39: The Grosvenor Estate in Mayfair.* Part 1: General history. London; Athlone Press; 1977. Pp xvi, 236.
118. Jones, F., 'Pontfaen,' *National Library of Wales J.* 20 (1977), 177—203.
119. Dewey, J. and S. *The book of Wallingford: an historical portrait.* Chesham; Barracuda Books; 1977. Pp 148.
120. Borer, M.C. *The city of London: a history.* London; Constable; 1977. Pp 324.
121. Jackson, A.A. (ed.). *Ashtead, a village transformed: a history of Ashtead from the earliest times to the present day.* Leatherhead and District Local History Soc.; 1977. Pp 237.
122. Aylmer, G.E.; Cant, R. (ed.). *A history of York minster.* Oxford; Clarendon; 1977. Pp xv, 586.
123. Haigh, D. *Old Park in the manor of Enfield.* [Barnet; the author]; 1977. Pp x, 146.
124. Corran, H.S. *The Isle of Man.* Newton Abbot; David & Charles; 1977. Pp 174.
125. Stockdale, E. *A study of Bedford prison, 1660—1877.* London; Phillimore; 1977. Pp xii, 238.
126. Viner, D., 'The Thames and Severn canal at Cirencester,' Bc8, 126—44.
127. Berrow, P. *Drawing the map of Romsey.* [Romsey]; Lower Test Valley Arch. Study Group; 1977. Pp 18.
128. Willmott, J. *The book of Bodmin: a portrait of the town.* Chesham; Barracuda Books; 1977. Pp 120.

(c) Collective Volumes

1. Benson, J.; Neville, R.G. (ed.). *Studies in the Yorkshire coal industry.* Manchester UP; 1976. Pp xii, 180.

2. Butt, J.; Ward, J.T. (ed.). *Scottish themes: essays in honour of Professor S.G.E. Lythe.* Edinburgh; Scottish Academic Press; 1976. Pp xvi, 189.

3. Emmison, F.G.; Stephens, R. (ed.). *Tribute to an antiquary: essays presented to Marc Fitch by some of his friends.* London; Leopard's Head Press; 1976. Pp xvi, 332.

4. Walker, D. (ed.). *A history of the Church in Wales.* Penarth; Church in Wales Publications; 1976. Pp xv, 221.

5. Simpson, M.A.; Lloyd, T.H. (ed.). *Middle class housing in Britain.* Newton Abbot; David & Charles; 1977. Pp 217.

6. Baker, D. (ed.). *Renaissance and renewal in Christian history* (Studies in Church History, vol. 14). Oxford; Blackwell; 1977. Pp xv, 428.

7. Cockburn, J.S. (ed.). *Crime in England, 1550–1800.* London; Methuen; 1977. Pp xiv, 364.

8. McWhirr, A. (ed.). *Studies in the archaeology and history of Cirencester.* Oxford; British Arch. Reports; 1976. Pp 100.

9. Cullen, L.M.; Smout, T.C. (ed.). *Comparative aspects of Scottish and Irish economic and social history, 1600–1900.* Edinburgh; Donald; [1977]. Pp viii, 252.

10. Minchinton, W.E. (ed.). *Population and marketing: two studies in the history of the south-west.* University of Exeter; 1976. Pp 139.

(d) Genealogy and Heraldry

1. Palgrave, D.A. *Heraldry at North Barningham church.* Doncaster; Palgrave Soc.; 1976. Pp 14.

2. Palgrave, D.A. *Archives at Flegg relating to the Palgraves.* Doncaster; Palgrave Soc.; 1975. Pp 20.

3. Graham, N.H. *The genealogist's consolidated guide to parish registers in the inner London area, 1538–1837* (revd. ed.). Orpington; the compiler; 1976. Pp 88.

4. Jones, R.A.; Harrington, D.W. *The memorial inscriptions of the nonconformist burial ground in Wincheap, Canterbury.* Kent Family History Soc.; 1976. Pp 36.

5. Palgrave-Moore, P.; Sayer, M.J. *A selection of revised and unpublished Norfolk pedigrees*, part 2. Norfolk and Norwich Genealogical Soc.; 1976. Pp 177.

6. White, H.L. *Monuments and their inscriptions: a practical guide.* London; Soc. of Genealogists; 1977. Pp 60.

7. Balfour Paul, J. *An ordinary of arms; vol. 2: contained in the public register of all arms and bearings in Scotland, 1902–1973.* Edinburgh; Lyon Office; 1977. Pp xvi, 525.

8. Wright, D. *Genealogy index, 1975.* Birmingham and Midland Soc. for Genealogy and Heraldry; 1976. Pp xii, 29.

9. Hamley, D.W. *The Hamley, Hambly, Hamlyn group of families:*

historical and genealogical notes. Norwich; D.W. & J.C. Hamley; [1977]. Pp 288.

10. Franklyn, C.A.H. *The genealogy of Anne the Queen [Anne Boleyn] and other English families* . . . Hassocks; the author; 1977. Pp 101.

11. Wagner, A.R.; Squibb, G.D., 'Deputy heralds,' Bc3, 229—64.

12. Barrow, G.B. *The genealogist's guide: an index to printed British pedigrees and family histories, 1950—1975.* London; Research Publishing Co.; 1977. Pp xv, 205.

13. Scott, S.A. *Monumental inscriptions (pre-1855) in the Upper Ward of Lanarkshire.* [Edinburgh]; Scottish Genealogy Soc.; 1977. Pp iii, 403.

C. ROMAN BRITAIN

(a) Archaeology

1. Taylor, A., et al. *Roman Malton and the Malton Museum.* [York; Yorkshire Museum; 1976]. Pp 14.

2. Thomas, C., 'Imported late-Roman mediterranean pottery in Ireland and western Britain: chronologies and implications,' *P. of the Royal Irish Academy* 76/C (1976), 245—55.

3. Fowler, P.J., 'Small settlements and their context in western Britain, first to fifth centuries A.D.,' ibid, 191—206.

4. Royal Commission on Historical Monuments (England). *Ancient and historical monuments in the county of Gloucester, vol. 1: Iron age and Romano-British monuments in the Gloucestershire Cotswolds.* London; HMSO; 1976. Pp lvi, 157.

5. Jones, M.J. *Roman fort-defences to AD 117, with special reference to Britain.* Oxford; British Arch. Reports; 1975. Pp 192.

6. Clack, P.A.G.; Gosling, P.F. *Archaeology in the north: report of the Northern Archaeological Survey.* Durham; The Survey; 1976. Pp xiii, 304.

7. Breeze, D.J., 'The line of the Antonine Wall at Falkirk,' *P. of the Soc. of Antiquaries of Scotland* 106 (1977 for 1974—5), 204—5.

8. Branigan, K. *The Roman villa in South-west England.* Bradford-on-Avon; Moonraker Press; 1977. Pp 127.

9. Smith, C., 'A Romano-British site at Binscombe, Godalming,' *Surrey Arch. Collections* 71 (1977), 13—42.

10. Painter, K.S. *The Mildenhall treasure.* London; British Museum Publications Ltd.; 1977. Pp 24.

11. Browne, D.M. *Roman Cambridgeshire.* Cambridge; Oleander Press; 1977. Pp 48.

12. Carrington, P., 'The planning and dating of the Roman legionary fortress at Chester,' *J. of the Chester Arch. Soc.* 60 (1977), 35—42.

13. Goodyear, F.H., 'The Roman fort at Chesterton, Newcastle-under-Lyme: report of the excavations of 1969–71,' *North Staffordshire J. of Field Studies* 16 (1976), 1–15.
14. Simpsons, F.G. (et al.). *Watermills and military works on Hadrian's Wall: excavations in Northumberland, 1907–1913.* Kendal; Titus Wilson; 1976. Pp xvi, 198.
15. Henig, M., 'Some notes on gems and finger rings in the Grosvenor Museum,' *J. of the Chester Arch. Soc.* 60 (1977), 43–8.
16. Lloyd-Morgan, G., 'Mirrors in Roman Chester,' ibid. 49–55.
17. Edwards, B.J.N., 'A Chester Mithraic figure recovered?,' ibid. 59–60.
18. Peacock, D.P.S. (ed.). *Pottery and early commerce: characterization and trade in Roman and later ceramics.* London; Academic Press; 1977. Pp xvi, 340.
19. Renfrew, C., 'The potential of ceramic studies,' Ca18, 1–20.
20. Peacock, D.P.S., 'Ceramics in Roman and medieval archaeology,' Ca18, 21–33.
21. Fulfold, M., 'Pottery and Britain's foreign trade in the later Roman period,' Ca18, 35–84.
22. Loughlin, N., 'Dales ware and Dales types: a contribution to the study of Roman coarse pottery,' Ca18, 85–162.
23. William, D.F., 'The Romano-British black-burnished industry: an essay on characterization by heavy mineral analysis,' Ca18, 163–220.
24. Laing, L. (ed.). *Studies in Celtic survival.* Oxford; British Archaeological Reports; 1977. Pp 123.
25. Faull, M.L., 'British survival in Anglo-Saxon Northumbria,' Ca24, 1–55.
26. Laing, L., 'Segontium and the post-Roman occupation of Wales,' Ca24, 57–60.
27. McWhirr, A., 'The Roman town plan [or Cirencester],' Bc8, 5–14.
28. Wacher, J., 'Late Roman developments [in Cirencester],' Bc8, 15–18.

(b) History

1. Sorrell, A. *Roman towns in Britain.* London; Batsford; 1976. Pp 80.
2. Davies, R.W., 'Roman Cumbria and the African connection,' *Klio* 59 (1977), 155–74.
3. Green, M.J. *A corpus of religious material from the civilian areas of Roman Britain.* Oxford; British Arch. Reports; 1976. Pp 321.
4. Dawson, G.J., 'Roads, bridges and the origin of Roman London,' *Surrey Arch. Collections* 71 (1977), 43–55.
5. Dumville, D., 'Sub-Roman Britain: history and legend,' *History* 62 (1977), 173–92.

D. ENGLAND 450–1066

(a) *General*

1. Biddle, M.; Barlow, F. (ed.). *Winchester in the early middle ages: an edition and discussion of the Winton Domesday.* Oxford; Clarendon Press; 1976 (i.e. 1977). Pp xxxiii, 612.
2. Witney, K.P. *The Jutish forest: a study of the Weald of Kent from 450 to 1380 A.D.* London; Athlone Press; 1976. Pp xvi, 339.
3. Barlow, F. (ed.). 'The Winton Domesday,' Da1, 1–142.
4. Biddle, M.; Keene, D.J., 'General survey and conclusions [on early medieval Winchester],' Da1, 449–508.
5. Biddle, M.; Keene, D.J., 'Winchester in the eleventh and twelfth centuries,' Da1, 241–441.
6. Dornier, A. (ed.). *Mercian Studies.* Leicester UP; 1977. Pp v, 254.
7. Clemoes, P. (ed.). *Anglo-Saxon England*, 6. Cambridge UP; 1977. Pp x, 316.
8. Blair, P.H. *An introduction to Anglo-Saxon England* (2nd ed.). Cambridge UP; 1977. Pp xvi, 380.
9. Smyth, A.P. *Scandinavian kings in the British Isles, 850–880.* Oxford UP; 1977. Pp xii, 307.
10. Sawyer, P.H.; Wood, I.N. *Early medieval kingship.* Leeds University Printing Service; 1977. Pp vii, 193.

(b) *Politics and Institutions*

1. John, E., 'War and society in the tenth century: the Maldon campaign,' *T. of the Royal Historical Soc.* 5th ser. 27 (1977), 173–95.
2. Alcock, L., 'Her . . . gefeaht wip Walas: aspects of the warfare of Saxons and Britons,' *B. of the Board of Celtic Studies* 27 (1977), 413–24.
3. Campbell, M.W., 'Hypothèses sur les causes de l'ambassade de Harold en Normandie,' *Annales de Normandie* 27 (1977), 243–65.
4. Davies, W., 'Annals and the origins of Mercia,' Da6, 17–30.
5. Kirby, D.P., Welsh bards and the border,' Da6, 31–42.
6. Hart, C., 'The kingdom of Mercia,' Da6, 43–62.
7. Phythian-Adams, C., 'Rutland reconsidered,' Da6, 63–86.
8. Barker, E.E., 'The last documents of King Athelstan,' Da7, 137–44.
9. Biddle, M., 'Hampshire and the origins of Wessex,' *Problems in Economic and Social Archaeology* (ed. G. de G. Sieveking, I.H. Longworth, K.E. Wilson; London, Duckworth, 1976), 323–42.
10. Lund, N., 'King Edgar and the Danelaw,' *Medieval Scandinavia* 9 (1976), 181–95.

11. Nelson, J.L., 'Inauguration rituals,' Da10, 50—71.
12. Dumville, D.N., 'Kingship, genealogies and regnal lists,' Da10, 72—104.
13. Wormald, C.P., *'Lex scripta* and *verbum regis*: legislation and Germanic kingship from Euric to Knut,' Da10, 105—38.

(c) Religion

1. Meyer, M.A., 'Women and the tenth century English monastic reform,' *Revue bénédictine* 87 (1977), 34—61.
2. Gallyon, M. *The early church in Northumbria.* Lavenham; T. Dalton; 1977. Pp 120.
3. Rodes, R.E. *This house I have built: a study of the legal history of establishment in England. Ecclesiastical administration in medieval England: the Anglo-Saxons to the Reformation.* Notre Dame/London; University of Notre Dame Press; 1977. Pp xvi, 287.
4. Dornier, A., 'The Anglo-Saxon monastery at Breedon-on-the-Hill,' Da6, 155—68.
5. Parsons, D., 'Brixworth and its monastery church,' Da6, 173—90.

(d) Economic Affairs/Numismatics

1. Blunt, C.E.; Pagan, H.E., 'Three tenth-century hoards: bath (1755), Kingbury (1761), Threadneedle Street (before 1924),' *British Numismatic J.* 45 (1975), 19—32.
2. Dykes, D.W. *Anglo-Saxon coins in the National Museum of Wales.* [Cardiff; The Museum; 1977]. Pp 31.
3. Metcalf, D.M., 'Monetary affairs in Mercia in the time of Aethelbald,' Da6, 87—107.
4. Gelling, M., 'Latin loan-words in Old English place-names,' Da7, 1—14.
5. Rumble, A., 'Hrepingas reconsidered,' Da6, 169—72.
6. Sawyer, P.H., 'Kings and merchants,' Da10, 139—58.

(e) Intellectual and Cultural

1. Stephens, J.N., 'Bede's Ecclesiastical History,' *History* 62 (1977), 1—14.
2. Brown, T.J.; Biddle, M.; Nixon, H.M.; Wormald, F., 'The manuscript of the Winton Domesday,' Da1, 520—50.
3. Wormald, C.P., 'The uses of literacy in Anglo Saxon England and its neighbours,' *T. of the Royal Historical Society.* 5th ser. 27 (1977), 95—114.
4. Boyd, W.J.P. *Aldred's marginalia: explanatory comments in the Lindisfarne Gospels.* University of Exeter; 1975. Pp x, 62.
5. Wheeler, H., 'Aspects of Mercian art: the book of Cerne,' Da6, 235—44.

6. Winterbottom, M., 'Aldhelm's prose style and its origins,' Da7, 39—76.
7. Law, V., 'The Latin and Old English glosses in the *ars Tatuini*,' Da7, 77—90.
8. Deshman, R., 'The Leofric Missal and tenth-century English art,' Da7, 145—74.
9. Gatch, M.McC., 'Old English literature and the liturgy: problems and potential,' Da7, 237—48.

(f) Society and Archaeology

1. Hall, R.A., 'The pre-conquest burgh of Derby,' *Derbyshire Arch. J.* 94 (1976 for 1974), 16—23.
2. Longley, D. 'Hanging-bowls, penannular brooches and the Anglo-Saxon connection'. Oxford; British Arch. Reports; 1975. Pp 49.
3. Holdsworth, P., 'Saxon Southampton: a new review,' *Medieval Archaeology* 20 (1976), 26—61.
4. Mayes, P.; Dean, M.J., 'An Anglo-Saxon cemetery at Baston, Lincolnshire', Sleaford; Soc. for Lincolnshire History and Archaeology; 1976. Pp 63.
5. Cox, B., 'The place-names of the earliest English records,' *English Place-Name Soc. J.* 8 (1976), 12—66.
6. Faull, M.L., 'The location and relationship of the Sancton Anglo-Saxon cemeteries,' *Antiquaries J.* 56 (1976), 227—33.
7. Biddle, M.; Keene, D.J., 'The early place-names of Winchester,' Da1, 231—40.
8. Feilitzen, O. von, 'The personal names and bynames of the Winton Domesday,' Da1, 143—229.
9. Sutermeister, H., 'Burpham: a settlement within Saxon defences,' *Sussex Arch. Collection* 114 (1976), 194—206.
10. Lang, J.T., 'The sculptors of the Nunburnholme cross,' *Arch. J.* 133 (1977 for 1976), 75—94.
11. Hinton, D.A. *Alfred's kingdom: Wessex and the south 800—1500.* London; Dent; 1977. Pp xii, 228.
12. Rahtz, P., 'The archaeology of west Mercian towns,' Da6, 107—30.
13. Cramp, R., 'Schools of Mercian sculpture,' Da6, 191—234.
14. Rahtz, P.; Bullough, D., 'The parts of an Anglo-Saxon mill,' Da7, 15—39.
15. Biddle, M.; Binns, A.; Cameron, J.M.; Metcalf, D.M.; Page, R.I.; Sparrow, C.; Warren, F.L., 'Sutton Hoo published: a review,' Da7, 249—65.
16. Addyman, P., 'Archaeology and Anglo-Saxon society,' *Problems in Economic and Social Archaeology* (ed. G. de G. Sieveking, I.H. Longworth, K.E. Wilson; London, Duckworth, 1976), 309—22.
17. Bond, C.J.; Hunt, A.M., 'Recent archaeological work in Pershore,'

> *Vale of Evesham Historical Soc. Research Papers* 6 (1977), 1—
> 76.

18. Phythian-Adams, C., 'Jolly cities, goodly towns: the current search for England's urban roots [review article],' *Urban History Yearbook* (1977), 30—9.
19. Slater, T., 'The town and its region in the Anglo-Saxon and medieval periods [Cirencester],' Bc8, 81—108.
20. Brown, D., 'Archaeological evidence for the Anglo-Saxon period [in Cirencester],' Bc8, 19—45.

E. ENGLAND 1066—1500

See also: Ab27; Ba5; Da1, 2, c3, f11, 18, 19

(a) General

1. Guth, D.J., 'Fifteenth-century England: recent scholarship and future directions,' *British Studies Monitor* 7/2 (1977), 3—50.
2. Goodman, A. *A History of England from Edward II to James I.* London; Longman; 1977. Pp xii, 467.
3. Morris, J. (ed.). *Domesday Book*: vols. 2 (Sussex), 20 (Bedfordshire), 23 (Warwickshire), 28 (Nottinghamshire). Chichester; Phillimore; 1976—7. Pp 224; 176; 160; 166.
4. Walmsley, J.R.F., 'Another Domesday text,' *Mediaeval Studies* 39 (1977), 109—20.

(b) Politics

1. Williams, D., 'The hastily drawn up will of William Catesby, esq., 25 August 1485,' *T. of the Leicestershire Arch. and Historical Soc.* 51 (1975—6), 43—51.
2. Davies, R.G., 'The episcopate and the political crisis in England of 1386—1388,' *Speculum* 51 (1976), 659—93.
3. Mason, E., 'William Rufus: myth and reality,' *J. of Medieval History* 3 (1977), 1—20.
4. Craig, M.A., 'A second daughter of Geoffrey of Brittany [d. 1186],' *B. of the Institute of Historical Research* 50 (1977), 112—15.
5. Studd, J.R., 'The Lord Edward and King Henry III,' ibid. 4—19.
6. Safford, E.W. *Itinerary of Edward I, part 3: Index.* London; List & Index Society, vol. 135; 1977. Pp 208.
7. Lander, J.R., 'The crown and the aristocracy in England 1450—1509,' *Albion* 8 (1976), 203—18.
8. Richmond, C., 'The nobility and the Wars of the Roses,' *Nottingham Mediaeval Studies* 21 (1977), 71—86.

9. Pollard, A.J., 'The tyranny of Richard III,' *J. of Medieval History* 3 (1977), 147–65.

10. Werckmeister, O.K., 'The political ideology of the Bayeux Tapestry,' *Studi medievali* 3rd ser. 17 (1976), 535–95.

11. Hollister, C.W., 'Magnates and *curiales* in early Norman England,' *Viator* 8 (1977), 63–81.

12. Türk, E. *Nugae Curialium: le règne d'Henri II Plantagenêt et l'éthique politique.* Geneva; Droz; 1977. Pp 229.

13. Linder, A., 'John of Salisbury's *Policraticus* in thirteenth-century England: the evidence of MS Cambridge, Corpus Christi College, 469,' *J. of the Warburg and Courtauld Institutes* 40 (1977), 276–82.

14. Waugh, S.L., 'The profits of violence: the minor gentry in the rebellion of 1321–1322 in Gloucestershire and Herefordshire,' *Speculum* 52 (1977), 843–69.

15. Stow, G.B. (ed.). *Historia vitae et regni Ricardi Secundi.* Philadelphia; University of Pennysylvania Press; 1977. Pp 228.

16. Genet, J.-P. (ed.). *Four English political tracts of the later middle ages.* London; Royal Historical Soc. (Camden 4th ser. vol. 18); 1977. Pp 229.

17. Cornwallis, Sir W. (ed. A.N. Kincaid). *The encomium of Richard III.* London; Turner and Decereux; 1977. Pp xiv, 65.

18. Edwards, A.S.G., 'The influence of Lydgate's *Fall of Princes* c. 1400–1559: a survey,' *Mediaeval Studies* 39 (1977), 424–39.

19. Kelly, H.A., 'English kings and the fear of sorcery,' ibid. 206–38.

20. Dockray, K.R., 'The troubles of the Yorkshire Plumptons in the wars of the Roses,' *History Today* 27 (1977), 459–66, 482.

21. Sayer, M., 'Norfolk involvement in dynastic conflict 1469–1471 and 1483–1487,' *Norfolk Archaeology* 36 (1977), 305–26.

(c) Constitution, Administration and Law

1. Elvey, E.M. (ed.). *The courts of the archdeaconry of Buckingham, 1483–1523.* Aylesbury; Buckinghamshire Record Soc.; 1975. Pp xxx, 449.

2. Hanawalt, B. (ed.). *Crime in East Anglia in the fourteenth century: Norfolk gaol delivery rolls, 1307–1316.* Norfolk Record Soc. vol. 44; 1976. Pp 150.

3. Byerly, B.F.; Byerly, C.R. (ed.). *Records of the Wardrobe and Household, 1285–1286.* London; HMSO; 1977. Pp xlvi, 309.

4. Palliser, D.M., 'Fifteenth-century borough representation: a comment,' *Northern History* 13 (1977), 265–6.

5. Harris, B.E. (ed.). *The great roll of the pipe for the third year of King Henry III, Michaelmas 1219 (Pipe Roll 63).* London; Pipe Roll Soc.; 1976. Pp xxvi, 314.

6. Cuttino, G.P., 'A chancellor of the Lord Edward,' *B. of the Institute of Historical Research* 50 (1977), 229–32.

7. Turner, R.V., 'Simon of Pattishall, Northamptonshire man, early common law judge,' *Northamptonshire Past and Present* 6 (1978), 5—14.

8. Turner, R.V., 'The origins or Common Pleas and King's Bench,' *American J. of Legal History* 21 (1977), 238—54.

9. Kimball, E.G., 'Commissions of the peace for urban jurisdictions in England, 1327—1485,' *P. of the American Philosophical Soc.* 121 (1977), 448—74.

10. Given, J.B. *Society and homicide in thirteenth-century England.* Stanford UP; 1977. Pp 262.

11. Hanawalt, B.A., 'Community conflict and social control: crime and justice in the Ramsey Abbery villages,' *Mediaeval Studies* 39 (1977), 402—23.

12. Kaye, J.M., 'Gaol delivery jurisdiction and the writ *de bono et malo*,' *Law Q.R.* 93 (1977), 259—72.

13. Griffiths, R.A., 'Queen Katherine of Valois and a missing statute of the realm,' ibid. 248—58.

14. Hand, G., 'The king's widow and the king's widows [see Ec13],' ibid. 506—7.

15. Griffiths, R.A., 'William Wawe and his gang, 1427,' *P. of the Hampshire Field Club* 33 (1976), 89—93.

16. Alford, J.A., 'Literature and law in medieval England,' *P. of the Modern Language Association of America* 92 (1977), 941—51.

17. Keen, M.H. *The outlaws of medieval legend* (revd. ed.). London; Routledge; 1977. Pp xxi, 235.

(d) *External Affairs*

1. Friedland, K. (ed.). *Frühformen englisch-deutscher Handels-partnerschaft.* Quellen und Darstellungen zur hansischen Geschichte; neue Folge, Bd. XXIII. Cologne/Vienna; Böhlau Verlag; 1976. Pp xii, 120.

2. Fowler, K.A., 'English diplomacy and the peace of Utrecht [of 1474],' Ed1, 9—24.

3. Neumann, G., 'Hansische Politik und Politiker bei den Utrechter Friedensverhandlungen [1473—4],' Ed1, 25—59.

4. Buszello, H., 'Die auswärtige Handelspolitik der englischen Krone im 15. Jahrhundert,' Ed1, 64—86.

5. Friedland, K., 'Hansische Handelspolitik und hansisches Wirtschaftssystem im 14. und 15. Jahrhundert,' Ed1, 87—99.

6. Irsigler, F., 'Anmerkungen zu den Kölner Wirtschaftsbeziehungen mit England im 15. Jahrhundert,' Ed1, 107—13.

7. Stoob, H., 'Hansische Westpolitik im frühen 14. Jahrhundert,' *Hansische Geschichtsblätter* 94 (1976), 1—17.

8. Forey, A.J., 'The military order of St Thomas of Acre,' *English Historical R.* 92 (1977), 481—503.

(e) *Religion*

1. Schmugge, L., 'Thomas Becket und König Heinrich II. in der Sicht des Radulfus Niger,' *Deutsches Archiv für Erforschung des Mittelalters*, 32 (1976), 572–9.
2. Hallam, E.M., 'Henry II as a founder of monasteries,' *J. of Ecclesiastical History* 28 (1977), 113–32.
3. Cheney, C.R. *Pope Innocent III and England.* Päpste und Papsttum, Bd. 9. Stuttgart; Hiersemann; 1976. Pp xii, 433.
4. Hockey, F. *Beaulieu, King John's Abbey: a history of Beaulieu Abbey, Hampshire, 1204–1538.* London; Pioneer Publications; 1976. Pp xiv, 251.
5. Brown, A., 'The financial system of Rochester cathedral priory: a reconsideration,' *B. of the Institute of Historical Research* 50 (1977), 115–20.
6. Erickson, C., 'The fourteenth-century Franciscans and their critics, I: The Order's growth and character,' *Franciscan Studies* 35 (1976 for 1975), 107–35.
7. Szittya, P.R., 'The antifraternal tradition in Middle English literature,' *Speculum* 52 (1977), 287–313.
8. Doyle, E., 'William Woodford, O.F.M., and John Wyclif's *De Religione*,' ibid. 329–36.
9. Windeatt, B.A., 'Julian of Norwich and her audience,' *R. of English Studies* new ser. 28 (1977), 1–17.
10. Saltman, A. (ed.). *The cartulary of the Wakebridge Chantries at Crich.* Derbyshire Arch. Soc.; 1976 for 1971. Pp 203.
11. Davies, R.G., 'Martin V and the English episcopate, with particular reference to his campaign for the repeal of the statute of provisors,' *English Historical R.* 92 (1977), 309–44.
12. Baker, D., 'Old wine in new bottles: attitudes to reform in fifteenth-century England,' Bc6, 193–211.
13. Clark, R. *The foundation of Dale Abbey in legend and chronicle.* Ilkeston and District Local History Soc.; 1977. Pp iv, 44.
14. Devine, M. (ed.). *The cartulary of Cirencester Abbey, Gloucestershire*, vol. 8. Oxford UP; 1977. Pp xv, 735–1182.
15. Greenway, D.E., 'Two bishops of Winchester: Henry of Blois and Peter des Roches,' *History Today* 27 (1977), 417–25, 481.
16. Foreville, R., 'La diffusion de culte de Thomas Becket dans la France de l'ouest avant la fin du XIIe siècle,' *Cahiers de civilisation médiévale, Xe–XIIe siècles* 19 (1976), 347–69.
17. Barratt, A., 'The sermons of Stephen Langton: a new manuscript,' *Recherches de théologie ancienne et médiévale* 63 (1976), 111–20.
18. Jennings, M., 'Higden's minor writings and the fourteenth-century Church,' *P. of the Leeds Philosophical and Literary Soc.* 16 (1977), 149–58.
19. Clark, J.P.H., 'The "lightsome darkness" — Aspects of Walter

Hilton's theological background,' *Downside R.* 95 (1977), 95–109.

20. Frankforter, A.D., 'The Reformation and the register: episcopal administration in late medieval England,' *Catholic Historical R.* 63 (1977), 204–24.

21. Field, P.J.C., 'Sir Robert Malory, prior of the Hospital of St John of Jerusalem in England (1432–1439/40),' *J. of Ecclesiastical History* 28 (1977), 249–64.

22. Gibson, M. *Lanfranc of Bec.* Oxford; Clarendon; 1978 [*recte* 1977]. Pp 266.

23. Smith, W.E.L. *The register of Richard Clifford bishop of Worcester, 1401–1407: a calendar.* Leiden; Brill; 1976. Pp 235.

24. Smith, D.M., 'A reconstruction of the York *sede vacante* register 1352–53,' *Borthwick Institute B.* 1 (1976), 75–86.

25. Willis, D., 'The conservation of the medieval cause papers of York,' ibid. 119–27.

26. McHardy, A.K. *The Church in London 1375–1392.* London Record Soc. (vol. 13); 1977. Pp 126.

27. Harper-Bill, C., 'A late medieval visitation – the diocese of Norwich in 1499,' *P. of the Suffolk Institute of Archaeology and History* 34 (1977), 35–47.

28. Harper-Bill, C., 'Bishop Richard Hill and the court of Canterbury, 1494–96,' *Guildhall Studies in London History* 3 (1977), 1–12.

29. Sayers, J.E., 'An Evesham manuscript containing the treatise known as "Actor et Reus" (Harley MS 3763),' *B. of Medieval Canon Law* new ser. 6 (1976), 75–81.

30. Thomson, R., 'Twelfth-century documents from Bury St Edmunds Abbey,' *English Historical R.* 92 (1977), 806–19.

31. Haines, R.M., 'A defence brief for Bishop Adam de Orleton,' *B. of the Institute of Historical Research* 50 (1977), 232–42.

32. Greatrex, J., 'A fourteenth-century injunction book from Winchester,' ibid. 242–6.

33. McHardy, A.K., 'Some late-medieval Eton College wills,' *J. of Ecclesiastical History* 28 (1977), 387–95.

34. Crook, E.J., 'A new version of Ranulph Hidgen's *Speculum Curatorum,' Manuscripta* 21 (1977), 41–9.

35. Bitterling, K., 'An abstract of John Kirk's "Instructions for parish priests" [Trinity College Dublin MS 211],' *Notes and Queries* new ser. 24 (1977), 146–8.

36. Cregg, J.Y., 'The exempla of "Jacob's Well": a study in the transmission of medieval sermon stories,' *Traditio* 33 (1977), 359–80.

37. Spencer, H., 'A fifteenth-century translation of a late twelfth-century sermon collection,' *R. of English Studies* new ser. 28 (1977), 257–67.

38. Patterson, L.W., 'Chaucerian confession: penitential literature and the Pardoner,' *Medievalia et Humanistica* 7 (1976), 153–73.

39. Barratt, A., 'The *De Institutione Inclusarum* of Ailred of Rievaulx and the Carthusian order,' *J. of Theological Studies* new ser. 28 (1977), 528—36.

40. Thomson, W.R., 'The image of the mendicants in the Chronicles of Matthew Paris,' *Archivum Franciscanum Historicum* 70 (1977), 3—34.

41. Harvey, M., 'Two *Questiones* on the great schism by Nicholas Fakenham, O.F.M.,' ibid. 97—127.

42. Hammer, C.I., 'The town-gown confraternity of St Thomas the Martyr in Oxford,' *Mediaeval Studies* 39 (1977), 466—76.

43. Orme, N., 'The Kalendar Brethren of the city of Exeter,' *Devonshire Association Report and T.* 109 (1977), 153—69.

44. Dunning, R.W., 'The minster at Crewkerne,' *Somerset Archaeology and Natural History* 120 (1976), 63—7.

45. Carley, J.P., 'An annotated edition of the list of sixty-three monks who entered Glastonbury Abbey during the abbacy of Walter de Moninton [1342—1375],' *Downside R.* 321 (1977), 306—15.

46. Renardy, C., 'Notes concernant le culte de saint Thomas Becket dans le diocèse de Liège aux XIIe et XIIIe siècles,' *Revue Belge de Philologie et d'Histoire* 55 (1977), 381—9.

47. Leff. G., 'Ockham and Wyclif on the eucharist,' *Reading Medieval Studies* 2 (1976), 1—13.

48. Aston, M., 'Lollardy and literacy,' *History* 62 (1977), 347—71.

49. Finucane, R.C. *Miracles and pilgrims: popular beliefs in medieval England.* London; Dent; 1977. Pp 248.

50. Bruce-Mitford, R.L.S., 'The chapter house vestibule graves at Lincoln and the body of St Hugh of Avalon,' Bc3, 127—40.

(f) Economic Affairs

1. Britnell, R.H., 'Agricultural technology and the margin of cultivation in the fourteenth century,' *Economic History R.* 2nd ser. 30 (1977), 53—66.

2. Postles, D., 'The demesne sheep flock at Hartington: a note,' *Derbyshire Arch. J.* 94 (1976 for 1974), 24—5.

3. Wright, S.M., 'Barton Blount: climatic or economic change?,' *Medieval Archaeology* 20 (1976), 148—52.

4. Lloyd, T.H. *The English wool trade in the middle ages.* Cambridge UP; 1977. Pp xi, 351.

5. Waites, B., 'The medieval ports and trade of north-east Yorkshire,' *Mariner's Mirror* 63 (1977), 137—49.

6. Bridbury, A.R., 'Before the Black Death,' *Economic History R.* 2nd ser. 30 (1977), 393—410.

7. Hatcher, J. *Plague, population and the English economy, 1348—1530.* London; Macmillan; 1977. Pp 95.

8. Harvey, B. *Westminster Abbey and its estates in the middle ages.* Oxford; Clarendon; 1977. Pp xii, 499.

9. Jones, E.D., 'Some economic dealings of Prior John the Almoner of Spalding,' *Lincolnshire History and Archaeology* 12 (1977), 41—7.

10. Farmer, D.L., 'Grain yields on the Winchester manors in the later middle ages,' *Economic History R.* 2nd ser. 30 (1977), 555—66.

11. Waites, B., 'Pastoral farming on the duchy of Lancaster's Pickering estate in the fourteenth and fifteenth centuries,' *Yorkshire Arch. Soc.* 49 (1977), 77—86.

12. Brown, A., 'London and north-west Kent in the later middle ages: the development of a land market,' *Archaeologia Cantiana* 92 (1977), 145—55.

13. Goose, N.R., 'Wage labour on the Kentish manor: Meopham 1307—75,' ibid. 203—23.

14. Mead, V.K., 'Evidence for the manufacture of amber beads in London in the 14th—15th century,' *T. of the London and Middlesex Arch. Soc.* 28 (1977), 211—14.

15. Woodward-Smith, N.; Schofield, J., 'A late 15th century account for a wharf at Vauxhall, London,' ibid. 278—91.

16. Stewart, I., 'The Bournemouth find (c. 1901) of coins of Henry I,' *Numismatic Chronicle* 7th ser. 17 (1977), 180—3.

17. Mayhew, N.J. (ed.). *Edwardian monetary affairs (1279—1344).* Oxford; British Archaeological Reports; 1977. Pp 186.

18. Metcalf, D.M., 'A survey of numismatic research into the pennies of the first three Edwards,' Ef17, 1—31.

19. Mate, M., 'Mint officials under Edward I and Edward II,' Ef17, 32—44.

20. Prestwich, M., 'Currency and economy of early fourteenth-century England,' Ef17, 45—58.

21. Rigold, S.E., 'Small change in the light of medieval site-finds,' Ef17, 59—80.

22. Palmer, N.J.; Mayhew, N.J., 'Medieval coins and jettons from Oxford excavations,' Ef17, 81—95.

23. Lloyd, T.H., 'Overseas trade and the English money supply in the fourteenth century,' Ef17, 96—124.

24. Mayhew, N.J.; Walker, D.R., 'Crockards and pollards: imitation and the problem of fineness in a silver coinage,' Ef17, 125—46.

25. Hadwin, J.F., 'Evidence on the possession of "treasure" from the lay subsidy rolls,' Ef17, 147—65.

26. Archibald, M.M., 'Wastage from currency: long-cross and the re-coinage of 1279,' Ef17, 167—86.

27. Taylor, A.J., 'Royal alms and oblations in the later 13th century,' Bc3, 93—125.

28. Evans, B., 'The collegiate church at Cirencester: a critical examination of the historical evidence,' Bc8, 46—60.

29. Smith, D., 'Medieval timber building: a surviving fragment [at Cirencester],' Bc8, 109—12.

30. Hidges, H., 'Some early medieval French wares in the British Isles: an archaeological assessment of the early French wine trade with Britain,' Ca18, 239—55.

31. Vince, A., 'The medieval and post medieval ceramic industry of the Malvern region: the study of a ware and its distribution,' Ca18, 257—305.

32. Raban, S. *The estates of Thorney and Crowland: a study in medieval monastic land tenure.* University of Cambridge Dept. of Land Economy; 1977. Pp 106.

(g) Social Structure and Population

1. Sayer, M.J., 'Twyford of Kirk Langley and Spondon: problems in the history of a medieval Derbyshire family,' *Derbyshire Arch. J.* 94 (1976 for 1974), 26—31.

2. Riden, P., 'An early 15th century Chesterfield rental,' ibid. 6—11.

3. Jones, A., 'Harvest customs and labourers' perquisites in southern England, 1150—1350,' *Agricultural History R.* 25 (1977), 14—22, 98—107.

4. Darby, H.C. *Domesday England.* Cambridge UP; 1977. Pp xiv, 416.

5. Walker, D.G., 'Gloucester and Gloucestershire in Domesday Book,' *T. of the Bristol and Gloucestershire Arch. Soc.* 95 (1977 for 1976), 107—16.

6. Soulsby, I.N., 'Richard Fitz Turold, lord of Penhallam, Cornwall,' *Medieval Archaeology* 20 (1976), 146—8.

7. Newman, J.E., 'Greater and lesser landowners and parochial patronage: Yorkshire in the thirteenth century,' *English Historical R.* 92 (1977), 280—308.

8. Harvey, P.D.A. (ed.). *Manorial records of Cuxham, Oxfordshire, circa 1200—1359.* London; HMSO; 1976. Pp xviii, 839.

9. Crook, D., 'The Spigurnels of Skegby,' *Nottingham Mediaeval Studies* 21 (1977), 50—70.

10. Breslow, B., 'The social status and economic interests of Richer de Refham, lord mayor of London,' *J. of Medieval History* 3 (1977), 135—45.

11. Jennings, J.M., 'The distribution of landed wealth in the wills of London merchants 1400—1450,' *Mediaeval Studies* 39 (1977), 261—80.

12. Not used.

13. Howell, C., 'Peasant inheritance customs in the Midlands, 1280—1700,' *Family and Inheritance: Rural Society in Western Europe* (ed. J. Goody, J. Thirsk, E.P. Thompson; Cambridge UP; 1976), 112—55.

14. Cornwall, J.C.K. 'Mediaeval peasant farmers,' *Records of Buckinghamshire* 20 (1975), 57—75.

15. Dewindt, E.B. *The LiberGersumarum of Ramsey Abbey: a calendar and index of B.L. Harley MS 445.* Leiden; Brill; 1976. Pp 455.

16. Raftis, J.A.; Hogan, M.P. *Early Huntingdonshire lay subsidy rolls.* Leiden; Brill; 1976. Pp 301.

17. Kristensson, G. *Studies on the early fourteenth-century population of Lindsey.* Lund; C.W.K. Gleerup (Scripta Minora Regiae Societatis Humaniorum Litterarum); 1977. Pp 39.

18. Lomas, R.A., 'Development in land tenure on the prior of Durham's estate in the later middle ages,' *Northern History* 13 (1977), 27—43.

19. Miles, D.; Rowley, T., 'Tusmore deserted village,' *Oxoniensia* 41 (1976), 309—15.

20. Cameron, A., 'The deserted medieval village of Sutton Passeys,' *T. of the Thoroton Soc.* 80 (1976), 47—62.

21. Brown, A.E., 'Chester on the Water: a deserted medieval hamlet,' *Northamptonshire Past and Present* 6 (1978), 15—19.

22. Burleigh, G.R., 'Further notes on deserted and shrunken medieval villages in Sussex,' *Sussex Arch. Collection* 114 (1976), 61—8.

23. Not used.

24. Brown, K.F., 'Two Walsall charters. 1 — The charter of William Ruffus to the burgesses of Walsall. 2 — Walsall borough charter, 1309,' *T. of the South Staffordshire Arch. and Historical Soc.* 17 (1975—6), 65—73.

25. Hall, R., 'An early Cockermouth charter,' *T. of the Cumberland and Westmorland Antiquarian and Arch. Soc.* 77 (1977), 75—81.

26. Dobson, R.B., 'Urban decline in late medieval England,' *T. of the Royal Historical Soc.* 5th ser. 27 (1977), 1—22.

27. Post, J.B., 'A fifteenth-century customary of the Southwark stews,' *J. of the Soc. of Archivists* 5 (1977), 418—28.

28. Sinclair Williams, C.L., 'The term "logh" in medieval Kentish documents,' *Archaeologia Cantiana* 92 (1977), 65—72.

29. Saltman, A. (ed.). *The Kniveton leiger.* London; HMSO; 1977. Pp xxxiv, 316.

30. Jefferies, P.J., 'Social mobility in the fourteenth century: the example of the Chelreys of Barkshire,' *Oxoniensia* 41 (1976), 324—36.

31. Faraday, M., 'Pre-parish register genealogy. 1 — Late medieval changes of residence,' *Genealogists' Magazine* 19 (1977), 129—30.

32. Sheppard, W.L., 'Pre-parish register genealogy. 2 — The ancestry of Sir Edward de St John of Londesborough,' ibid. 130—3.

33. Latta, C. *The commandery: the hospital of St Wulstan, Worcester.* Worcester; The City; 1977. Pp 32.

34. Gelling, P.S., 'Celtic continuity in the Isle of Man,' Ca24, 77—82.

(h) Naval and Military

1. Rose, S., 'Henry V's *Grace Dieu* and mutiny at sea: some new evidence,' *Mariner's Mirror* 63 (1977), 3—6.
2. Chibnall, M., 'Mercenaries and the *familia regis* under Henry I,' *History* 62 (1977), 15—23.
3. Runyan, T.J., 'Ships and mariners in later medieval England,' *J. of British Studies* 16 (1977), 1—17.
4. Sherborne, J.W., 'English barges and balingers of the late fourteenth century,' *Mariner's Mirror* 63 (1977), 109—14.
5. Hubbard, J.T.W., ' "En otros tiempos . . . ": did the men of Bristol discover Newfoundland in 1481?,' *American Neptune* 37 (1977), 157—63.
6. Howard, G.F., 'The date of the Hastings Manuscript ships [Pierpont Morgan MS M.775],' *Mariner's Mirror* 63 (1977), 215—18.
7. Glasgow, T., 'The date of the Hastings Manuscript ships [see Eh6],' *ibid.* 367—8.
8. Ritchie, N., 'Sir John Hawkwood, the first Anglo-Florentine,' *History Today* 27 (1977), 637—46.
9. Sherborne, J.W., 'The cost of English warfare with France in the later fourteenth century,' *B. of the Institute of Historical Research* 50 (1977), 135—50.
10. Morley, B.M., 'Hylton Castle,' *Arch. J.* 133 (1976), 118—34.
11. Williams, F. *Pleshey Castle, Essex (XII—XVI century): excavations in the bailey, 1959—1963.* Oxford; British Arch. Reports; 1977. Pp 251.
12. Rodwell, K.A., 'Excavations on the site of Banbury Castle,' *Oxoniensia* 41 (1976), 90—147.
13. Palmer, N., 'Excavations on the outer city wall of Oxford in St Helen's Passage and Hertford College,' *ibid.* 148—60.
14. Streeten, A.D.F., 'Excavations at Lansdowne Road, Tonbridge, 1972 and 1976,' *Archaeologia Cantiana* 92 (1977), 105—18.

(i) Intellectual and Cultural

1. Staines, D., 'Havelok the Dane: a thirteenth-century handbook for princes,' *Speculum* 51 (1976), 602—23.
2. Britton, D., 'Manuscripts associated with Kirby Bellars priory,' *T. of the Cambridge Bibliographical Soc.* 6 (1976), 267—84.
3. De la Mare, A.C., 'A fragment of Augustine in the hand of Theodericus Werken,' *ibid.* 285—90.
4. Doyle, E., 'A bibliographical list by William Woodford, O.F.M.,' *Franciscan Studies* 35 (1976 for 1975), 93—106.
5. Gál, G., 'Opiniones Ricardi Rufi Cornubiensis a censore reprobatae,' *ibid.* 136—93.
6. Aston, T.H., 'Oxford's medieval alumni,' *Past & Present* 74 (1977), 3—40.

7. Herrmann, E., 'Spätmittelalterliche englische Pseudoprophetien,' *Archiv für Kilturgeschichte* 57 (1975), 87–116.

8. Strohm, P., 'Chaucer's audience,' *Literature & History* 5 (1977), 26–41.

9. Nixon, H.M., 'Caxton, his contemporaries and successors in the book trade from Westminster documents,' *Library* 5th ser. 31 (1976), 305–26.

10. Moran, J. *Wynkyn de Worde, father of Fleet Street* (2nd revd. ed.). London; Wynkyn de Worde Soc.; 1976. Pp 60.

11. Edwards, F. *Ritual and drama: the medieval theatre.* Guildford; Lutterworth Press; 1976. Pp 127.

12. Maddison, F.; Pelling, M.; Webster, C. (ed.). *Essays on the life and work of Thomas Linacre, c. 1460–1524.* Oxford; Clarendon Press; 1977. Pp liii, 416.

13. Clough, C.C., 'Thomas Linacre, Cornelio Vitelli, and humanistic studies at Oxford,' Ei12, 1–23.

14. Thomson, D.F.S., 'Linacre's Latin Grammars,' Ei12, 24–35.

15. Schmitt, C.B., 'Thomas Linacre and Italy,' Ei12, 36–75.

16. Durling, R.J., 'Linacre and medieval humanism,' Ei12, 76–106.

17. Fletcher, J.M., 'Linacre's lands and lectureships,' Ei12, 107–97.

18. Webster, C., 'Thomas Linacre and the foundation of the College of Physicians,' Ei12, 198–222.

19. Lewis, R.G., 'The Linacre Lectureships subsequent to their foundation,' Ei12, 223–64.

20. Pelling, M., 'The refoundation of the Linacre Lectureships in the nineteenth century,' Ei12, 265–89.

21. Barber, G., 'Thomas Linacre: a bibliographical survey of his works,' Ei12, 290–336.

22. Pelling, M., 'Published references to Thomas Linacre,' Ei12, 337–53.

23. Hill, M., 'An iconography of Thomas Linacre,' Ei12, 354–74.

24. Pagel, W., 'Medieval humanism — a historical necessity in the era of the Renaissance,' Ei12, 375–86.

25. Arngart, O., 'Book-hand and court-hand: a question of co-ordination,' *Speculum* 52 (1977), 337–40.

26. Orlando, T.A., 'Roger Bacon and the *Testimonia gentilium de secta christiana*,' *Recherches de théologie ancienne et médiévale* 63 (1976), 202–18.

27. Kaluza, Z., 'La prétendue discussion de Thomas Bradwardine avec Thomas de Buckingham: Témoignage de Thomas de Cracovie,' ibid. 219–36.

28. Tyson, D.B., 'The epitaph of Edward the Black Prince,' *Medium Aevum* 46 (1977), 98–104.

29. Partner, N.F. *Serious entertainments: the writing of history in twelfth-century England.* Chicago/London; University of Chicago Press; 1977. Pp xi, 289.

30. Zinn, G.A., 'The influence of Hugh of St Victor's *Chronicon* on

the *Abbreviationes chronicorum* of Ralph of Diceto,' *Speculum* 52 (1977), 38—61.

31. Stow, G.B., 'Thomas Walsingham, John Malvern, and the *Vita Ricardi Secundim* 1377—1381: a reassessment,' *Mediaeval Studies* 39 (1977), 490—7.

32. Foster, B. (ed.). *The Anglo-Norman 'Alexander'*. Vol. 1: texts and variants; London; Anglo-Norman Text Soc.; 1976. Pp 300.

33. Metlitzki, D. *The matter of Araby in Medieval England*. New Haven/London; Yale UP; 1977. Pp xiii, 320.

34. Thomson, R.M., 'Geoffrey of Wells, De Infancia sancti Edmundi (BHL 2392),' *Analecta Bollandiana* 95 (1977), 25—42.

35. Lapidge, M., 'The medieval hagiography of St Ecgwine,' *Vale of Evesham Historical Soc. Research Papers* 6 (1977), 77—93.

36. Martin, J., 'John of Salisbury's manuscripts of Frontinus and of Gellius,' *J. of the Warburg and Courtauld Institutes* 40 (1977), 1—26.

37. Rouse, R.H., 'New light on the circulation of the A-text of Seneca's Tragedies [New College MS 21],' ibid. 283—6.

38. Hunt, R.W., 'The preface to the *Speculum ecclesiae* of Giraldus Cambrensis,' *Viator* 8 (1977), 189—213.

39. Otte, J.K., 'The role of Alfred of Sareshel (Alfredus Anglicus) and his commentary on the *Metheora* in the reacquisition of Aristotle,' ibid. 197—209.

40. Dales, R.C., 'Adam Marsh, Robert Grosseteste, and the Treatise on the Tides,' *Speculum* 52 (1977), 900—1.

41. Karadjole, M., 'Une correction de catalogues à propos de Roger Bacon,' *Recherches de théologie ancienne et médiévale* 64 (1977), 216—19.

42. Kitchel, M.J., 'Walter Burley's doctrine of the soul: another view,' *Mediaeval Studies* 39 (1977), 387—401.

43. Evans, G.R., ' "Interior homo": two great monastic scholars on the soul: St Anselm and Ailred of Rievaulx,' *Studia Monastica* 19 (1977), 57—73.

44. Evans, R.R., 'St Anselm and knowing God,' *J. of Theological Studies* new ser. 28 (1977), 430—44.

45. Evans, G.R., 'St Anselm's technical terms of rhetoric,' *Latomus* 36 (1977), 171—9.

46. Bestul, T.H., 'The Verdun Anselm, Ralph of Battle, and the formation of the Anselmian apocrypha,' *Revue Bénédictine* 87 (1977), 383—9.

47. Ward, B. *Anselm of Canterbury, a monastic scholar*. Oxford; S.L.G. Press; 1977. Pp 23.

48. Lawrence, C.H., 'The origin of the chancellorship at Oxford,' *Oxoniensia* 41 (1976), 316—23.

49. Orme, N.I., 'Evesham schools before the Reformation,' *Vale of Evesham Historical Soc. Research Papers* 6 (1977), 95—100.

Ei50

50. Keen, M., 'Chivalrous culture in fourteenth-century England,'
    La3, 1—24.
51. Hull, P.L., 'Thomas Chiverton's book of obits, part IV,' *Devon
    and Cornwall Notes and Queries* 33 (1977), 337—41.
52. Braddy, H., 'Chaucer, Alice Perrers and Cecily Chaumpaigne,'
    Speculum 52 (1977), 906—11.
53. Peterson, C.; Wilson, E., 'Hoccleve, the Old Hall manuscript,
    Cotton Nero A.x, and the *Pearl* poet,' *R. of English Studies* new
    ser. 28 (1977), 49—56.
54. Wilson, E., 'A middle English manuscript at Coughton Court,
    Warwickshire, and B.L. Harley MS 4012,' *Notes and Queries*
    new ser. 24 (1977), 295—303.
55. Stern, K., 'The London "Thornton" miscellany, II,' *Scriptorium*
    30 (1976), 201—18.
56. Brewer, D.S.; Owen, A.E.B. (ed.). *The Thornton Manuscript
    (Lincoln Cathedral MS 91).* Scolar Press; 1977. Pp 668.
57. Beadle, R.; Owen, A.E.B. (ed.). *The Findern Manuscript (Cam-
    bridge University Library MS Ff.1.6).* Scolar Press; 1977. Pp 338.
58. Ker, N.R. (intr.). *The Winchester Malory: a facsimile.* London;
    Oxford UP (EETS suppl. series 4); 1976. Pp 484.
59. Fisher, J.H., 'Chancery and the emergence of standard written
    English in the fifteenth century,' *Speculum* 52 (1977), 870—99.
60. Benskin, M., 'Local archives and middle English dialects,' *J. of the
    Soc. of Archivists* 5 (1977), 500—14.
61. Ayto, J., 'Marginalia in the manuscript [Cotton Faustina B.iii] of
    the *Life of St Edith*: a new light on early printing,' *The Library*
    5th ser. 32 (1977), 28—36.
62. Blake, N.F., 'A new approach to William Caxton [review article],'
    Book Collector 26 (1977), 380—5.
63. Greatrex, J.G., 'Humanistic script in a monastic register: an out-
    ward and visible sign?,' Bc6, 187—91.

(j) *The Visual Arts*

1. Royal Commission on Historical Monuments (England). *Ancient
   and historical monuments in the city of Salisbury (excluding the
   Cathedral Close).* London; HMSO; 1977. Pp 7.
2. Routh, P.E. *Medieval effigial alabaster tombs in Yorkshire.*
   Ipswich; Boydell Press; 1976. Pp 155.
3. Rigold, S.E., 'Structural aspects of medieval timber bridges:
   addenda,' *Medieval Archaeology* 20 (1976), 152—3.
4. Green, L., 'Merton Priory: twelfth century extension,' *Surrey
   Archaeological Collections* 71 (1977), 95—100.
5. Armitage, P.L.; Goodall, J.A., 'Medieval horned and polled sheep:
   the archaeological and iconographical evidence,' *Antiquaries J.*
   57 (1977), 73—89.
6. Rouse, E.C.; Varty, K., 'Medieval paintings of Reynard the Fox

36

in Gloucester Cathedral and some other related examples,' ibid. 104–17.

7. Young, P.A., 'The origin of the Herlufsholm ivory crucifix figure,' *Burlington Magazine* 119 (1977), 12–19.

8. Cooper, J.K.D., 'A re-assessment of some English late gothic and early "Renaissance" plate,' ibid. 408–12, 475–6.

9. Fernie, E.C., 'Alexander's frieze on Lincoln minster,' *Lincolnshire History and Archaeology* 12 (1977), 19–28.

10. King, D.J., 'An antiphon to St Edward in Taversham church,' *Norfolk Archaeology* 36 (1977), 387–91.

11. Lang, J.T., 'The St Helena Cross, Church Kelloe, Co. Durham,' *Archaeologia Aeliana* 5th ser. 5 (1977), 105–19.

12. Hewett, C.; Tatton-Brown, T., 'New structural evidence regarding Bell Harry Tower and the south-east spire at Canterbury,' *Archaeologia Cantiana* 92 (1977), 129–36.

13. Fernie, E.C., 'The romanesque piers of Norwich cathedral,' *Norfolk Archaeology* 36 (1977), 383–6.

14. Roberts, E., 'Moulding analysis and architectural research: the late middle ages,' *Architectural History* 20 (1977), 5–13.

15. Williams, R.A.H., 'An excavation at Neville Castle, Kirkby Moorside, North Yorkshire, 1974,' *Yorkshire Arch. J.* 49 (1977), 87–96.

16. Jones, S.R., 'West Bromwich (Staffs.) manor house,' *T. of the South Staffordshire Arch. and Historical Soc.* 17 (1977), 1–63.

17. Thompson, M., 'The construction of the manor at South Wingfield, Derbyshire,' *Problems of Economic and Social Archaeology: papers presented to Grahame Clark* (ed. G. de G. Sieveking, I.H. Longworth, K.E. Wilson; London; Duckworth; 1976), 417–38.

18. Child, P.; Laithwaite, M., 'Little Rull: a late medieval farmhouse near Cullompton,' *Devon Arch. Soc. P.* 33 (1975), 303–10.

19. Draper, J.C.. 'A fifteenth-century timber building at Segensworth farm, Titchfield, Hampshire,' *P. of the Hampshire Field Club* 33 (1976), 11–12.

20. Alcock, N.W.; Woodward, P.J., 'Cruck-frame buildings in Bedfordshire,' *Bedfordshire Arch. J.* 11 (1976), 51–68.

21. Gibson, A.V.B., 'A base cruck wall at Offley,' *Hertfordshire Archaeology* 4 (1974–76), 153–57.

22. Gibson, A.V.B., 'The medieval aisled barn at Parkbury Farm, Radlett: thirteenth-century rafters re-used,' ibid. 158–63.

23. Stevens, J., 'Recent discoveries in St Mary's parish church,' *Société Jersiaise Annual B.* 22 (1977), 67–8.

24. Fadden, K., 'An investigation beneath the floor of the church of St Andrew, Ampthill,' *Bedfordshire Arch. J.* 11 (1976), 77–9.

25. Blair, W.J., 'A monastic fragment at Wadham College, Oxford,' *Oxoniensia* 41 (1976), 161–7.

26. J.U.W., 'The Newmarch tomb in Whatton church, Nottinghamshire,' *The Coat of Arms* new ser. 2 (1977), 149–52.

27. Knight, S.; Keen, L., 'Medieval floor tiles from Guisborough priory, Yorkshire,' *Yorkshire Arch. J.* 49 (1977), 65—75.
28. Alvey, R.C., 'Medieval inlaid tiles from Lambley church, Notts.,' *T. of the Thoroton Soc.* 80 (1976), 82.
29. Hassall, J., 'Medieval pottery and a possible kiln site at Everton,' *Bedfordshire Arch. J.* 11 (1976), 69—75.
30. Barton, K.J., 'Medieval and post-medieval pottery from Gorcy Castle,' *Société Jersiaise Annual B.* 22 (1977), 69—82.
31. Zarnecki, G., 'English 12th-century sculpture and its resistance to St. Denis,' Bc3, 83—92.
32. Andersen, J. *The witch on the wall: medieval erotic sculpture in the British isles.* Copenhagen; Rosenkilde & Bagger; 1977. Pp 173.
33. Hinton, D.A., 'Fashions in floor-tiles,' Ca18, 307—12.
34. Hinton, D.A., ' "Rudely made earthen vessels" of the twelfth to fifteenth centuries A.D.,' Ca18, 221—38.

(k) Topography

1. Everitt, A., 'River and wold: reflections on the historical origin of regions and pays,' *J. of Historical Geography* 3 (1977), 1—19.
2. Rahtz, P.A. *Excavations at St Mary's Church, Deerhurst, 1971—73.* London; Council for British Archaeology; 1976. Pp iv, 59.
3. Hall, C.P.; Ravensdale, J.R. (ed.). *The west fields of Cambridge.* Cambridge Antiquarian Records Soc.; 1976. Pp xii, 168.
4. Hall, C.P., 'Application of field-names in the Cambridge west fields,' *J. of the English Place-Name Soc.* 9 (1977), 12—18.
5. Langton, J., 'Late medieval Gloucester: some data from a rental of 1455,' *T. of the Institute of British Geographers* new ser. 2 (1977), 259—77.
6. Le Patourel, H.E.J., 'Les sites fossoyés (moated sites) et leurs problèmes: l'organisation de la recherche en Grande-Bretagne,' *Revue du nord* 58 (1976), 571—92.
7. Turner, D.J., 'Moated site near Moat Farm, Hookwood, Charlwood,' *Surrey Arch. Collections* 71 (1977), 57—87.
8. Turner, D.J., 'Moated sites in Surrey: a provisional list,' ibid. 89—94.
9. Ketteringham, L.L., 'Excavations at the church of St John the Evangelist, Coulsdon,' ibid. 101—10.
10. Shearman, P., 'The topography of medieval Ewell and Cuddington: a reply,' ibid. 139—44.
11. Cloake, J., 'The Charterhouse of Sheen,' ibid. 145—98.
12. Darby, H.C. *Medieval Cambridgeshire.* Cambridge; Oleander Press; 1977. Pp 48.
13. Allen, J. *Heardred's Hill: a history of the parishes of Hartshill and Oldbury, North Warwickshire.* Part 3: Lords of the manor: the Hardreshulles of Hardreshulle, 1125 A.D. to 1367 A.D. Nuneaton; the author; 1977. Pp 53.
14. Hindle, B.P., 'Medieval roads in the diocese of Carlisle,' *T. of the*

Cumberland and Westmorland Antiquarian and Arch. Soc. 77
(1977), 83—95.

15. Bull, L., 'The ancient saltway from Droitwich to Princes Risborough,' *Records of Buckinghamshire* 20 (1975), 87—92.

16. Crook, D., 'Clipstone Park and "Peel",' *T. of the Thoroton Soc.*
80 (1976), 35—46.

17. Tinsley, H.M., 'Monastic woodland clearance on the Dieulacres
estate (North Staffordshire),' *North Staffordshire J. of Field
Studies* 16 (1976), 16—22.

18. Parfitt, J.H.; Rigold, S.E., 'A moated site at Moat Farm, Leigh,
Kent,' *Archaeologia Cantiana* 92 (1977), 173—201.

19. Lambrick, G.; Woods, H., 'Excavations on the second site of the
Dominican priory, Oxford,' *Oxoniensia* 41 (1976), 168—231.

20. Gilyard-Beer, R., 'Ipswich Blackfriars,' *P. of the Suffolk Institute
of Archaeology and History* 34 (1977), 15—23.

21. Blatchly, J.; Wade, K., 'Excavations at Ipswich Blackfriars in
1898 and 1976,' ibid. 25—34.

22. Fairclough, G.; Alvey, R.C., 'Excavations of two medieval and
post-medieval sites at Newark, 1975,' *T. of the Thoroton Soc.*
80 (1976), 1—34.

23. Simco, A., 'A medieval site at Rook Tree Lane, Stotfold,' *Bedfordshire Arch. J.* 11 (1976), 35—42.

24. Simco, A., 'Work at Newnham priory, Bedford,' ibid. 80—1.

25. Samuels, J., 'Cherry Lane, Barrow-upon-Humber, South Humberside,' *Lincolnshire History and Archaeology* 12 (1977), 29—40.

26. Black, G., 'The redevelopment of 20 Dean's Yard, Westminster
Abbey, 1975—77,' *T. of the London and Middlesex Arch. Soc.*
28 (1977), 190—210.

27. Taylor, P., 'A knight's fee at Acton, in the manor of Fulham,'
ibid. 316—22.

28. Sherlock, D., 'Horsham St Faith Priory: a further note,' *Norfolk
Archaeology* 36 (1977), 386—7.

29. Greene, P.; Hough, P., 'Excavation in the medieval village of
Norton 1974—1976 (part one),' *J. of the Chester Arch. Soc.* 60
(1977), 61—93.

30. Miles, H. and T., 'Pilton, North Devon: excavating within a
medieval village,' *Devon Arch. Soc. P.* 33 (1975), 267—95.

31. Steane, J.M.; Bryant, G.F.; Webster, P.A., 'Excavations at the
deserted medieval settlement at Lyveden,' *J. of the Northampton
Museums and Art Gallery* 12 (1975), 3—160.

32. Miles, T.J., 'The shrunken medieval town of Colyton,' *Devon
Arch. Soc. P.* 33 (1975), 297—302.

33. Keene, D.J., 'Thirteenth-century surveys of Winchester,' Da1,
509—19.

34. Cunliffe, B. *Excavations at Portchester Castle.* Vol. 3: Medieval,
the outer bailey and its defences. London; Soc. of Antiquaries
of London; 1977. Pp ix, 253.

35. Seymour, D.J. *Torre Abbey: an account of its history, buildings, cartularies and lands.* [Torquay; the author] ; 1977. Pp xvi, 303.

F. ENGLAND AND WALES, 1500–1714

See also: Aa1, 3, c1; Ba5; Ec1

(a) *General*

1. Thompson, R. (ed.). *Samuel Pepys' 'penny merriments': being a collection of chapbooks* [etc]. London; Constable; 1976. Pp 302.
2. Crummy, P.; Moyes, R.H., 'Portreeve's House, Colchester, and a method of modernizing Essex houses in the sixteenth and seventeenth centuries,' *Post-Medieval Archaeology* 10(1976), 89–103.
3. Warmington, R., 'Rebuilding of "Le Belle" inn, Andover, 1534,' ibid. 131–41.
4. Sylvester, R.S.; Marc'hadour, G. (ed.). *Essential articles for the study of Thomas More.* Hamden, Conn.; Archon Books; 1977. Pp xxiv, 676.
5. Clark, P.; Slack, P. *English towns in transition, 1500–1700.* London; Oxford UP; 1976. Pp vii, 176.
6. Fisher, R.M., 'Thomas Cromwell, dissolution of the monasteries, and the Inns of Court,' *J. of the Soc. of Public Teachers of Law* 15 (1977), 103–17.
7. Hoare, J., 'The death of Nell Gwynne,' *History Today* 36 (1977), 396–9.
8. Parkinson, C.N., 'Charles I's dwarf,' ibid. 380–4.
9. Elton, G.R. *Reform and Reformation: England 1509–1558.* London; Arnold; 1977. Pp viii, 423.
10. Downie, J.A., 'The attack on Robert Harley, M.P., by the Lewis brothers of Harpton Court in the streets of New Radnor, 2 October 1963,' *National Library of Wales J.* 20 (1977), 40–5.
11. Milward, R.J. *History of Wimbledon, part 3: Wimbledon in the time of the civil war.* [London; the author] ; 1976. Pp 165.
12. Deane, F.B. *Bramall Hall: the story of an Elizabethan manor house.* Stockport Metropolitan Borough; 1977. Pp x, 124.
13. Shuttleworth, J.M. (ed.). *The life of Edward, first lord Herbert of Cherbury.* London; Oxford UP; 1976. Pp xxviii, 156.
14. Drewett, P., 'The excavation of the Great Hall at Bolingbroke Castle, Lincolnshire, 1973,' *Post-Medieval Archaeology* 10 (1976), 1–24.
15. Ungerer, G. (ed.). *A Spaniard in Elizabethan England: the correspondence of Antonio Perez's exile*, vol. 2. London; Tamesis, 1976. Pp 450.

16. Hughes, J.J., 'The missing "Last Words" of Gilbert Burnet in July 1687,' *Historical J.* 20 (1977), 221–8.
17. Rowe, M.M. (ed.). *Tudor Exeter: tax assessments, 1489–1595, including the military survey, 1522.* Exeter; Devon & Cornwall Record Soc.; 1977. Pp xix, 106.
18. Crawford, P., ' "Charles Stuart, that Man of Blood",' *J. of British Studies* 16 (1977), 41–61.
19. Ollard, R.L. *The war without an enemy: a history of the English civil wars.* London; Hodder & Stoughton; 1976. Pp 224.
20. Copley, G.J. (ed.). *Camden's 'Britannia': Kent; Surrey and Sussex* (2 vols.). London; Hutchinson; 1977. Pp xxxii, 96; xxxii, 80.
21. Clark, P. *English provincial society from the Reformation to the Revolution: religion, politics and society in Kent, 1500–1640.* Hassocks; Harvester; 1977. Pp xiv, 503.
22. Moss, D.E., 'Roger Ascham,' *History Today* 27 (1977), 651–7.
23. Taswell, W., 'The plague and the fire: reminiscences of Restoration times by William Taswell,' *ibid.* 812–16.
24. Jarvis, R.C., 'Books of rates,' *J. of the Soc. of Archivists* 5 (1977), 515–26.
25. Clark, P. *English provincial society from the Reformation to the Revolution.* Hassocks; Harvester Press; 1977. Pp xiii, 504.
26. Kenyon, J.P. *The Stuarts: a study in English kinship* (revd. ed.). London; Severn House; 1977. Pp 223.
27. Richardson, R.C. *The debate on the English Revolution.* London; Methuen; 1977. Pp xi, 195.
28. Plowden, A. *Marriage with my kingdom: the courtships of Elizabeth I.* London; Macmillan; 1977. Pp 216.
29. Durant, D.N. *Bess of Hardwick: portrait of an Elizabethan dynast.* London; Weidenfeld & Nicolson; 1977. Pp xiii, 274.
30. Ellis, P.B. *The great fire of London: an illustrated account.* London; New English Library; 1976. Pp 126.
31. Pope, D. *Harry Morgan's way: the biography of Sir Henry Morgan, 1635–1684.* London; Secker & Warburg; 1977. Pp xx, 379.
32. Powell, K.; Cook, C. *English historical facts, 1485–1603.* London; Macmillan; 1977. Pp vii, 228.
33. Donno, E.S. (ed.) *An Elizabethan in 1582: the diary of Richard Madox, fellow of All Souls.* London; Hakluyt Soc.; 1976. Pp xvi, 365.
34. Wilson, D. *The world encompassed: Drake's great voyages 1577–1580.* London; Hamilton; 1977. Pp xiii, 240.
35. MacCulloch, D. (ed.). *The chorography of Suffolk.* Ipswich; Boydell Press; 1976. Pp x, 170.
36. Drake, G., 'Annotated bibliography for the life of Algernon Percy, 10th earl of Northumberland,' *Colorado College Studies* 13 (1975), 5–14.

(b) *Political*

1. Gruenfelder, J.K., 'The lord wardens and elections, 1604–1628,' *J. of British Studies* 16 (1976–7), 1–23.
2. Russell, C., 'The examination of Mr Mallory after the parliament of 1621,' *B. of the Institute of Historical Research* 50 (1977), 125–32.
3. Tyacke, N., 'Wroth, Cecil and the parliamentary session of 1604,' ibid. 120–5.
4. Ham, R.E., 'The autobiography of Sir James Croft,' ibid. 48–57.
5. Morton, A.L., 'The plebeian left in the English Revolution,' *Wissenschaftliche Zeitschrift der Wilhelm-Pieck-Universität Rostock* 25 (1976), 393–402.
6. Hill, B.W. *The growth of parliamentary parties, 1689–1742.* London; Allen & Unwin; 1976. Pp 265.
7. Horwitz, H. *Parliament, policy and politics in the reign of William III.* Manchester UP; 1977. Pp xiii, 385.
8. Holmes, G.S. *The electorate and the national will in the first age of party* [inaugural lecture]. Lancaster; The University; 1976. Pp 33.
9. Pam, D.O. *The rude multitude: Enfield and the civil war.* Enfield; Edmonton Hundred Historical Soc.; 1977. Pp 17.
10. Tittler, R. *Nicholas Bacon: the making of a Tudor statesman.* London; Cape; 1976. Pp 256.
11. Dockray, K.R., 'The troubles of the Yorkshire Plumptons,' *History Today* 27 (1977), 459–66, 482.
12. Cotton, A.N.B., 'Cromwell and the self-denying ordinance,' *History* 62 (1977), 211–31.
13. Russell, C., 'The foreign policy debate in the House of Commons in 1621,' *Historical J.* 20 (1977), 289–309.
14. Morrill, J.S., 'Provincial squires and "middling sorts" in the Great Rebellion,' ibid. 229–36.
15. Lehmberg, S.E. *The later parliaments of Henry VIII, 1536–1547.* Cambridge UP; 1977. Pp ix, 379.
16. Swanson, R.N., 'The second Northamptonshire election of 1701,' *Northamptonshire Past and Present* 6 (1978), 29–31.
17. Schwoerer, L.G., 'Press and parliament in the Revolution of 1689,' *Historical J.* 20 (1977), 5454–67.
18. Nourse, G.B., 'Richard Cromwell's house of commons,' *B. of the John Rylands University Library of Manchester* 60 (1977), 95–113.
19. Robinson, W.R.B., 'Sir George Herbert of Swansea, (d. 1570),' *B. of the Board of Celtic Studies* 27 (1977), 303–9.
20. Rondet, C., 'Fidélités et clientèles dans l'Angleterre d'Elizabeth et des Stuarts,' *Revue du Nord* 59 (1977), 317–41.
21. Bard, N.P., 'The ship money case and William Fiennes, viscount Saye and Sele,' *B. of the Institute of Historical Research* 50 (1977), 177–84.

22. Snyder, H.L., 'A new parliamentary list for 1711,' ibid. 185—93.
23. Kenyon, J.P. *Revolution principles: the politics of party, 1689—1720.* Cambridge UP; 1977. Pp viii, 248.
24. Stieg, M.F. (ed.). *The diary of John Harington, M.P., 1646—53: with notes of his charges.* [Yeovil] ; Somerset Record Soc.; 1977. Pp viii, 121.
25. Howell, R. *Cromwell.* London; Hutchinson; 1977. Pp xii, 269.
26. Chapman, H.W. *Four fine gentlemen.* London; Constable; 1977. Pp 301.
27. Bradshaw, B., 'Cromwellian reform and the origins of the Kildare rebellion,' *T. of the Royal Historical Soc.* 5th ser. 27 (1977), 69—93.
28. Bruce, M.L. *The making of Henry VIII.* London; Collins; 1977. Pp 254.
29. Cornwall, J. *Revolt of the peasantry 1549.* London; Routledge; 1977. Pp xi, 254.
30. Swales, R.J.W., 'The Howard interest in Sussex elections, 1529—1558,' *Sussex Arch. Collections* 114 (1976), 49—60.
31. Land, S.K. *Kett's rebellion.* Ipswich; Boydell Press; 1977. Pp 184.
32. Edwards, P.S., 'The parliamentary representation of Welsh boroughs in the mid-sixteenth century,' *B. of the Board of Celtic Studies* 27 (1977), 425—39.
33. Gruenfelder, J.K., 'Yorkshire borough elections, 1603—1640,' *Yorkshire Arch. Soc.* 49 (1977), 101—14.
34. Hitchcock, J., 'The misconduct of Lord Latimer, 1553—1560,' ibid. 97—100.
35. Adams, S.L., 'Captain Thomas Gainsford, the "Vox Spiritus" and the *Vox Populi*,' *P. of the Institute of Historical Research* 49 (1976), 141—4.
36. Ham, R.E. *The country and the kingdom: Sir Herbert Croft and the Elizabethan state.* Washington; UP of America; 1977. Pp x, 301.

(c) Constitution, Administration and Law

1. Schoeck, R.J., 'The place of Sir Thomas More in legal history and tradition: a sketch with some observations,' *Moreana* 51 (1976), 83—94.
2. Jensen, J.V., 'The staff of the Jacobean privy council,' *Huntingdon Library Q.* 40 (1976), 11—44.
3. McGurk, J.J.N., 'Royal purveyance in the shire of Kent, 1590—1614,' *B. of the Institute of Historical Research* 50 (1977), 58—68.
4. Tittler, R., 'The incorporation of boroughs, 1540—1558,' *History* 62 (1977), 24—42.
5. Morrill, J.S., 'English local government in the early modern period [review article] ,' *Archives* 13 (1977), 41—7.

6. Robinson, W.R.B., 'The charter granted to Chepstow by Charles, earl of Worcester, in 1524,' *National Library of Wales J.* 20 (177), 85—94.

7. Cockburn, J.S. (ed.). *Calendar of assize records: Hertfordshire indictments, Elizabeth I.* London; HMSO; 1975. Pp vii, 268.

8. Guy, J.A. *The cardinal's court: The impact of Thomas Wolsey in star chamber.* Hassocks; Harvester Press; 1977. Pp x, 191.

9. Nenner, H. *By colour of law: legal culture and constitutional politics in England, 1660—1689.* Chicago; University of Chicago Press; 1977. Pp xx, 251.

10. Roberts, C., 'The constitutional significance of the financial settlement of 1690,' *Historical J.* 20 (1977), 59—76.

11. Deab, W., 'The law of criminal procedure in *The Contention between Liberality and Prodigality*,' *Renaissance and Reformation* new ser. 1 (1977), 59—71.

12. Davis, J. *The case of the pretended marriage: Hide v. Emerton, 1674—1683.* Aldbury; Church Farm House Publications; 1976. Pp 38.

13. Langbein, J.H. *Torture and the law of proof: Europe and England in the ancient regime.* Chicago; University of Chicago Press; 1977. Pp x, 229.

14. Smith, A.G.R. *Servant of the Cecils: the life of Sir Michael Hickes, 1543—1612.* London; Cape; 1977. Pp 221.

15. Green, D.G., 'The court of the Marshalsea in late Tudor and Stuart England,' *American J. of Legal History* 20 (1976), 267—81.

16. Cockburn, J.S. (ed.). *Western Circuit assize orders, 1629—1648: a calendar.* London; Royal Historical Soc. (Camden 4th series, 17); 1976. Pp xiv, 352.

17. Cook, S.G., 'The Congregational Independents and the Cromwellian constitutions,' *Church History* 46 (1977), 335—57.

18. Elton, G.R., 'Mid-Tudor finance [review article],' *Historical J.* 20 (1977), 737—40.

19. Guy, J.A., 'Thomas More as successor to Wolsey,' *Thought (Fordham University Q.)* 52 (1977), 275—92.

20. Spence, R.T., 'The pacification of the Cumberland borders, 1593—1628,' *Northern History* 13 (1977), 59—160.

21. Ham, R.E., 'The four-shire controversy,' *Welsh Historical R.* 8 (1977), 381—99.

22. Swales, R.J.W., 'The ship-money levy of 1628,' *B. of the Institute of Historical Research* 50 (1977), 164—76.

23. Hawkins, M. *Unpublished state papers of the English Civil War and Interregnum* [introduction to parts 1—5]. Hassocks; Harvester Press; 1977. Pp 80.

24. Sherwood, R.E. *The court of Oliver Cromwell.* London; Croom Helm; 1977. Pp 196.

25. Knafla, L.A. *Law and politics in Jacobean England: the tracts of Lord Chancellor Ellesmere.* Cambridge UP; 1977. Pp xxvii, 355.

26. Ward, P.L. (ed.). *William Lambarde's notes on the procedure and privileges of the house of commons (1584).* House of Commons Library Document No. 10. London; HMSO; 1977. Pp 96.
27. Graves, M.A.R., 'Freedom of peers from arrest: the case of Henry second lord Cromwell,' *American J. of Legal History* 21 (1977), 1–14.
28. Foster, E.R., 'The house of lords and ordinances 1641–1649,' ibid. 157–73.
29. Woods, R.L., 'Politics and precedent: Wolsey's parliament of 1523,' *Huntington Library Q.* 40 (1977), 297–312.
30. Streitberger, W.R., 'A letter from Edmund Tilney to Sir William More,' *Surrey Arch. Collections* 71 (1977), 225–31.
31. Baker, J.H. *The Reports of Sir John Spelman,* vol. 1. London; Selden Soc.; 1977. Pp li, 238.
32. Boyer, L.M., 'The justice of the peace in England and America from 1506 to 1776: a bibliographic history,' *Q. J. of the Library of Congress* 34 (1977), 315–26.
33. Ives, E.W. (ed.). *Letters and accounts of William Brereton of Malpas.* The Record Soc. of Lancashire and Cheshire, vol. CXVI; 1976. Pp ix, 290.
34. Baker, J.H., 'Criminal courts and procedure at common law, 1550–1800,' Bc7, 15–48.
35. Cockburn, J.S., 'The nature and incidence of crime in England 1559–1625: a preliminary survey,' Bc7, 49–71.
36. Macfarlane, A.D.J., 'Witchcraft in Tudor and Stuart Essex,' Bc7, 72–89.
37. Sharpe, J.A., 'Crime and delinquency in an Essex parish 1600–1640,' Bc7, 90–109.
38. Ingram, M.J., 'Communities and courts: law and disorder in early-seventeenth-century Wiltshire,' Bc7, 110–34.
39. Curtis, T.C., 'Quarter sessions appearances and their background: a seventeenth-century regional study,' Bc7, 135–54.
40. Snow, V.F. (ed.). *Parliament in Elizabethan England: John Hooker's Order and Usage.* New Haven/London; Yale UP; 1977. Pp xiv, 221.
41. Cole, M.J., 'Checklist of holdings of the Yale Center for Parliamentary History,' *Albion* 9 (1977), 2–39.

(d) External Affairs

1. Refai, G.Z., 'Sir George Oxinden and Bombay, 1662–1669,' *English Historical R.* 92 (1977), 573–81.
2. Marshall-Cornwall, J., 'An English arctic expedition, 1533,' *History Today* 27 (1977), 741–6.
3. Barrie, V., 'La prohibition du commerce avec la France dans la politique anglaise à la fin du XVIIème siècle,' *Revue du Nord* 59 (1977), 343–64.

4. McJimsey, R.D., 'Concepts of English foreign policy, 1689—1697,' *Colorado College Studies* 13 (1975), 27—38.
5. Hollaender, A.E.J., 'Mr Resident George Stepney and the "Pietas Austriaca", 1693,' Bc3, 217—27.

(e) *Religion*

1. Tolmie, M., 'Thomas Lambe, soapboiler, and Thomas Lambe, merchant, general baptists,' *Baptist Q.* 27 (1977), 4—13.
2. Hurwich, J.J., 'Dissent and catholicism in English society: a study of Warwickshire, 1660—1720,' *J. of British Studies* 16 (1976—7), 24—58.
3. Chambers, B., 'The first French New Testament printed in England,' *Bibliothèque d'humanisme et renaissance* 39 (1977), 143—8.
4. King, J.N., 'Freedom of the press, protestant propaganda and Protector Somerset,' *Huntington Library Q.* 40 (1976), 1—10.
5. Backus, I., 'Laurence Tomson (1539—1608) and Elizabethan puritanism,' *J. of Ecclesiastical History* 28 (1977), 17—27.
6. Willis, A.J. (ed.). *Church life in Kent: being church records of the Canterbury diocese, 1559—1563.* London; Phillimore; 1975. Pp viii, 97.
7. Dunn, T.F., 'The development of the text of Pole's *De Unitate Ecclesiae,' Papers of the Bibliographical Soc. of America* 70 (1976), 455—68.
8. Haigh, C.A., 'Puritan evangelism in the reign of Elizabeth I,' *English Historical R.* 92 (1977), 30—58.
9. Cross, M.C. *Church and people, 1450—1660: the triumph of the laity in the English Church.* Hassocks; Harvester; 1976. Pp 272.
10. Sheldrake, P., 'Thomas More and authority,' *Month* 238 (1977), 122—5, 134.
11. Luoma, J.K., 'Restitution or Reformation? Cartwright and Hooker on the Elizabethan Church,' *Historical Magazine of the Protestant Episcopal Church* 46 (1977), 85—106.
12. Clark, P., 'Josias Nicholls and religious radicalism, 1553—1639,' *J. of Ecclesiastical History* 28 (1977), 133—50.
13. Bowker, M., 'The Henrician Reformation and the parish clergy,' *B. of the Institute of Historical Research* 50 (1977), 30—47.
14. Bond, R.B., 'Cranmer and the controversy surrounding publication of *Certayne Sermons or Homilies* (1547),' *Renaissance and Reformation* 12 (1976), 28—35.
15. Sundstrom, R.A., 'French huguenots and the civil list, 1696—1727: a study of alien assimilation in England,' *Albion* 8 (1976), 219—35.
16. Gruffyd, R.G. *'In that gentle country — ': the beginnings of puritan nonconformity in Wales.* Bridgend; Evangelical Library of Wales; 1976. Pp 31.

17. Buchanan, C.O. *What did Cranmer think he was doing?* Bramcote; Grove Books; 1976. Pp 32.
18. Kalu, O.U., 'Bishops and puritans in early Jacobean England: a perspective on methodology,' *Church History* 45 (1976), 469–89.
19. Hilton, J.A., 'Catholicism in Elizabethan Durham,' *Recusant History* 14 (1977), 1–8.
20. Parmiter, G. de C., 'Plowden, Englefield and Sandford, II: 1585–1609,' ibid. 9–25.
21. Evetts-Secker, J., 'Fuga Saeculi or Holy Hatred of the World: John Donne and Henry Hawkins,' ibid. 40–52.
22. Clarke, D.M., 'Conformity certificates among the king's bench records: a calendar,' ibid. 53–63.
23. Newman, P.R., 'Catholic royalist activists in the north, 1642–46,' ibid. 26–38.
24. Elliott, Brian, 'The earl Quakers of Monk Bretton, 1657–1700: a study of dissent in a south Yorkshire village,' *T. of the Hunter Arch. Soc.* 10 (1977), 260–72.
25. Shane, A.L., 'Rabbi Jacob Judah Leon (Templo) of Amsterdam (1603–1675) and his connection with England,' *T. of the Jewish Historical Soc. of England* 25 (1977 for 1973–5), 120–36.
26. Samuel, E.R. 'David Gabay's 1660 letter from London,' ibid. 38–42.
27. More, T. *Treatise on the Passion; Treatise on the Blessed Body; Instruction and prayers* (ed. G.E. Haupt). New Haven/London; Yale UP; 1976. Pp clxxxiv, 364.
28. More, T. *A dialogue of comfort against tribulation* (ed. L.L. Martz and F. Manley). New Haven/London; Yale UP; 1976. Pp clxvii, 566.
29. More, T. *De Tristitia Christi* (2 parts; ed. C.H. Miller). New Haven/London; Yale UP; 1976. Pp xiv, 1192.
30. Lupton, L. *A history of the Geneva bible, vol. 8: Faith; a supplementary volume containing a study of a poetic agent, Henry Lok.* London; Olive Tree; 1976. Pp 223.
31. Beddard, R.A., 'Sheldon and Anglican recovery,' *Historical J.* 19 (1976), 1005–17.
32. Guttentag, G.D., 'The beginnings of the Newcastle Jewish community,' *T. of the Jewish Historical Soc. of England* 25 (1977 for 1973–5), 1–24.
33. Blethen, H.I., 'Episcopacy and stability in the Restoration settlement,' *Historical Magazine of the Protestant Episcopal Church* 16 (1977), 209–14.
34. Duffy, E., 'A rubb-up for Old Soares: Jesuits, Jansenists, and the English secular clergy, 1705–1715,' *J. of Ecclesiastical History* 28 (1977), 291–317.
35. Foster, S., 'The faith of a separatist layman: the authorship, con-

47

text and significance of *The Cry of a Stone*,' *William and Mary Q.* 3rd ser. 34 (1977), 375—403.

36. Rechtien, J.G., 'Antithetical literary structures in the Reformation theology of Walter Travers,' *Sixteenth-Century J.* 8/1 (1977), 51—60.
37. Black, T., 'Thomas Cromwell's patronage of preaching,' ibid. 37—50.
38. VanderSchaaf, M.E., 'Archbishop Parker's efforts toward a Bucerian discipline in the Church of England,' ibid. 85—103.
39. Hilton, J.A., 'Catholicism in Jacobean Durham,' *Recusant History* 14 (1977), 78—85.
40. Forster, A.M.C., 'The oath tendered [i.e. of supremacy],' ibid. 86—96.
41. Hodgetts, M., 'Elizabethan priest-holes, VI: the escape of Charles II,' ibid. 97—126.
42. Sutherland, N.M., 'The English refugees at Geneva, 1555—1559,' *History Today* 27 (1977), 779—87.
43. White, B.R., 'Early Baptist letters (1),' *Baptist Q.* 27 (1977), 142—9.
44. Kelley, D.R., 'The conscience of the king's "good servant" [Thomas More],' *Thought (Fordham University Q.)* 52 (1977), 293—9.
45. Martz, L.L., 'Thomas More: the sacramental life,' ibid. 300—18.
46. Seaver, P., 'Le puritanisme: communauté et continuité dans l'Angleterre pré-révolutionnaire,' *Revue du Nord* 59 (1977), 299—316.
47. Gwynn, R.D., 'James II in the light of his treatment of Huguenot refugees in England, 1685—1686,' *English Historical R.* 112 (1977), 820—33.
48. Hilton, J.A., 'Catholicism in Elizabethan Northumberland,' *Northern History* 13 (1977), 44—58.
49. Zell, M.L., 'The use of religious preambles as a measure of religious belief in the sixteenth century,' *B. of the Institute of Historical Research* 50 (1977), 246—9.
50. Jenkins, G.H., 'Popular beliefs in Wales from the Restoration to Methodism,' *B. of the Board of Celtic Studies* 27 (1977), 440—62.
51. Heal, F.; O'Day, R. (ed.). *Church and society in England, Henry VIII to James I.* London; Macmillan; 1977. Pp vi, 206.
52. Heal, F.; O'Day, R., 'Introduction,' Fe51, 1—14.
53. Cross, M.C., 'Churchmen and royal supremacy,' Fe51, 15—34.
54. Palliser, D.M., 'Popular reactions to the Reformation during the years of uncertainty 1530—1570,' Fe51, 35—56.
55. Luxton, I., 'The Reformation and popular culture,' Fe51, 57—77.
56. R. Houlbrooke, 'The Protestant episcopate 1547—1603: the pastoral contribution,' Fe51, 78—98.
57. Heal, F., 'Economic problems of the Church,' Fe51, 99—118.

58. Kitching, C., 'The disposal of monastic and chantry lands,' Fe51, 119—136.
59. O'Day, R., 'Ecclesiastical patronage,' Fe51, 137—55.
60. Sheils, W.J., 'Religion in provincial towns,' Fe51, 156—76.
61. Anderson, A.B., 'A study in the sociology of religious persecution: the first Quakers,' *J. of Religious History* 9 (1977), 247—62.
62. Tolmie, M. *The triumph of the saints: the separate churches of London, 1616—1649.* Cambridge UP; 1977. Pp xii, 251.
63. Shuffelton, F. *Thomas Hooker, 1586—1647.* Princeton UP; 1977. Pp xii, 324.
64. Emmison, F.G., 'Tithes, perambulations and sabbath-breach in Elizabethan Essex,' Bc3, 177—215.
65. Walker, D., 'The Reformation in Wales,' Bc4, 54—78.
66. Jones, R.T., 'Relations between anglicans and dissenters: the promotion of piety 1670—1730,' Bc4, 79—102.
67. Dunning, R.D., 'Revival at Glastonbury, 1530—9,' Bc6, 213—22.
68. Collinson, P., ' "A magazine of religious patterns": an Erasmian topic transposed in English protestantism,' Bc6, 223—49.
69. Duffy, E., 'Primitive Christianity revived: religious renewal in Augustan England,' Bc6, 287—300.
70. Fletcher, A., 'Concern for renewal in the root and branch debates of 1641,' Bc6, 279—86.
71. Patterson, W.B., 'The anglican reaction [to the Lutheran Concord of 1576],' *Discord, Dialogue and Concord: Studies in the Lutheran Reformation's Formula of Concord* (ed. L.W. Spitz, W. Lohff; Philadelphia, Fortune Press, 1977), 150—65.
72. Manning, R.B., 'The making of a protestant aristocracy: the ecclesiastical commissioners of the diocese of Chester,' *B. of the Institute of Historical Research* 49 (1976), 60—79.
73. Fisher, R.M., 'Reform, repression and unrest at the Inns of Court, 1518—1558,' *Historical J.* 20 (1977), 783—801.
74. Milward, P. (ed.). *Religious controversies of the Elizabethan age: a survey of printed sources.* London; Scolar Press; 1977. Pp xv, 202.

(f) Economic Affairs

1. Jewell, C.A., 'The impact of America on English agriculture,' *Agricultural History* 50 (1976), 125—36.
2. Shipley, N.R., 'Thomas Sutton: Tudor-Stuart moneylender,' *Business History R.* 50 (1976), 456—76.
3. Shimwell, D.W., 'Sheep grazing intensity in Edale, Derbyshire, 1692—1747, and its effect on blanket pest erosion,' *Derbyshire Arch. J.* 94 (1976 for 1974), 35—40.
4. Bettey, J.H., 'The development of water meadows in Dorset during the seventeenth century,' *Agricultural History R.* 25 (1977), 37—43.

5. Walker, I.C., 'Churchwarden clay tobacco-pipes and the Southorn pipemaking family of Broseley, Shropshire,' *Post-Medieval Archaeology* 10 (1976), 142—9.

6. Charters, J.A., 'Road carrying in England in the seventeenth century: myth and reality,' *Economic History R.* 2nd ser. 30 (1977), 73—94.

7. Samuel, E.R., 'Sir Francis Child's jewellery business,' *Three Banks R.* 113 (1977), 43—55.

8. Kerridge, E., 'The coal industry in Tudor and Stuart England: a comment,'; D.C. Coleman, 'The coal industry: a rejoinder,' *Economic History R.* 2nd ser. 30 (1977), 340—5.

9. Holderness, B.A. *Pre-industrial England: economy and society, 1500—1750.* London; Dent; 1976. Pp 244.

10. Phillips, C.B., 'Iron-mining in Restoration Furness: the case of Sir Thomas Preston — a comment,' *Recusant History* 14 (1977), 39.

11. Thompson, R.H., 'Gloucester farthings, 1657—1662,' *British Numismatic J.* 45 (1975), 77—91.

12. Challis, C.E., 'Mint officials and moneyers of the Tudor period,' ibid. 51—76.

13. Woodward, D., 'Ships, masters and shipowners of the Wirral, 1550—1650,' *Mariner's Mirror* 63 (1977), 233—47.

14. Ramsay, G.D., 'Clothworks, Merchant Adventurers and Richard Hakluyt,' *English Historical R.* 92 (1977), 504—21.

15. Vanes, J. *The port of Bristol in the sixteenth century.* Bristol Branch of the Hist. Ass.; 1977. Pp 26.

16. Burke, V., 'The economic consequences of recusancy in Elizabethan Worcestershire,' *Recusant History* 14 (1977), 71—7.

17. Woodward, D., 'Ships, masters and shipowners of the Wirral, 1550—1650,' *Maritime History* 5 (1977), 1—25.

18. Chartres, J.A. *Internal trade in England, 1500—1700.* London; Macmillan; 1977. Pp 79.

19. Beckett, J.V., 'English landownership in the later seventeenth and eighteenth centuries: the debate and the problem,' *Economic History R.* 2nd ser. 30 (1977), 567—81.

20. Jarrett, M.G.; Wrathmell, S., 'Sixteenth- and seventeenth-century farmsteads: West Whelpington, Northumberland,' *Agricultural History R.* 25 (1977), 108—19.

21. Hopkinson, G.E., 'The development of the south Yorkshire and north Derbyshire coalfield, 1500—1775,' Bc1, 1—30.

22. Woodward, W.D., 'A comparative study of the Irish and Scottish livestock trade in the seventeenth century,' Bc9, 147—64.

23. Arnold, C.J., 'The clay tobacco pipe industry: an economic study,' Ca18, 313—36.

24. Tittler, R., 'The English fishing industry in the sixteenth century: the case of Great Yarmouth,' *Albion* 9 (1977), 40—60.

(g) Social History (General)

1. Brinkworth, E.R.C.; Gibson, J.S.W. (ed.). *Banbury wills and inventories, part 2: 1621–1650.* Banbury Historical Soc.; 1976. Pp vi, 193.

2. Clark, P., 'The ownership of books in England, 1560–1640: the example of some Kentish townsfolk,' *Schooling and Society*, ed. L. Stone (Baltimore; Johns Hopkins UP; 1976), 95–114.

3. Thomas, D., 'Leases in reversion on the crown's lands', *Economic History R.* 2nd ser. 30 (1977), 67–72.

4. Stone, L., 'Ages of admission to educational institutions in Tudor and Stuart England,' *History of Education* 6 (1977), 9.

5. Gibson, J.S.W., 'Trouble over sheep-pens [at Banbury],' *Cake & Cockhorse* 7 (1976–7), 35–48.

6. Bard, N., 'Local influence and family connections of the first viscount Saye and Sele,' ibid. 67–87.

7. Heselton, K.Y. *Sunbury household effects, 1673–1724* [probate inventories]. Sunbury-on-Thames; Local History Soc.; 1976. Pp 16.

8. May, P. (ed.). *Newmarket inventories, 1662–1715.* Newmarket; the editor; 1976. Pp iv, 44.

9. Simpson, D.H. *Twickenham society in Queen Anne's reign from the letters of Isabella Wentworth.* Twickenham Local History Soc.; 1976. Pp 34.

10. Thomas, K.V. *Rule and misrule in the schools of early modern England.* Reading; The University; 1976. Pp 35.

11. McMullen, N., 'The education of the English gentlewoman 1540–1640,' *History of Education* 6 (1977), 87–101.

12. Cressy, D., 'Levels of illiteracy in England, 1530–1730,' *Historical J.* 20 (1977), 1–23.

13. Manning, R.B., 'Violence and social conflict in mid-Tudor rebellions,' *J. of British Studies* 16/2 (1977), 18–40.

14. York, B.A., 'The origins of Kettering grammar school,' *Northamptonshire Past and Present* 6 (1978), 21–7.

15. Gibson, J.S.W., 'A century of tavern-keeping, Part I: The Stokes family at the Unicorn and Three Tuns [Banbury],' *Cake & Cockhorse* 7 (1977), 103–15.

16. Haynes, A., 'Italian immigrants in England, 1550–1603,' *History Today* 27 (1977), 526–34.

17. Shapiro, S.C., 'Feminists in Elizabethan England,' ibid. 703–11.

18. Haem, M., 'La répression du banditisme en Grande-Bretagne aux XVIIème et XVIIIème siècles,' *Revue du Nord* 59 (1977), 365–75.

19. Russell, E., 'The influx of commoners into the University of Oxford before 1581: an optical illusion?,' *English Historical R.* 112 (1977), 721–45.

20. Gentles, I., 'The purchasers of Northamptonshire crown lands, 1649—1660,' *Midland History* 3 (1976), 206—32.

21. Phillips, C.B., 'The royalist composition papers and the landed income of the gentry: a note of warning from Cumbria,' *Northern History* 13 (1977), 161—74.

22. Blackwood, B.G., 'The catholic and protestant gentry of Lancashire during the civil war period,' *T. of the Historic Soc. of Lancashire and Cheshire* 126 (1977 for 1976), 1—29.

23. McConica, J.K., 'The social relations of Tudor Oxford,' *T. of the Royal Historical Soc.* 5th ser. 27 (1977), 115—34.

24. Salgado, G. *The Elizabethan underworld.* London; Dent; 1977. Pp 221.

25. Cornwall, J., 'Sussex wealth and society in the reign of Henry VIII,' *Sussex Arch. Collections* 114 (1976), 1—27.

26. Brent, C.E., 'Rural unemployment and population in Sussex between 1550 and 1640,' ibid. 27—48.

27. Wrightson, K., 'Aspects of social differentiation in rural England, c. 1580—1660,' *J. of Peasant Studies* 5 (1977), 33—47.

28. Berker, J., 'William and Rebecca George (Powell) and their town house, now Gloucester House, 60 Dyer Street [Cirencester],' Bc8, 113—25.

(h) Social Structure and Population

1. Ripley, P., 'Trade and social structure of Gloucester, 1600—1640,' *T. of the Bristol and Gloucestershire Arch. Soc.* 1977 (for 1976), 117—23.

2. Kettle, A.J. (ed.). *A list of families in the archdeaconry of Stafford.* Staffordshire Record Soc.; 1976. Pp xxvi, 216.

3. Jones, G. *The gentry and the Elizabethan state.* Swansea; C. Davies; 1977. Pp 114.

4. Alcock, N.W. *Stoneleigh villagers, 1597—1650.* Coventry; University of Warwick; 1975. Pp viii, 58.

5. Howard, A.J.; Stoate, T.L. (ed.). *The Devon muster roll for 1569.* Bristol; T.L. Stoate; 1977. Pp xix, 283.

6. Shammas, C., 'The determinants of personal wealth in seventeenth-century England and America,' *J. of Economic History* 37 (1977), 675—89.

7. Stone, L. *The family, sex and marriage in England, 1500—1800.* London; Weidenfeld & Nicolson; 1977. Pp xxxi, 800.

8. Thirsk, J., 'The European debate on customs of inheritance, 1500—1700,' *Family and inheritance: rural society in western Europe 1200—1800*, ed. J. Goody, J. Thirsk, E.P. Thompson (Cambridge UP; 1977), 177—91.

9. Spufford, M., 'Peasant inheritance customs and land distribution in Cambridgeshire from the sixteenth to the eighteenth centuries,' ibid. 156—76.

10. Holmes, 'Gregory King and the social structure of pre-industrial England,' *T. of the Royal Historical Society* 5th ser. 27 (1977), 41–68.

11. *Deanery of Walsall. Walsall parish register: Walsall baptisms 1646–1675, marriages 1662–1754.* [Dudley]; Staffordshire Parish Registers Soc.; 1975. Pp 155.

12. Yates, E.M. *Tudor Greatham: a social geography of a Hampshire village.* [London; King's College Dept. of Geography]; 1977. Pp 60.

13. Bestall, J.M.; Fowkes, D.V. (ed.). *Chesterfield wills and inventories, 1521–1603.* Matlock; Derbyshire Record Soc.; 1977. Pp xxxiv, 348.

14. McGrath, P.; Williams, M.E. (ed.). *Bristol wills, 1546–1593.* University of Bristol; 1975. Pp ix, 90.

(i) Naval and Military

1. Millar, G.J., 'Mercenaries under Henry VIII, 1544–46,' *History Today* 27 (1977), 173–82.

2. Webb, S.S., 'Army and empire: English garrison government in Britain and America, 1569 to 1763,' *William and Mary Q.* 3rd ser. 34 (1977), 1–31.

3. Scouller, R.E.,. 'The Peninsula in the war of the Spanish Succession,' *J. of the Soc. for Army Historical Research* 55 (1977), 35–53.

4. Burg, R.R., 'Legitimacy and authority: a case study of pirate commanders in the seventeenth and eighteenth centuries,' *American Neptune* 37 (1977), 40–9.

5. Frey, L.; Frey, M., 'The Anglo-Prussian war of 1704,' *Canadian J. of History* 11 (1976), 283–94.

6. Barbary, J. *Puritan and Cavalier: the English civil war.* London; Gollancz; 1977. Pp 192.

7. Bence-Jones, M. *The cavaliers.* London; Constable; 1976. Pp xi, 206.

8. Ridley, J. *The roundheads.* London; Constable; 1976. Pp xi, 276.

9. Hastings, M. *Montrose: the king's champion.* London; Gollancz; 1977. Pp 384.

10. Senior, C.M. *A Nation of pirates: English piracy in its heyday.* Newton Abbot; David & Charles; 1976. Pp 166.

11. Glasgow, T., jr., 'Vice Admiral Woodhouse and shipkeeping in the Tudor navy,' *Mariner's Mirror* 63 (1977), 253–63.

12. Gentles, I., 'Arrears of pay and the army revolt of 1647,' *War and Society* (ed. B. Bond and I. Roy; London, Croom Helm) 1 (1976), 44–66.

13. Roy, I., 'The English civil war and English society,' ibid. 24–43.

14. Cowan, E.J. *Montrose, for covenant and king.* London; Weidenfeld & Nicholson; 1977. Pp ix, 326.

15. Morley, B.M. *Henry VIII and the development of coastal defence.* London; HMSO; 1976. Pp 44.
16. Thurlow, W., 'Charles I at York,' *History Today* 27 (1977), 495—504.
17. Martin, C.J.M., 'Spanish Armada tonnages,' *Mariner's Mirror* 63 (1977), 365—7.
18. Lander, R.J., 'An assessment of the numbers, sizes and types of English and Spanish ships mobilized for the Armada campaign,' ibid. 359—64.
19. Ashley, M. *General Monck.* London; Cape; 1977. Pp viii, 316.
20. Priestley, E.J., 'The Portsmouth captains [courts martial],' *J. of the Soc. for Army Historical Research* 55 (1977), 153—60.

(j) Political Thought and the History of Ideas

1. Norena, C.G., 'Juan Luis Vives and Henry VIII,' *Renaissance and Reformation* 12 (1976), 85—8.
2. Allen, W.S., 'The tone of More's farewell to *Utopia*: a reply to J.H. Hexter,' *Moreana* 51 (1976), 108—18.
3. Sylvester, R.S., 'Editing Thomas More,' ibid. 26—37.
4. Mulligan, L.; Graham, J.K.; Richards, J., 'Winstanley: a case for the man as he said he was,' *J. of Ecclesiastical History* 28 (1977), 57—75.
5. Smith, E.O., jr., 'Crown and commonwealth: a study in the official Elizabethan doctrine of the prince,' *T. of the American Philosophical Soc.* 66 (1976), pp. 51.
6. Bartlett, K., 'The decline and abolition of the master of grammar: an early victory of humanism at the university of Cambridge,' *History of Education* 6 (1977), 1—8.
7. Jacob, J.R., 'Boyle's circle in the Protectorate: Revelation, politics and the millenium,' *J. of the History of Ideas* 38 (1977), 131—40.
8. Thompson, M.P., 'The idea of conquest in controversies over the 1688 revolution,' ibid. 33—46.
9. Buck, P., 'Seventeenth-century political arithmetic: civil strife and vital statistics,' *Isis* 68 (1977).
10. Kupperman, K., 'English perceptions of treachery, 1583—1640: the case of the American "savages",' *Historical J.* 20 (1977), 263—87.
11. Schedler, G., 'Hobbes on the basis of political obligation,' *J. of the History of Philosophy* 15 (1977), 165—70.
12. Goldie, M., 'Edmund Bohun and *Jus Gentium* in the Revolution debate,' *Historical J.* 20 (1977), 569—86.
13. Wooden, W.W., 'Anti-scholastic satire in Sir Thomas More's *Utopia*,' *Sixteenth Century J.* 8 (1977), 29—45.
14. Feather, J., 'The publication of John Harrington's *Commonwealth of Oceana*,' *The Library* 5th ser. 32 (1977), 262—8.

15. Scarisbrick, J.J., 'Thomas More: the king's good servant,' *Thought (Fordham University Q.)* 52 (1977), 249—68.
16. Raphael, D.D. *Hobbes: morals and politics.* London; Allen & Unwin; 1977. Pp 104.
17. Pocock, J.G.A. (ed.). *The political works of John Harrington.* Cambridge UP; 1977. Pp xviii, 878.

(k) Culture and Science

1. Lancashire, I., 'The auspices of *The World and the Child*,' *Renaissance and Reformation* 12 (1976), 96—105.
2. Ward, J.M., 'Tessier and the "Essex circle",' *Renaissance Q.* 29 (1976), 378—84.
3. Abernathy, G.R., 'Sir Richard Temple and the Stowe Library,' *Huntington Library Q.* 40 (1976), 45—58.
4. Clark, S., 'Wisdom literature of the seventeenth century: a guide to the contents of the "Bacon-Tottel" commonplace books; Part I,' *T. of the Cambridge Bibliographical Soc.* 6 (1976), 291—305.
5. Wilson, E.M., 'Three printed ballad texts from Birmingham,' ibid. 339—45.
6. McKenzie, D.F., 'Richard Bentley's design for the Cambridge University Press c. 1696,' ibid. 322—7.
7. Massa, D., 'Giordano Bruno's ideas in seventeenth-century England,' *J. of the History of Ideas* 38 (1977), 227—42.
8. Snyder, H.L., 'A further note on the circulation of newspapers in the reign of Queen Anne,' *Library* 5th ser. 31 (1976), 387—9.
9. Binns, J., 'STC Latin books: evidence for printing-house practice,' *Library* 5th ser. 32 (1977), 1—27.
10. Whiteside, D.T. (ed.). *The mathematical papers of Isaac Newton, vol. 7: 1691—1695.* Cambridge UP; 1976. Pp xlviii, 706.
11. Harvey, W. *An anatomical disputation concerning the movement of the heart and blood in living creatures* (translated and edited by G. Whitteridge). Oxford; Blackwell Scientific; 1976. Pp lxii, 142.
12. Oldenburg, H. *Correspondence, vol. 11: May 1674—September 1675.* London; Mansell; 1977.
13. Pagel, W. *New light on William Harvey.* Basel/London; Karger; 1976. Pp ix, 189.
14. Van Eerde, K.S. *John Ogilby and the taste of his times.* Folkestone; Dawson; 1976. Pp 183.
15. Gardiner, J.K., 'Elizabethan psychology and Burton's *Anatomy of Melancholy*,' *J. of the History of Ideas* 38 (1977), 373—88.
16. Wooden, W.W., 'The art of partisan biography: George Cavendish's *Life of Wolsey*,' *Renaissance and Reformation* new ser. 1 (1977), 24—35.
17. Soubeille, G., 'L'amitié de Th. More et de Salmon Macrin,' *Moreana* 54 (1977), 11—21.

18. Bennett, J.S., 'God, Satan and King Charles: Milton's royal portraits,' *Publications of the Modern Language Association* 92 (1977), 441–57.

19. Delany, P., '*King Lear* and the decline of feudalism,' ibid. 429–40.

20. Pebworth, T.-L., 'Sir Henry Wotton's 'Dazel'd Thus, with Height of Place" and the appropriation of political poetry in the earlier seventeenth century,' *Papers of the Bibliographical Soc. of America* 71 (1977), 151–69.

21. Strong, R. *The cult of Elizabeth: Elizabethan portraiture and pageantry.* London; Thames & Hudson; 1977. Pp 227.

22. Kaufman, P.I., 'John Colet and Erasmus' *Enchiridion*,' *Church History* 46 (1977), 296–312.

23. Knowles Middleton, W.E., 'What did Charles II call the fellows of the Royal Society?,' *Notes and Records of the Royal Soc. of London* 32 (1977), 13–16.

24. Rose, P.L., 'Erasmians and mathematicians at Cambridge in the early sixteenth century,' *Sixteenth Century J.* 8 (1977), 47–59.

25. Shuttleworth, J.M., 'Edward, Lord Herbert of Cherbury (1583–1648),' *National Library of Wales J.* 20 (1977), 151–68.

26. Ker, N., 'The library of John Jewel,' *The Bodleian Library Record* 9 (1977), 256–65.

27. Crum, M., 'Common-place books of Bishop William Lloyd, 1627–1717,' ibid. 265–73.

28. Walters, G.; Emery, F.V., 'Edward Lhuyd, Edmund Gibson, and the printing of Camden's *Britannica*,' *The Library* 5th ser. 32 (1977), 109–37.

29. Zell, M.L., 'An early press in Canterbury?,' ibid. 155–6.

30. Thompson, C.R., 'The humanism of More reappraised,' *Thought (Fordham University Q.)*, 52 (1977), 233–48.

31. Burke, P., 'Popular culture in seventeenth century London,' *London J.* 3 (1977), 143–62.

32. Yewbrey, G., 'A redated manuscript of John Dee,' *B. of the Institute of Historical Research* 50 (1977), 249–53.

33. Downie, J.A., 'William Stephens and the *Letter to the Author of the Memorial of the State of England* reconsidered,' ibid. 253–9.

34. Hill, J.E.C. *Milton and the English revolution.* London; Faber; 1977. Pp xviii, 541.

35. Not used.

36. Scheller, R.W., 'An unknown letter by Rubens: on the death of Buckingham,' *Burlington Magazine* 119 (1977), 647.

37. Fisher, R.M., 'Thomas Cromwell, humanism and educational reform, 1530–40,' *B. of the Institute of Historical Research* 50 (1977), 151–63.

38. Logan, F.D., 'The origins of the so-called Regius professorships: an aspect of the Renaissance in Oxford and Cambridge,' Bc6, 271–8.

39. Jones, F., 'Kilgetty: a Pembrokeshire mansion,' *Archaeologia Cambrensis* 125 (1977 for 1976), 127–39.
40. Levine, J.M. *Doctor Woodward's Shield: history, science and satire in Augustan England.* Berkeley/London; University of California Press; 1977. Pp x, 362.
41. Cowling, T.G. *Isaac Newton and astrology.* Leeds UP; 1977. Pp 21.

G. BRITAIN 1714–1815

See also: Aa4, 7, 9, b29; Fe2, f2, i2, 12

(a) General

1. Calder-Marshall, A. *The grand century of the lady.* London; Gordon & Cremonesi; 1976. Pp 184.
2. Whitworth, R., 'William Augustus, duke of Cumberland,' *History Today* 27 (1977), 82–91.
3. Bragg, M. *John Peel: the man, the myth and the song.* Carlisle; Cumbria Weekly Digest; 1976. Pp 88.
4. Cross, A., 'A Russian engineer in eighteenth-century Britain: the journal of N.I. Korsakov, 1776–7,' *Slavonic and East European R.* 55 (1977), 1–20.
5. Gillen, M. *Royal duke: Augustus Frederick, duke of Sussex (1773–1843).* London; Sidgwick & Jackson; 1976 (i.e. 1977). Pp 268.
6. Andrews, A. *The king who lost America: George II and independence.* London; Jupiter Books; 1976. Pp 184.
7. Pollock, J. *Wilberforce.* London; Constable; 1977. Pp xvi, 368.
8. Clarke, J. *The price of progress: Cobbett's England, 1780–1835.* London; Hart-Davis MacGibbon; 1977. Pp vii, 200.
9. Low, D.A. *That sunny dome: a portrait of Regency Britain.* London; Dent; 1977. Pp xv, 208.
10. Macnaghten, A. *Windsor and Eton in Georgian times.* [Ascot; the author]; 1976. Pp 99.
11. Money, J. *Experience and Identity: Birmingham and the West Midlands, 1760–1800.* Manchester UP; 1977. Pp viii, 312.
12. Speck, W.A. *Stability and Strife: England 1714–1760.* London; Arnold; 1977. Pp viii, 311.
13. Lustig, I.S., 'The friendship of Johnson and Boswell: some biographical considerations,' *Studies in Eighteenth Century Culture* 6 (ed. R.S. Rosbottom; University of Wisconsin Press; 1977), 199–224.
14. Cowie, L.W., 'Holy Thursday,' *History Today* 27 (1977), 513–19.

(b) Politics

1. Thomas, M., 'The rioting crowd in Derbyshire in the 18th century,' *Derbyshire Arch. J.* 95 (1976 for 1975), 37—47.
2. Berens, J.E., ' "Good news from a far country": a note on divine providence and the Stamp Act crisis,' *Church History* 45 (1976), 308—15.
3. Ditchfield, G.M., 'Debates on the Test and Corporation Acts, 1787—90: the evidence of the division lists,' *B. of the Institute of Historical Research* 50 (1977), 69—81.
4. Lancien, D., 'La formation des parties politiques britanniques modernes vue à travers l'étude des structures partisanes: mérites et limites d'une approche de la réalité politique,' *Revue historique* 257 (1977), 26—80.
5. Press, C., 'The Georgian political print and democratic institutions,' *Comparative Studies in Society and History* 19 (1977), 216—38.
6. Speck, W.A., 'The whig schism under George I,' *Huntington Library Q.* 40 (1977), 171—9.
7. Willis, R.E., ' "A handful of violent people": the nature of the Foxite opposition, 1794—1801,' *Albion* 8 (1976), 236—54.
8. Davies, K.G. (ed.). *Documents of the American Revolution 1776—1783, Colonial Office series.* Vol. 12: Transcripts, 1776; vol. 13: Calendar, 1777—1778; vol. 14: Transcripts, 1777; vol. 15: Transcripts, 1778; vol. 16: Calendar, 1779—1780; vol. 17: Transcripts, 1779. Dublin; Irish UP; 1976. Pp vi, 301; vi, 481; vi, 299; vi, 320; vi, 550; vi, 291.
9. Edwards, O.D.; Shepperson, G. (ed.). *Scotland, Europe and the American Revolution.* Edinburgh University Student Publications, 1976. Pp 138.
10. Colley, L.J., 'The Loyal Brotherhood and the Cocoa Tree: the London organization of the Tory party, 1727—1760,' *Historical J.* 20 (1977), 77—95.
11. May, W.E., 'The *Gaspée* affair,' *Mariner's Mirror* 63 (1977), 129—35.
12. Elliott, M., 'The "Despard conspiracy" reconsidered,' *Past and Present* 75 (1977), 46—61.
13. Hannay, P., 'Portrait of Lord Althorp, 1782—1845,' *History Today* 27 (1977), 796—804.
14. McCann, T.J., 'Crocket and the Sussex county by-election of 1741,' *Sussex Arch. Collection* 114 (1976), 121—5.
15. Thomis, M.I.; Holt, P. *Threats of revolution in Britain, 1789—1848.* London; Macmillan; 1977. Pp 147.
16. Walker, F.A., 'The Grenville-Fox "junction" and the problem of peace,' *Canadian J. of History* 12 (1977), 51—63.
17. Walvin, J.A., 'The English Jacobins, 1789—1799,' *Historical Reflections/Réflexions Historiques* 4 (1977), 91—109.

18. Myers, M., 'Politics from the outside: Mary Wollstonecraft's first *Vindication,' Studies in Eighteenth Century Culture* 6 (ed. R.C. Rosbottom; University of Wisconsin Press; 1977), 113–32.
19. Colley, L.J., 'The Mitchell election division, 24 March 1755,' *B. of the Institute of Historical Research* 49 (1976), 80–107.

(c) Constitution, Administration and Law

1. Faller, L.B., 'In contrast to Defoe: the Rev. Paul Lorrain, historian of crime,' *Huntington Library Q.* 40 (1976), 59–78.
2. Whiting, J.R.S. *Prison reform in Gloucestershire, 1776–1820: a study of the work of Sir George Onesiphorus Paul, Bart.* London; Phillimore; 1975. Pp xxii, 287.
3. Bennett, H., 'A murder victim discovered: clothing and other finds from an early 18th-century grave on Arnish Moor, Lewis,' *P. of the Soc. of Antiquaries of Scotland* 106 (1977 for 1974/5), 172–82.
4. Mason, F. *Wolverhampton, the town commissioners, 1777–1848: their story in their minutes and the files of the 'Wolverhampton Chronicle'.* Wolverhampton Public Libraries; 1976. Pp 71.
5. Beattie, J.M., 'Crime and the courts in Surrey 1736–1753,' Bc7, 155–86.
6. Malcolmson, R.W., 'Infanticide in the eighteenth century,' Bc7, 186–209.
7. Munsche, P.B., 'The game laws in Wiltshire 1750–1800,' Bc7, 210–28.
8. Sheehan, W.J., 'Finding solace in eighteenth-century Newgate,' Bc7, 229–45.
9. Linebaugh, P., 'The ordinary of Newgate and his *Account*,' Bc7, 246–69.
10. Whetstone, A.E., 'The reform of the Scottish sheriffdoms in the eighteenth and early nineteenth centuries,' *Albion* 9 (1977), 61–71.

(d) External Affairs

1. Brown, W., ' "Victorious in defeat": the American loyalists in Canada,' *History Today* 27 (1977), 92–100.
2. Barnett, R.D., 'Diplomatic aspects of the Sephardi influx from Portugal in the early eighteenth century,' *T. of the Jewish Historical Soc. of England* 25 (1977 for 1973/5), 210–21.
3. Pemble, J. *The Raj, the Indian Mutiny and the kingdom of Oudh, 1804–1859.* Hassocks; Harvester Press; 1977. Pp xi, 303.
4. Blanning, T.C.W., ' "That Horrid Electorate" or "Ma patrie germanique"? George III, Hanover, and the Fürstenbund of 1785,' *Historical J.* 20 (1977), 311–44.
5. Rice, G.W., 'British consuls and diplomats in the mid-eighteenth

century: an Italian example,' *English Historical R.* 92 (1977), 834—46.

6. Schweizer, K.W., 'Lord Bute, Newcastle, Prussia and the Hague overtures: a re-examination,' *Albion* 9 (1977), 72—97.

(e) *Religion*

1. Baker, D.S., 'Charles Wesley and the American war of independence (ctd.),' *P. of the Wesley Historical Soc.* 40 (1976), 165—82.
2. Heitzenrater, R.P., 'Mary Wesley's marriage,' ibid. 153—63.
3. Oliver, R.C.B., 'David Davies, rector of Barkham in Berkshire, 1782—1819,' *National Library of Wales J.* 19 (1976), 362—94.
4. Stell, C.F., 'The Eastern Association of Baptist churches, 1775—1782,' *Baptist Q.* 27 (1977), 14—26.
5. Jones, R.T. *John Elias: prince among preachers.* Bridgend; Evangelical Library of Wales; 1975. Pp 33.
6. Nuttall, G.F., 'Questions and answers: an eighteenth-century correspondence,' *Baptist Q.* 27 (1977), 82—90.
7. Royle, E. (ed.). *The infidel tradition: from Paine to Bradlaugh.* London; Macmillan; 1976. Pp xvii, 228.
8. Shaftesley, J.M.; Rosenbaum, M., 'Jews in English regular freemasonry, 1717—1860,' *T. of the Jewish Historical Soc. of England* 25 (1977 for 1973/5), 150—209.
9. Waddy, J.L. *The bitter sacred cup: the Wednesbury riots, 1743—44.* London; Pinhorns; 1976. Pp ix, 46.
10. Whitefield, G. *Letters of George Whitfield, for the period 1734—1742.* Edinburgh; Banner of Truth Trust; 1976 [facsimile reprint of vol. 1 of 1771 ed. of W.'s works]. Pp xiii, 570.
11. Williams, J.A. (ed.). *Post-Reformation Catholicism in Bath*, vol. 2: Registers, 1780—1825. London; Catholic Record Soc.; 1976. Pp xiv, 244.
12. Doster, G.R., 'Discipline and ordination at Berkhamsted General Baptist Church, 1712—1718,' *Baptist Q.* 27 (1977), 128—38.
13. Grant, F.L., 'The revolution in religious rhetoric: John Wesley and the evangelical impact on England,' *The Historian* 39 (1977), 439—54.
14. Hill, A.M., 'The successors of the Remnant: a bicentenary account of St. Mark's Unitarian Church, Edinburgh. Part I: before 1776 until 1822,' *T. of the Unitarian Historical Soc.* 16 (1977), 101—23.
15. Mather, F.C., 'Church, parliament and penal laws: some Anglo-Scottish interactions in the eighteenth century,' *English Historical R.* 92 (1977), 540—72.
16. Oddy, J.A., 'The dissidence of William Richards,' *Baptist Q.* 27 (1977), 118—27.

17. Addy, J., 'Bishop Porteus' visitation of the diocese of Chester, 1778,' *Northern History* 13 (1977), 175–98.
18. Baker-Jones, D.L., 'The letters of the Reverend David Griffiths, Nevern, 1756–1834,' *National Library of Wales J.* 20 (1977), 169–76.
19. Binfield, C. *So down to prayers: studies in English nonconformity, 1780–1920.* London; Dent; 1977. Pp xiv, 296.
20. Bollen, J.D., 'English Christianity and the Australian colonies, 1788–1860,' *J. of Ecclesiastical History* 28 (1977), 361–85.
21. Champion, L.G., 'The letters of John Newton to John Ryland,' *Baptist Q.* 27 (1977), 157–63.
22. Ditchfield, G.M., 'The campaign in Lancashire and Cheshire for the repeal of the Test and Corporation Acts, 1787–1790,' *T. of the Historic Soc. of Lancashire and Cheshire* (1977 for 1976), 109–38.
23. Foreman, H., 'Baptists and the charity school movement,' *Baptist Q.* 27 (1977), 150–6.
24. Goldthorpe, L.M., 'John Wesley's visits to the upper Calder valley,' *T. of the Halifax Antiquarian Soc.* (1977 for 1975), 55–74.
25. Jones, O.W., 'The Welsh Church in the eighteenth century,' Bc4, 103–20.
26. Davies, E.T., 'The Church in the industrial revolution,' Bc4, 121–43.
27. Rosman, D.M., ' "What has Christ to do with Apollo?"; evangelism and the novel, 1800–20,' Bc6, 301–11.
28. Laird, A., 'The English College, Rome, under Italian secular administration,' *Recusant History* 14 (1977), 127–47.
29. Luehrs, R.B., 'The early deism of Anthony Collins,' *Studies in Eighteenth Century Culture* 6 (ed. R.C. Rosbottom; University of Wisconsin Press, 1977), 59–77.

(f) Economic Affairs

1. Lindsay, J.M., 'Forestry and agriculture in the Scottish Highlands, 1700–1850: a problem in estate management,' *Agricultural History R.* 25 (1977), 23–36.
2. Longfield, A.K. (Mrs Lask), 'Irish linen for Spain and Portugal: James Archbold's latters 1771–79,' *P. of the Royal Irish Academy* 76/C (1976), 13–22.
3. Playne, E.; de Boer, G. (ed.). *Lonsdale documents.* Durham; Surtees Soc.; 1976. Pp viii, 158.
4. McCahill, M.W., 'Peers, patronage and the industrial revolution, 1760–1800,' *J. of British Studies* 16 (1976), 84–107.
5. Martin, R.A., 'Kettering inclosure 1804–5,' *Northamptonshire Past and Present* 5 (1977), 413–26.
6. Moss, D.J., 'Birmingham and the campaigns against the Orders-in-

Council and East India Company charter, 1812–13,' *Canadian J. of History* 11 (1976), 173–88.

7. Press, J. *The merchant seamen of Bristol, 1747–1789.* Bristol Branch of the Historical Association; 1976. Pp 23.

8. Turnbull, G.L., 'Provincial road carrying in England in the eighteenth century,' *J. of Transport History* new ser. 4 (1977), 17–39.

9. Fearon, J.H.; Hurst, C.W. (ed.). *Parish accounts for the 'town' of Bodicote, Oxfordshire, 1700–1822.* Banbury Historical Soc.; 1975. Pp xxvi, 34.

10. Colyer, R., 'The Hafod estate under Thomas Johnes and Henry Pelham, fourth duke of Newcastle,' *Welsh History R.* 8 (1977), 257–84.

11. Donnachie, I., 'Sources of capital and capitalization in the Scottish brewing industry, c. 1750–1830,' *Economic History R.* 2nd ser. 30 (1977), 269–83.

12. Forbes, D. (ed.). *The Sutherland clearances, 1806–1820: a documentary survey.* Ayr; Craigie College of Education; 1976. Pp 52.

13. Freeman, M.D., 'Assessing potential milling capacity in Hampshire, c. 1750–1914,' *Industrial Archaeology R.* 1 (1976–7), 47–62.

14. Atkins, P.J., 'London's intra-urban milk supply, circa 1790–1914,' *T. of the Institute of British Geographers* new ser. 2 (1977), 383–99.

15. Jeremy, D.J., 'Damming the flood: British government efforts to check the outflow of technicians and machinery 1780–1843,' *Business History R.* 51 (1977), 1–34.

16. Marshall, P.J. *East India fortunes: the British in Bengal in the eighteenth century.* Oxford; Clarendon Press; 1976. Pp ix, 284.

17. Miller, S.T., 'The iron bridge at Sunderland: a revision,' *Industrial Archaeology R.* 1 (1976–7), 70–2.

18. Neal, L.D., 'Interpreting power and profit in economic history: a case study of the Seven Years' War,' *J. of Economic History* 37 (1977), 20–35.

19. Palmer, M. & D., 'Moira furnace [Leicestershire],' *Industrial Archaeology R.* 1 (1976–7), 63–9.

20. Skempton, A.W., 'The engineers of Sunderland harbour 1718–1817,' ibid. 103–25.

21. Steele, I.K., 'A London trader and the Atlantic empire: Joseph Cruttenden, apothecary, 1710 to 1717,' *William and Mary Q.* 3rd ser. 34 (1977), 281–97.

22. Thomis, M.I. *Responses to industrialisation: the British experience, 1780–1850.* Newton Abbot; David & Charles; 1976. Pp 194.

23. Tucker, D.G., 'The slate quarries at Easdale, Argyllshire, Scotland,' *Post-Medieval Archaeology* 10 (1976), 118–30.

24. Anstey, R.; Hair, P.E.H. (ed.). *Liverpool, the African slave trade and abolition: essays to illustrate current knowledge and*

research. [Widnes]; Historic Soc. of Lancashire and Cheshire; 1976. Pp ix, 244.

25. Anstey, R.; Hair, P.E.H., 'Introduction,' Gf24, 1—13.

26. Johnson, M., 'The Atlantic slave trade and the economy of West Africa,' Gf24, 14—38.

27. Minchinton, W.E., 'The slave trade of Bristol with the British mainland colonies in North America 1699—1770,' Gf24, 39—59.

28. Richardson, D., 'Profits in the Liverpool slave trade: the accounts of William Davenport, 1757—1784,' Gf24, 60—90.

29. Lamb, D.P., 'Volume and tonnage of the Liverpool slave trade 1772—1807,' Gf24, 90—112.

30. Klein, H.S.; Engerman, S.L., 'Slave mortality on British ships 1791—1797,' Gf24, 113—25.

31. Drake, B.K., 'The Liverpool-African voyage c. 1790—1807: commercial problems,' Gf24, 126—56.

32. Anstey, R., 'The historical debate on the abolition of the British slave trade,' Gf24, 157—66.

33. Drescher, S., 'Capitalism and abolition: values and forces in Britain 1783—1814,' Gf24, 167—95.

34. Sanderson, F.E., 'The Liverpool abolitionists,' Gf24, 196—238.

35. Crafts, N.F.R., 'Industrial revolution in England and France: some thoughts on the question, "Why was England first?",' *Economic History R.* 2nd ser. 30 (1977), 429—41.

36. Freeman, M.J., 'The carrier system of south Hampshire, 1775—1851,' *J. of Transport History* new ser. 4 (1977), 61—85.

37. Gittins, L., 'Soapmaking and the excise laws, 1711—1853,' *Industrial Archaeology R.* 1 (1977), 265—75.

38. Pawson, E. *Transport and economy: the turnpike roads of eighteenth century Britain.* London; Academic Press; 1977. Pp xx, 407.

39. Porteous, J.D. *Canal ports: the urban achievement of the canal age.* London; Academic Press; 1977. Pp xvii, 249.

40. Wallace, A.F.; Jeremy, D.J., 'William Pollard and the Arkwright patents,' *William and Mary Q.* 3rd ser. 34 (1977), 404—25.

41. Acaster, E.J.T., 'The private banking of the Leslie-Melvilles,' *Three Banks R.* 115 (1977), 40—51.

42. Brent, J., 'The Pooles of Chailey and Lewes: the establishment and influence of a gentry family, 1732—1739,' *Sussex Arch. Collection* 114 (1976), 69—80.

43. Chapman, J., 'Land purchasers at enclosure: evidence from West Sussex,' *Local Historian* 12 (1977), 337—41.

44. Chapman, S.D., 'The foundation of the English Rothschilds: N.M. Rothschild as a textile merchant 1799—1811,' *Textile History* 8 (1977), 99—115.

45. Firth, G., 'The origins of Low Moor Ironworks, Bradford, 1788—1800,' *Yorkshire Arch. Soc.* 49 (1977), 127—39.

46. Farrant, J.H., 'The seaboard trade of Sussex,' *Sussex Arch. Collection* 114 (1977), 97—120.

47. Gatty, R. *Portrait of a merchant prince: James Morrison, 1789—1857.* Northallerton; [Pamela Gatty; 1977]. Pp 326.

48. Gill, M.A.V., 'The latter days of the York assay office,' *Yorkshire Arch. Soc.* 49 (1977), 115—25.

49. Ince, L., 'The Neath Abbey ironworks,' *Industrial Archaeology* 11—12 (1977), 21—37.

50. Johnstone, W.J.D., 'The precipitation and fall of Messrs. Douglas, Heron and Company,' *Three Banks R.* 116 (1977), 52—69.

51. Malet, H. *Bridgewater, the canal duke, 1736—1803.* Manchester UP; 1977. Pp 224.

52. Martins, S.W., 'The farm buildings of the agricultural revolution,' *Local Historian* 12 (1977), 407—23.

53. Schofield, M.M., 'The slave trade from Lancashire and Cheshire ports outside Liverpool, c. 1750—c. 1790,' *T. of the Historic Soc. of Lancashire and Cheshire* 126 (1977 for 1976), 30—72.

54. Shyllon, F. *John Ramsay: the unknown abolitionist.* Edinburgh; Canongate Publishing; 1977. Pp viii, 144.

55. Singleton, F.J., 'The flax merchants of Kirkham,' *T. of the Historic Soc. of Lancashire and Cheshire* (1977 for 1976), 73—108.

56. Smith, W.J., 'The cost of building Lancashire loomhouses and weavers' workshops: the account book of James Brandwood of Turton, 1794—1814,' *Textile History* 8 (1977), 56—76.

57. Trinder, B. (ed.). *'The most extraordinary district in the world' — Ironbridge and Coalbrookdale: an anthology of visitors' impressions of Ironbridge, Coalbrookdale and the Shropshire coalfield.* London; Phillimore; 1977. Pp x, 125.

58. Turner, M., 'Enclosure commissioners and Buckinghamshire parliamentary enclosure,' *Agricultural History R.* 25 (1977), 120—9.

59. Tyson, N., 'John Carr, a Georgian bridge builder,' *Industrial Archaeology* 11—12 (1977), 74—83.

60. Wells, R.A.E., 'Dearth and distress in Yorkshire 1793—1802,' *Borthwick Papers* no. 52 (1977), Pp. 49.

61. Wilde, P.D., 'Power supplies and the development of the silk industry in the southwest Pennines,' *North Staffordshire J. of Field Studies* 16 (1976), 47—56.

62. Edwards, A.C. *The account books of Benjamin Mildmay, earl Fitzwalter.* London; Regency Press; 1977. Pp 213.

63. McAloon, T., 'A minor Scottish merchant in general trade: the case of Edward Burd, 1728—39,' Bc2, 17—27.

64. Duckham, B.F., 'English influences in the Scottish coal trade, 1700—1815,' Bc2, 28—45.

65. Jackson, G., 'Government bounties and the establishment of the Scottish whaling trade 1750—1800,' Bc2, 46—66.

66. Butt, J., 'Capital and enterprise in the Scottish iron industry 1780—1840,' Bc2, 67—79.

67. Smouth, T.C., 'Famine and famine-relief in Scotland,' Bc9, 21–31.
68. Durie, A.J., 'The Scottish linen industry in the eighteenth century: some aspects of expansion,' Bc9, 88–99.
69. Butt, J., 'The Scottish cotton industry during the industrial revolution,' Bc9, 116–28.
70. Devine, T.M., 'Colonial commerce and the Scottish economy, c. 1730–1815,' Bc9, 177–90.
71. Campbell, R.H., 'The Scottish improvers and the course of agrarian change in the eighteenth century,' Bc9, 204–15.
72. Hyde, C.K. *Technological change and the British iron industry, 1700–1870.* Princeton UP; 1977. Pp xvi, 283.

(g) Social Structure and Population

1. Burchall, M.J. *Sussex military marriages, 1750–1812; part 1.* Brighton; Sussex Family History Group; 1975. Pp 64.
2. Edwards, W.J., 'National marriage data: a re-aggregation of John Rickman's marriage returns,' *Local Population Studies* 17 (1976), 25–41.
3. Wrigley, E.A., 'Checking Rickman,' ibid. 9–15.
4. Martin, J.M., 'Marriage and economic stress in the Felden of Warwickshire during the eighteenth century,' *Population Studies* 31 (1977), 519–35.
5. Newton, R., 'Exeter 1770–1870,' Bc5, 12–43.
6. Flinn, M.W., 'Malthus, emigration and potatoes in the Scottish north-west, 1770–1870,' Bc9, 47–64.
7. Crafts, N.F.R., 'Some aspects of the interactions between population growth and economic circumstances in the eighteenth century,' Bc10, 49–63.
8. Clapp, B., 'Wembworthy: a Devon parish in the eighteenth century,' Bc10, 65–72.
9. Chater, A.O., 'Early Cardiganshire gravestones: Part I,' *Archaeologia Cambrensis* 125 (1977 for 1976), 140–61.
10. Barnsby, G.J. *The working class movement in the Black Country, 1750–1867.* Wolverhampton; Integrated Publishing Series; 1977. Pp 233.

(h) Naval and Military

1. Gardiner, R., 'The frigate designs of 1755–57,' *Mariner's Mirror* 63 (1977), 51–69.
2. Johnson, R.E. *Sir John Richardson: arctic explorer, natural historian, naval surgeon.* London; Taylor & Francis; 1976. Pp xii, 209.
3. Kennedy, L. *Nelson and his captains* (revd. ed.). London; Fontana; 1976. Pp 353.

4. *The Craven muster roll.* North Yorkshire County Council; 1976. Pp 226.

5. Craster, J.M. (ed.). *'Fifteen rounds a minute': the Grenadiers at war, August to December 1914.* London; Macmillan; 1976. [Really section I.]

6. Cooper, J. *Fort Pitt: some notes on the history of a Napoleonic fort, military hospital and technical school.* Maidstone; Kent County Library; 1976. Pp 35.

7. Woodford, L.W. (ed.). *A young surgeon in Wellington's army: the letters of William Dent.* Old Woking; Unwin Brothers Ltd.; 1976. Pp 68.

8. Edwardes, M. *Clive, the heaven-born general.* London; Hart-Davis MacGibbon; 1977. Pp ix, 211.

9. Bradford, E. *Nelson: the essential hero.* London; Macmillan; 1977. Pp 368.

10. David, A.C.F., 'Broughton's schooner and the Bounty mutineers,' *Mariner's Mirror* 63 (1977), 207–13.

11. Glover, M., 'Writing news and keeping coffee-houses,' [military intelligence in the Peninsular war] *History Today* 27 (1977), 452–8.

12. Glover, M. *Wellington's army in the Peninsula, 1808–1814.* Newton Abbot; David & Charles; 1977. Pp 192.

13. Hinchcliffe, G., 'A royal visit to the Fleet, 1735,' *Mariner's Mirror* 63 (1977), 187–9.

14. Jones, A.G.E., 'Sir Thomas Slade 1703/4–1771,' ibid. 224–6.

15. McAteer, W., 'Admiral Sir Charles Adam,' ibid. 264–72.

16. Parkinson, C.N. *Britannia rules: the classic age of naval history, 1793–1815.* London; Weidenfeld & Nicolson; 1977. Pp viii, 199.

17. Patterson, A.T., 'A protégé of Pellew' [John Cree Smyth], *Mariner's Mirror* 63 (1977), 273–8.

18. Rogers, H.C.B. *The British army of the eighteenth century.* London; Allen & Unwin; 1977. Pp 252.

19. Thomas, E.G., 'The old poor law and maritime apprenticeship,' *Mariner's Mirror* 63 (1977), 153–61.

20. Thurburn, R.G., 'The capture of Minorca, 1708,' *J. of the Soc. for Army Historical Research* 55 (1977), 65–72.

21. Watkin, R., 'Captain Hugh Crow: a Liverpool Guineaman,' *Mariner's Mirror* 63 (1977), 177–85.

22. Condon, M.E., 'Freight rates and the British transport service during the war against revolutionary France 1793–1802,' *Maritime History* 5 (1977), 26–33.

23. Feldbaek, O., 'The Anglo-Danish convoy conflict of 1800,' *Scandinavian J. of History* 2 (1977), 161–82.

24. Kup, A.P., 'Sir Charles McCarthy (1768–1824), soldier and administrator,' *B. of the John Rylands University Library of Manchester* 60 (1977), 52–94.

25. Friendly, A. *Beaufort of the Admiralty: the life of Sir Francis Beaufort, 1774–1857*. London; Hutchinson; 1977. Pp 362.

26. Lavery, B., 'The origins of the 74-gun ship,' *Mariner's Mirror* 63 (1977), 335–50.

27. O'Donoghue, Y. *William Roy, 1726–1790*. London; British Museum Publications; 1977.

28. Severn, D., 'Nelson's Hardy,' *History Today* 27 (1977), 505–12.

29. Sullivan, F.B., 'The Royal Academy at Portsmouth 1729–1806,' *Mariner's Mirror* 63 (1977), 311–26.

30. Webb, P.L.C., 'The rebuilding and repair of the fleet 1783–93,' *B. of the Institute of Historical Research* 50 (1977), 194–209.

31. Glover, M., 'The Lavalette affair, 1815,' *History Today* 27 (1977), 600–5.

32. Pocock, T. *Remember Nelson: the life of Captain Sir William Hoste*. London; Collins; 1977. Pp 256.

(i) Intellectual and Cultural

1. Chalmers, G.S. *Reading easy, 1800–50: a study of the teaching of reading with a list of the books which were used and a selection of facsimile pages*. London; The Broadsheet King; 1976. Pp 185.

2. Hyde, M., 'The Thrales of Streatham Park; II: the *Family Book* (IV) 1777–1778,' *Harvard Library B.* 25 (1977), 63–100.

3. Kaestle, C.F., ' "Between the Scylla of brute ignorance and the Charybdis of a literary education": elite attitudes towards mass schooling in early industrial England and America,' *Schooling and Society*, ed. L. Stone (Baltimore; Johns Hopkins UP; 1976), 177–91.

4. Laquer, T.W., 'Working-class demand and the growth of English elementary education, 1750–1850,' ibid. 192–205.

5. Landon, H.C.R. *Haydn in England, 1791–1795*. London; Thames & Hudson; 1976. Pp 640.

6. Rabicoff, R.; McKitterick, D.J., 'John Nichols, William Bowyer, and Cambridge University Press in 1765,' *T. of the Cambridge Bibliographical Soc.* 6 (1976), 328–38.

7. Stephens, M.D.; Roderick, G.W., 'Education and the dissenting academies,' *History Today* 27 (1977), 47–54.

8. Watson, R., 'Thomas Jefferson's visit to England, 1786,' ibid. 3–13.

9. Pavia, E., 'Vicende italiane di "The true intellectual System of the Universe" di Ralph Cudworth,' *Critica Storica* 13 (1976), 124–67.

10. Brownell, M.R. *Alexander Pope and the arts of Georgian England*. Oxford; Clarendon; 1977.

11. Chartres, J.A., 'The capital's provincial eyes: London's inns in the early eighteenth century,' *London J.* 3 (1977), 24–39.

12. Chitnis, A.C. *The Scottish Enlightenment: a social history.*
    London; Croom Helm; 1976. Pp 279.

13. David, A.C.F. *The surveyors of the 'Bounty': a preliminary study
    of the hydrographic surveys of William Bligh, Thomas Hayward
    and Peter Heywood and the charts published from them.*
    Taunton; the author; 1976. Pp iii, 96.

14. Gray, J., ' "A hot-bed of genius": some reflections on the literati
    of Adam Smith's Scotland,' *T. of the Royal Soc. of Canada* 4th
    ser. 14 (1976), 255—76.

15. Haywood, P. *Joseph Johnson, publisher, 1738—1809.* [Aberyst-
    wyth] ; College of Librarianship; 1976. Pp 63.

16. Hyde, M., 'The Thrales of Streatham Park, III: the death of Thrale
    and remarriage of his widow,' *Harvard Library B.* 25 (1977),
    193—241.

17. Withey, L.E., 'Catharine Macaulay and the uses of history: ancient
    rights, perfectionism, propaganda,' *J. of British Studies* 16
    (1976), 59—83.

18. Lenman, B.P.; Kenworthy, J.B., 'Dr David Skene and the Scottish
    Enlightenment,' *Aberdeen University R.* 47 (1977), 32—44.

19. Pattie, T.S., 'An unexpected affect of the change of the calendar
    in 1752,' *British Library J.* 2 (1976), 27—8.

20. Ray, G.N. *The illustrator and the book in England from 1790 to
    1914.* New York; Pierpont Morgan Library; 1976. Pp xxxiii, 336.

21. Stubbings, F., 'Anthony Askew's *Liber amicorum,*' *T. of the
    Cambridge Bibliographical Soc.* 6 (1976), 306—21.

22. Walters, G., 'Thomas Pennant's map of Scotland, 1777: a study
    in sources, and an introduction to George Paton's role in the
    history of Scottish cartography,' *Imago Mundi* 28 (1976), 121—8.

23. Watson, J.W., 'Adam Smith, *Wealth of Nations,* and Edinburgh
    New Town,' *T. of the Royal Soc. of Canada* 4th ser. 14 (1976),
    241—54.

24. Worman, I. *Thomas Gainsborough: a biography, 1727—1788.*
    Lavenham; Dalton; 1976. Pp 148.

25. Foner, E. *Thomas Paine and revolutionary America.* London;
    Oxford UP; 1977. Pp xxi, 326.

26. Haggar, R.G.; Adams, E. *Mason porcelain and ironstone, 1796—
    1853: Miles Mason and the Mason manufactories.* London; Faber;
    1977. Pp 135.

27. Johnson, P.; Money, E. *The Nasmyth family of painters.* Leigh-on-
    Sea; F. Lewis; 1977. Pp 64.

28. Lindsay, J. *Hogarth: his art and his world.* London; Hart-Davis
    MacGibbon; 1977. Pp x, 277.

29. Marshall, D. *Fanny Kemble.* London; Weidenfeld & Nicolson;
    1977. Pp vii, 280.

30. Steintrager, J. *Bentham.* London; Allen & Unwin; 1977. Pp 133.

31. Wilson, T.; Skinner, A.S. (ed.). *The market and the state: essays in
    honour of Adam Smith.* Oxford; Clarendon; 1976. Pp xi, 359.

32. Chard, L.F., 'Bookseller to publisher: Joseph Johnson and the English book trade,' *The Library* 5th ser. 31 (1977), 138–54.

33. Clark, J.P. *The philosophical anarchism of William Godwin.* Princeton UP; 1977. Pp ix, 343.

34. Cole, H. *Beau Brummell.* London; Granada; 1977. Pp 240.

35. Conolly, L.W. *The censorship of English drama, 1737–1824.* San Marino, Calif.; Huntington Library; 1976. Pp xii, 223.

36. Darcy, C.P. *The encouragement of the fine arts in Lancashire, 1760–1860.* Manchester UP (Chetham Soc.); 1976. Pp vi, 180.

37. Hunt, E. *Robert Lucas Pearsall: the 'compleat gentleman' and his music (1795–1856).* Amersham; the author; 1977. Pp viii, 140.

38. Hyde, M., 'The Thrales of Streatham Park, IV; the Thrale daughters and their children,' *Harvard Library B.* 25 (1977), 332–73.

39. Kilcup, R.W., 'Burke's historicism,' *J. of Modern History* 49 (1977), 394–410.

40. Levey, M. *A royal subject: portraits of Queen Charlotte.* London; National Gallery; 1977. Pp 24.

41. McLaverty, J. *Pope's printer, John Wright: a preliminary study.* Oxford Bibliographical Soc.; 1976. Pp iv, 52.

42. Maxted, I. *The London book trades, 1775–1800: a preliminary checklist of members.* Folkestone; Dawson; 1977. Pp xxxv, 257.

43. Murphy, M.J. *Cambridge newspapers and opinion, 1780–1850.* Cambridge; Oleander Press; 1977. Pp 143.

44. Nash, M. *The provoked wife: the life and times of Susannah Cibber.* London; Hutchinson; 1977. Pp xii, 369.

45. Nelson, J.M., 'Ideology in search of a context: eighteenth-century British political thought and the loyalists of the American Revolution [review article],' *Historical J.* 20 (1977), 741–9.

46. Reynolds, R.R., 'Mrs. Piozzi's "Scotch journey", 1789,' *B. of the John Rylands University Library of Manchester* 60 (1977), 114–34.

47. St Clair, W. *Trelawny: the incurable romancer.* London; Murray; 1977. Pp xii, 235.

48. Mossner, E.C.; Ross, I.S. (ed.). *The correspondence of Adam Smith.* Oxford; Clarendon; 1977. Pp xxx, 441.

49. Stroud, B. *Hume.* London; Routledge; 1977. Pp xii, 280.

50. Temperley, N. *Jonathan Gray and church music in York, 1740–1840.* [York; St Anthony's Press]; 1977. Pp 30.

51. Townsend, M., 'Cobbett's views on schools,' *History Today* 27 (1977), 566–72.

52. Wilton, A. *British watercolours, 1750–1850.* Oxford: Phaidon; 1977. Pp 208.

53. Dobai, J. *Die Kunstliteratur des Klassizismus und der Romantik in England; vol. 3: 1790–1840.* Bern; Berteli Verlag; 1977. Pp 1593.

54. Gilbert, A.N., 'Sexual deviation and diasater during the Napoleonic wars,' *Albion* 9 (1977), 98–113.
55. Downes, K. *Vanbrugh.* London; Zwemmer; 1977. Pp xiv, 291.

(j) Science

1. Inkster, I., 'Science and society in the metropolis: a preliminary examination of the social and institutional context of the Askesian Society of London, 1796–1807,' *Annals of Science* 34 (1977), 1–32.
2. Laycock, W.S. *The lost science of John 'Longitude' Harrison.* Ashford (Kent); Brant Wright Associates; 1976. Pp 159.
3. McClintock, D. *The life of Joshua Gosselin of Guernsey, 1739– 1813: greffier and soldier, antiquary and artist, plantsman and natural historian.* [St Peter Port] ; Toucan Press; 1976. Pp 32.
4. Masters, A. *Bedlam.* London; Joseph; 1977. Pp 206.
5. Porter, R. *The making of geology: earth science in Britain, 1660–1815.* Cambridge UP; 1977. Pp xi, 288.

H. BRITAIN 1815–1914

See also: Aa37, b31; Gb13, 15, e19, 20, 27, f1, 9, 11, 13, 15, 22, 26, 72, h25, i1, 3, 4, 20, 35; Ib16, c1, j1, 14

(a) General

1. Trevor-Roper, H.R. *A hidden life: the enigma of Sir Edmund Backhouse.* London; Macmillan; 1976. Pp viii, 316.
2. Richardson, J., 'Queen Victoria's jubilees,' *History Today* 27 (1977), 349–57.
3. Gardiner, L. *Bartholomew, 150 years.* Edinburgh; J. Bartholomew; 1976. Pp 112.
4. Alexander, J. *Whom the gods love: Boyd Alexander's expedition from the Niger to the Nile 1904–7, and his last journey, 1908– 10.* London; Heinemann; 1977. Pp 310.
5. Olsen, D.J. *The growth of Victorian London.* London; Batsford; 1976. Pp 384.
6. Delgado, A. *The annual outing and other excursions.* London; Allen & Unwin; 1977. Pp 173.
7. Young, J.A. *Southbourne on Sea, 1870–1901.* Dorset County Council; 1976. Pp 14.
8. Chadwick, S. *A bold and faithful journalist: Joshua Hobson, 1810–1876.* Huddersfield; Kirklees Libraries and Museums Service; 1976. Pp 82.

9. Woodruff, J. *John Woodruff's journal, 1851—56.*] Upchurch; Keith Chave; 1976]. Pp 67.
10. Lloyd, A. *The great prize fight.* London; Cassell; 1977. Pp xii, 188.
11. Marriott, P.J. *Oxford's legendary son, the young Lawrence of Arabia, 1888—1910.* [Oxford; the author; 1977]. Pp viii, 100.
12. Brown, L.M., 'The treatment of the news in mid-Victorian newspapers,' *T. of the Royal Historical Soc.* 5th ser. 27 (1977), 23—39.
13. Robertson, M. *Wimbledon, 1877—1977.* London; Barker; 1977. Pp xii, 180.
14. Poulsen, C. *Victoria Park: a study in the history of East London.* London; Journeyman Press; 1976. Pp 120.
15. Huxley, E. *Scott of the Antarctic.* London; Weidenfeld & Nicolson; 1977. Pp xiv, 303.
16. Bristow, P. *The Mansfield brew.* Ringwood; Navigator Publishing; 1976. Pp 188.
17. Oates, M., 'A royal visit in 1863,' *T. of the Halifax Antiquarian Soc.* (1977 for 1975), 25—7.
18. Porrit, A., 'Samuel Henry Hamer,' ibid. 75—91.
19. Teversham, T.F. *Reminiscence: a recording of some aspects of Sawston life between 1886 and 1942.* Sawston; [Ronald Bircham] ; 1976. Pp 29.
20. Gilbert, H. *The life of Lord Mount Stephen, vol. 2: 1891—1921, the end of the road.* Aberdeen UP; 1977. Pp xiii, 442.
21. Turton, 'Crewe New Town in 1851,' *North Staffordshire J. of Field Studies* 16 (1976), 57—72.
22. Wagner, A.R., Papers of a middling family: Bell of Belford, Hull and Henley in Arden,' Bc3, 265—304.
23. Freeman, S. *Isabella and Sam: the story of Mrs Beeton.* London; Gollancz; 1977. Pp 336.
24. Florance, A. *Queen Victoria at Osborne.* [Newport, I.o.W.; the author] ; 1977. Pp viii, 90.
25. Jenkins, D. and H. *Isambard Kingdom Brunel, engineer extraordinary.* Hove; Priory Press; 1977. Pp 96.

(b) Politics

1. Temmel, M.R., 'Gladstone's resignation of the Liberal leadership, 1874—1875,' *J. of British Studies* 16 (1976), 153—77.
2. Rossi, J.P., ' "The Nestor of his Party" — Gladstone, Hartington and the Liberal leadership crisis: November 1879—January 1880,' *Canadian J. of History* 11 (1976), 189—99.
3. Hogarth, C.E., 'Derby and Derbyshire elections 1837—47,' *Derbyshire Arch. J.* 95 (1976 for 1974), 48—58.
4. Williams, T.C. *Robert Owen* [in Welsh]. Swansea; Hughes a'i Fen; 1975. Pp 43.

5. Gilbert, B.B., 'David Lloyd George: land, the budget, and social reform,' *American Historical R.* 81 (1976), 1058—66.
6. Howard, C.; Gordon, P., 'The first Balmoral journal of Dudley Ryder, viscount Sandon (later third earl of Harrowby), 6—14 November 1879,' *B. of the Institute of Historical Research* 50 (1977), 82—109.
7. McHugh, J., 'The Belfast labour dispute and riots of 1907,' *International R. of Social History* 22 (1977), 1—20.
8. Godfrey, C.; Epstein, J., 'Interviews of Chartist prisoners 1840—1841,' *Soc. for the study of Labour History* 34 (1977), 27—34.
9. Watmough, P.A., 'The membership of the Social Democratic Federation 1885—1902,' ibid. 35—40.
10. Cookson, J.E., 'Canning's Pantheon,' *History* 62 (1977), 43—8.
11. Newbould, D.C., 'William IV and the dismissal of the Whigs, 1834,' *Canadian J. of History* 11 (1976), 311—30.
12. Fraser, D. *Urban politics in Victorian England: the structure of politics in Victorian cities.* Leicester UP; 1976. Pp 324.
13. Tholfsen, T.R. *Working class radicalism in mid-Victorian England.* London; Croom Helm; 1976. Pp 332.
14. Vincent, J. *The formation of the British Liberal Party, 1857—1868* (2nd ed.). Hassocks; Harvester Press; 1976. Pp li, 300.
15. Moore, D.C. *The politics of deference: a study of the mid-nineteenth century English political system.* Hassocks; Harvester Press; 1976. Pp ix, 529.
16. Ziegler, P. *Melbourne: a biography of William Lamb, 2nd viscount Melbourne.* London; Collins; 1976. Pp 412.
17. Crosby, T.L. *Sir Robert Peel's administration, 1841—1846.* Newton Abbot; David & Charles; 1976. Pp 190.
18. Harvie, C. *The lights of liberation: university liberals and the challenge of democracy.* London; Allen Lane; 1976. Pp 343.
19. Brooke, J.; Gandy, J. (ed.). *Wellington: Political correspondence. I: 1833—November 1834.* London; HMSO; 1975 [i.e. 1976]. Pp v, 776.
20. Kriegel, A.D. (ed.). *The Holland House diaries, 1831—1840: the diary of Henry Richard Vassall Fox, third lord Holland, with extracts from the diary of Dr John Allen.* London; Routledge; 1977. Pp lxiv, 513.
21. Lovell, J. *British trade unions, 1875—1933.* London; Macmillan; 1977. Pp 75.
22. Davis, R.W. *Disraeli.* London; Hutchinson; 1976. Pp xiii, 231.
23. Campbell, J. *Lloyd George: the Goat in the wilderness, 1922—1931.* London; Cape; 1977. Pp xii, 389.
24. Pinney, T. (ed.). *The letters of Thomas Babington Macaulay, vol. 4: September 1841—December 1848.* Cambridge UP; 1977. Pp xii, 407.
25. Hogarth, C.E., 'The 1835 election in Derbyshire,' *Derbyshire Arch. J.* 94 (1976 for 1974), 45—59.

26. Thomis, M., 'The guilt of Thomas Bacon of Pentrich,' ibid. 41—4.
27. Cregier, D.M. *Bounder from Wales: Lloyd George's career before the first World War*. Colombia/London; Univ. of Missouri Press; 1976. Pp ix, 292.
28. Hamburger, J. *Macaulay and the Whig tradition*. Chicago/London; Univ. of Chicago Press; 1976. Pp xiii, 274.
29. Holton, B. *British syndicalism, 1900—1914: myth and realities*. London; Pluto Press; 1976. Pp 232.
30. Bealey, F. *The Post Office Engineering Union: the history of the Post Office Engineers, 1870—1970*. London; Bachman & Turner; 1976. Pp 432.
31. Haynes, W.J., 'Class and class conflict in the early nineteenth century: Northampton shoemakers and the Grand National Consolidated Trades' Union,' *Literature and History* 5 (1977), 73—94.
32. Kapp, Y. *Eleanor Marx; vol. 2: The crowded years (1884—1898)*. London; Lawrence & Wishart; 1976. Pp 775.
33. Pelling, H. *A history of British trade unionism* (3rd ed.). London; Macmillan; 1976. Pp xiii, 326.
34. Brown, K. *John Burns*. London; Royal Historical Society; 1977. Pp 217.
35. Judd, D. *Radical Joe: a life of Joseph Chamberlain*. London; Hamilton; 1977. Pp xvi, 310.
36. Phillips, Gregory D., 'The "Diehards" and the myth of the "Backwoodsmen",' *J. of British Studies* 16/2 (1977), 105—20.
37. Garrard, J.A., 'Parties, members and voters after 1867: a local study,' *Historical J.* 20 (1977), 145—64.
38. Rossi, J.P., 'English catholics, the Liberal party and the general election of 1880,' *Catholic Historical R.* 63 (1977), 411—27.
39. Milne, M., 'Strikes and strike-breaking in north-east England, 1815—44: the attitude of the local press,' *International R. of Social History* 22 (1977), 226—40.
40. Anand, V.S.; Ridley, F.A. *The Cato Street conspiracy*. London; Medusa Press; 1977. Pp 120.
41. Aronson, T. *Victoria and Disraeli: the making of a romantic partnership*. London; Cassell; 1977. Pp xii, 212.
42. Knott, S. *The electoral crucible: the politics of London, 1900—1914*. London; Greene & Co.; [1977]. Pp iii, 194.
43. Richardson, J. *Victoria and Albert: a study of a marriage*. London; Dent; 1977. Pp 233.
44. Wasson, E.A., 'The coalitions of 1827 and the crisis of Whig leadership,' *Historical J.* 20 (1977), 587—606.
45. Munson, J.E.B., 'The Unionist coalition and education, 1895—1902,' ibid. 607—46.
46. Howard, C.H.D.; Gorden, P., 'The Osborne journals, second Balmoral journal, and notes of events of Dudley Ryder, Viscount Sandon (later third earl of Harrowby), 1879—96,' *B. of the Institute of Historical Research* 50 (1977), 210—17.

47. Lowe, W.J., 'Lancashire Fenianism, 1864—71,' *T. of the Historical Soc. of Lancashire and Cheshire* (1977 for 1976), 156—85.

48. Clarke, P.F., 'Liberals, Labour and the franchise,' *English Historical R.* 92 (1977), 582—90.

49. Griffiths, P., 'Pressure groups and parties in late Victorian England,' *Midland History* 3 (1976), 191—205.

50. Sutherland, J., 'Thackeray, the Oxford election and the Sunday question,' *Bodleian Library Record* 9 (1977), 274—9.

51. Fraser, D., 'Voluntaryism and West Riding politics in the mid-nineteenth century,' *Northern History* 13 (1977), 199—231.

52. Foster, D., 'The politics of uncontested elections: North Lancashire, 1832—1865,' ibid. 232—47.

53. Palmer, S.H., 'Before the bobbies: the Caroline riots of 1821,' *History Today* 27 (1977), 637—44.

54. Powell, J.E. *Joseph Chamberlain.* London; Thames & Hudson; 1977. Pp 160.

55. Mitchell, D. *Queen Christabel: a biography of Christabel Pankhurst.* London; Macdonald & Jane's; 1977. Pp x, 397.

56. Stevenson, J. (ed.). *London in the age of reform.* Oxford; Blackwell; 1977. Pp xxvi, 214.

57. Lewenhak, S. *Women and trade unions: an outline history of women in the British trade union movement.* London; Benn; 1977. Pp xii, 308.

58. Crosby, T.L. *English farmers and the politics of protection, 1815—1852.* Hassocks; Harvester Press; 1977. Pp 224.

59. Cromwell, V. *Revolution or evolution: British government in the nineteenth century.* London; Longman; 1977. Pp x, 230.

60. Craig, F.W.S. (ed.). *British parliamentary election results, 1832—1885.* London; Macmillan; 1977. Pp xvii, 692.

61. Gash, N. *The conservatives: a history from their origins to 1965.* London; Allen & Unwin; 1977. Pp 492.

62. Clinton, A. *The trade union rank and file: trades councils in Britain, 1900—40.* Manchester UP; 1977. Pp x, 262.

63. Bennett, D. *King without a crown: Albert, prince consort of England, 1819—1861.* London; Heinemann; 1977. Pp xvii, 430.

64. Pemberton, J.E. *Politics and public libraries in England and Wales, 1850—1970.* London; Library Association; 1977. Pp 160.

65. Prest, J. *Politics in the age of Cobden.* London; Macmillan; 1977. Pp 165.

66. Hilton, B. *Corn, cash, commerce.* Oxford UP; 1977. Pp 350.

67. Garrard, J. *Leaders and politics in nineteenth century Salford: a historical analysis of urban political power.* University of Salford; 1977. Pp 96.

68. Benson, J., 'The establishment of the West Riding of Yorkshire Miners' Permanent Relief Fund,' Bc1, 92—108.

69. Ward, J.T., 'Some aspects of working class conservatism in the nineteenth century,' Bc2, 141—57.

70. Edsall, N.C., 'A failed national movement: the Parliamentary and Financial Reform Association, 1848–54,' *B. of the Institute of Historical Research* 49 (1976), 108–31.
71. Matthew, H.C.G., 'H.H. Asquith's political journalism,' ibid. 146–51.
72. Harvey, C.F., 'The political diaries of Sir John Trelawny,' ibid. 144–6.
73. Weeks, J. *Coming out: homosexual politics in Britain from the nineteenth century to the present.* London; Quartet Books; 1977. Pp x, 278.

(c) Constitution, Administration and Law

1. Chowdharay-Best, G., 'A note on the temporary civil servant,' *Public Administration* 54 (1976), 333–40.
2. Schneider, F.D., 'The Anglican quest for authority: Convocation and the imperial factor, 1850–60,' *J. of Religious History* 9 (1976), 139–57.
3. Boyce, D.G.; Stubbs, J.O., 'F.S. Oliver, Lord Selbourne and Federalism,' *J. of Imperial and Commonwealth History* 5 (1976–7), 53–81.
4. Nelson, P., 'Leicester suburban school boards,' *History of Education* 6 (1977), 53–63.
5. Dimoldenberg, P. *The evolving role of the state and its impact on the development of Bermondsey, 1850–1975.* Oxford Polytechnic (Townplanning Dept.); 1977. Pp 112.
6. Gibson, J.S. *Deacon Brodie: father to Jekyll and Hyde.* Edinburgh; P. Harris; 1977. Pp 158.
7. Spring, E., 'Landowners, lawyers and land law reform in nineteenth-century England,' *American J. of Legal History* 21 (1977), 40–59.
8. Philips, D., 'The Black Country magistracy, 1835–60,' *Midland History* 3 (1976), 161–90.
9. Lloyd, C., 'The blockade of the smugglers,' *History Today* 27 (1977), 765–71.
10. Webster, E., 'Royal Commission on rivers, November 1866,' *T. of the Halifax Antiquarian Soc.* (1977 for 1975), 1–9.
11. Dunbabin, J.P.D., 'British local government reform: the nineteenth century and after,' *English Historical R.* 92 (1977), 777–805.
12. Neville, R.G., 'In the wake of Taff Vale: the Denaby and Cadeby miners' strike and conspiracy case, 1902–6,' Bc1, 145–62.

(d) External Affairs

1. Turnbull, P., 'Ferrozeshah and the Sikh war, December 1849,' *History Today* 27 (1977), 31–40.

2. Geiger, J.O., 'A scholar meets John Bull: Edward Everett as United States minister to England, 1841—1845,' *New England Q.* 49 (1976), 577—95.

3. Farley, M.F., 'Commissioner Lin and opium,' *History Today* 27 (1977), 73—81.

4. Waller, R., 'The Massai and the British 1895—1905: the origins of an alliance,' *J. of African History* 17 (1976), 529—53.

5. Summerton, N.W., 'Dissenting attitudes to foreign relations, peace and war, 1840—1890,' *J. of Ecclesiastical History* 28 (1977), 151—78.

6. Randall, A., 'Lord Odo Russell and Bismarck,' *History Today* 27 (1977), 240—8.

7. Gruner, W.D., ' "British interest" und Friedenssicherung: zur Interaktion von britischer Innen= und Aussenpolitik im frühen 19. Jahrhundert,' *Historische Zeitschrift* 224 (1977), 92—104.

8. Wong, J.T., 'The building of an informal British empire in China in the middle of the nineteenth century,' *B. of the John Rylands Library* 59 (1977), 472—85.

9. Turton, E.R., Lord Salisbury and the Macdonald expedition,' *J. of Imperial and Commonwealth History* 5 (1976—7), 35—52.

10. Pla, J. *The British in Paraguay, 1850—1870* (translated by B.C. MacDermot). Richmond, Surrey; Richmond Publishing Co.; 1976. Pp xxix, 277.

11. Cohen, S.A. *British Policy in Mesopotamia, 1903—1914.* London; Ithaca Press; 1976. Pp vii, 361.

12. Farwell, B. *The great Boer war.* London; Allen Lane; 1977. Pp xiv, 495.

13. Jennings, L.C., 'France, Great Britain, and the repression of the slave trade, 1841—1845,' *French Historical Studies* 10 (1977), 101—25.

14. Kennedy, P.M., 'The theory and practice of imperialism [review article],' *Historical J.* 20 (1977), 761—9.

15. Hinsley, F.H. (ed.). *British foreign policy under Sir Edward Grey.* Cambridge UP; 1977. Pp viii, 702.

16. Robbins, K.G., 'The foreign secretary, the cabinet, parliament and the parties,' Hd15, 3—21.

17. Steiner, Z., 'The foreign office under Sir Edward Grey, 1905—1914,' Hd15, 22—69.

18. Robbins, K.G., 'Public opinion, the press and pressure groups,' Hd15, 70—88.

19. Parry, C., 'Foreign policy and international law,' Hd15, 88—110.

20. Hamilton, K.A., 'Great Britain and France, 1905—1911,' Hd15, 113—32.

21. Williams, B., 'Great Britain and Russia, 1905 to the 1907 Convention,' Hd15, 133—47.

22. Kent, M., 'Constantinople and Asiatic Turkey,' Hd15, 148—64.

23. Bridge, F.R., 'Relations with Austria-Hungary and the Balkan states, 1905—1908,' Hd15, 165—77.
24. Sweet, D.W., 'The Bosnian crisis,' Hd15, 178—92.
25. Steinberg, J., 'The German background to Anglo-German relations, 1905—1914,' Hd15, 193—215.
26. Sweet, D.W., 'Great Britain and Germany, 1905—1911,' Hd15, 216—35.
27. Sweet, D.W.; Langhorne, R.T.B., 'Great Britain and Russia, 1907—1914,' Hd15, 238—55.
28. Crompton, R.J., 'The Balkans, 1909—1914,' Hd15, 256—70.
29. Dockrill, M.L., 'British policy during the Agadir crisis of 1911,' Hd15, 271—87.
30. Langhorne, R.T.B., 'Great Britain and Germany, 1911—1914,' Hd15, 288—314.
31. Lowe, C.J., 'Grey and the Tripoli war, 1911—1912,' Hd15, 315—23.
32. Hamilton, K.A., 'Great Britain and France, 1911—1914,' Hd15, 324—41.
33. Ekstein, M.G., 'Great Britain and the Triple Entente on the eve of the Sarajevo crisis,' Hd15, 342—8.
34. Edwards, E.W., 'Great Britain and China, 1905—1911,' Hd15, 351—61.
35. Nish, I.H., 'Great Britain, Japan, and north-east Asia, 1905—1911,' Hd15, 362—7.
36. Edwards, E.W., 'China and Japan, 1911—1914,' Hd15, 368—81.
37. Calvert, P.A.R., 'Great Britain and the New World, 1905—1914,' Hd15, 382—94.
38. Ekstein, M.G.; Steiner, Z., 'The Sarajevo crisis,' Hd15, 397—410.
39. Richardson, R.G. (ed.). *Nurse Sarah Anne [Terrot]: with Florence Nightingale at Scutari.* London; Murray; 1977. Pp 183.
40. Steeds, D.; Nish, I.H. *China, Japan, and 19th century Britain.* Dublin; Irish UP; 1977. Pp 136.
41. Llewellyn, A. *The siege of Delhi.* London; Macdonald & Jane's; 1977. Pp vi, 182.
42. Gillard, D. *The struggle for Asia, 1828—1914: a study in British and Russian imperialism.* London; Methuen; 1977. Pp x, 214.
43. Brent, P. *Black Nile: Mungo Park and the search for the Niger.* London; Gordon & Cremonesi; 1977. Pp 200.
44. Chanock, M. *Unconsummated union: Britain, Rhodesia and South Africa, 1900—45.* Manchester UP; 1977. Pp xi, 289.
45. Philips, C.H. (ed.). *The correspondence of Lord William Cavendish Bentinck, governor-general of India 1828—1835.* Oxford UP; 1977. 2 vols; pp. xlix, 1483.
46. Platt, D.C.M. *Business imperialism, 1840—1930.* Oxford; Clarendon; 1977. Pp 466.
47. Mewes, K., 'Handelspolitische Aspekte in den deutsch-englischen

Beziehungen 1878—1882,' *Wissenschaftliche Zeitschrift der Wilhelm-Pieck Universität Rostock* 25/10 (1976), 789—97.

48. Jenkins, B. *Britain and the war for the Union, vol. 1.* Montreal/London; McGill-Queen's UP; 1974. Pp x, 315.

49. Gruner, W.D., 'Europäischer Friede als nationales Interesse: Die Rolle des Deutschen Bundes in der britischen Politik 1814—1832,' *Bohemia* 18 (1977), 96—128.

50. Tulloch, H., 'Changing British attitudes towards the United States in the 1880s,' *Historical J.* 20 (1977), 825—40.

(e) Religion

1. Pinnington, J.E., 'The debate on the continental churches,' *Downside R.* 95 (1977), 49—61.

2. Pfaff, W., 'Anglo-American patristic translations 1866—1900,' *J. of Ecclesiastical History* 28 (1977), 39—56.

3. Roe, G.; Hutchings, A. *J.B. Dykes (1823—1876), priest and musician.* [Durham; St Oswald's Parochial Church Council; 1976]. Pp 25.

4. Martin, B.W. *John Keble: Priest, professor and poet.* London; Croom Helm; 1976. Pp 191.

5. Payne, E.A., 'The rise and decline of the Downs Chapel, Clapton,' *Baptist Q.* 27 (1977), 34—44.

6. Chambers, D., 'The Church of Scotland's nineteenth century foreign missions scheme: evangelical or moderate revival?,' *J. of Religious History* 9 (1976), 115—38.

7. Porter, A., 'Cambridge, Keswick and late nineteenth-century attitudes in Africa,' *J. of Imperial and Commonwealth History* 5 (1976—7?), 5—34.

8. Tamke, S.S., 'Separating the sheep from the goats: Victorian didactic hymns,' *Albion* 8 (1976), 255—73.

9. Pals, D., 'The reception of "Ecce Homo",' *Historical Magazine of the Protestant Episcopal Church*, 46 (1977), 63—84.

10. Hayes, A.J., 'The extinct Methodist societies of south-east Scotland: 1. Dunfermline,' *P. of the Wesley Historical Soc.* 41 (1977), 12—21.

11. Scotland, N.A.D., 'Methodism and the "Revolt of the Field" in East Anglia, 1872—96,' ibid. 2—11.

12. Jacob, A.M., 'Aaron Levy Green, 1821—1883,' *T. of the Jewish Historical Soc. of England* 25 (1977 for 1973/5), 87—106.

13. Schiefen, R.J., ' "Anglo-Gallicanism" in nineteenth-century England,' *Catholic Historical R.* 63 (1977), 14—44.

14. Yeo, S. *Religion and voluntary organisations in crisis.* London; Croom Helm; 1976. Pp xii, 426.

15. Obelkevich, J. *Religion and rural society: South Lindsey, 1825—1875.* Oxford; Clarendon Press; 1976. Pp xiii, 353.

16. Northcott, C. *Slavery's martyr: John Smith of Demerara and the*

emancipation movement, 1817–24. London; Epworth Press; 1976. Pp 136.

17. Jones, I.G.; Williams, D. (ed.). *The religious census of 1851: a calendar of the returns relating to Wales; vol. 1: South Wales.* Cardiff; Univ. of Wales Press; 1976. Pp xxv, 698.

18. Vickers, J.A. *Thomas Coke and world Methodism.* Bognor Regis; World Methodist Historical Soc.; 1976. Pp 20.

19. Johnson, D.A., 'Did the nineteenth-century English Church fail to heed the signs of the time?,' *Historical Magazine of the Protestant Episcopal Church* 46/2 (1977), 227–49.

20. Hayes, A.J., 'The extinct Methodist societies of south-east Scotland: 2, Haddington,' *P. of the Wesley Historical Soc.* 61 (1977), 43–52.

21. Scotland, N.A.D., 'Methodism and the "revolt of the field" in East Anglia, 1872–96 (continued),' ibid. 39–42.

22. Newton, J.A. *Search for a saint: Edward King.* London; Epworth Press; 1977. Pp 128.

23. Harrison, F.M.W., 'The Nottinghamshire Baptists and education,' *Baptist Q.* 27 (1977), 94–109.

24. Chadwick, W.O., 'Lord Acton at the first Vatican Council,' *J. of Theological Studies* new ser. 28 (1977), 465–97.

25. Perry, P.J., 'Edward Girdlestone 1805–84: a forgotten evangelical,' *J. of Religious History* 9 (1977), 292–301.

26. Steele, E.D., 'Infidels and churchmen [review article],' *Northern History* 13 (1977), 280–2.

27. Sellers, I. *Nineteenth-century nonconformity.* London; Arnold; 1977. Pp ix, 102.

28. Machin, G.I.T. *Politics and the Churches in Great Britain, 1832 to 1868.* Oxford; Clarendon; 1977. Pp 448.

29. Jackman, S.W. *Nicholas Cardinal Wiseman: a Victorian prelate and his writings.* [Dublin]; Five Lamps Press; 1977. Pp 143.

30. Cox, J.E. *Rev. William Buckler: rector of St Mary Major, Ilchester, 1837–1876.* St Peter Port; Toucan Press; 1977. Pp 137–44.

31. Dessain, C.S.; Gornall, T. (ed.). *The letters and diaries of John Henry Newman, vol. 31: The last years, January 1885 to August 1890; with a supplement of addenda to volumes XI–XXX.* Oxford; Clarendon; 1977. Pp 130.

32. Thatcher, B.M., 'The episcopal church in Helensburgh in the mid-nineteenth century,' Bc2, 98–123.

33. Jones, O.W., 'The Welsh church in the nineteenth century,' Bc4, 144–63.

34. White, G., 'New names for old things: Scottish reaction to early tractarianism,' Bc6, 329–37.

35. Barkley, J.M., 'The renaissance of public worship in the Church of Scotland, 1865–1905,' Bc6, 339–50.

36. Kent, J., 'A late nineteenth century nonconformist renaissance,' Bc6, 351–60.

37. Vidler, A.R., 'An abortive renaissance: Catholic modernists in Sussex,' Bc6, 377–92.

(f) *Economic Affairs*

1. O'Brien, D.P., 'Torrens, McCulloch and Disraeli,' *Scottish J. of Political Economy* 24 (1977), 1–18.
2. Gatrell, V.A.C., 'Labour, power and the size of firms in Lancashire cotton in the second quarter of the nineteenth century,' *Economic History R.* 2nd ser. 30 (1977), 95–139.
3. Boyns, T., 'The mines of Llywernog,' *National Library of Wales J.* 19 (1976), 430–52.
4. Cunningham, T.M., 'Factors influencing the growth of Peterborough, 1850–1900,' *Northamptonshire Past and Present* 5 (1977), 427–36.
5. Greenall, R.L., 'The history of boot and shoemaking at Long Buckley,' ibid. 437–47.
6. Lewis, E.D., 'The Cymer (Rhondda) explosion,' *T. of the Honourable Soc. of Cymmrodorion* 1976, 119–61.
7. Holmes, G.M., 'The South Wales coal industry, 1850–1914,' ibid. 162–207.
8. Peake, F.A., 'Heanor in the 19th century,' *Derbyshire Arch. J.* 95 (1976 for 1974), 59–66.
9. Thorne, H.D. *Rails to Portpatrick.* Prescot; Stephenson & Sons; 1976. Pp xvi, 261.
10. Coleman, T. *The liners: a history of the North Atlantic crossing.* London; Allen Lane; 1976. Pp 232.
11. Aspinall, B., 'Glasgow trams and American politics 1894–1914,' *Scottish Historical R.* 56 (1977), 64–84.
12. Ó Gráda, C., 'The beginnings of the Irish creamery system, 1880–1914,' *Economic History R.* 2nd ser. 30 (1977), 284–305.
13. Roberts, E., 'Working-class standards of living in Barrow and Lancaster, 1890–1914,' ibid. 306–21.
14. Perrone, N., 'Il manifesto dell' imperialismo américano nelle borse di Londra e Parigi: reazioni alla dottrina di Monroe,' *Belfagor* 32 (1977), 321–7.
15. Thorne, R.G., 'Thomas Phillips of Milford, emigrant extraordinary,' *National Library of Wales J.* 20 (1977), 1–13.
16. Rashid, S., 'Richard Whately and Christian political economy at Oxford and Dublin,' *J. of the History of Ideas* 38 (1977), 147–55.
17. Schmitz, C.J., 'An account of Mendip calamine mining in the early 1870s,' *Somerset Archaeology and Natural History* 120 (1976), 81–3.
18. Gordon, B. *Political economy in parliament, 1819–1823.* London; Macmillan; 1976. Pp x, 246.
19. Holmes, G.M. *Britain and America: a comparative economic his-*

tory, 1850–1939. Newton Abbot; David & Charles; 1976. Pp 224.

20. Moss, M.S.; Hume, J.R. *Workshop of the British empire: engineering and shipbuilding in the west of Scotland.* London; Heinemann; 1977. Pp xvi, 192.

21. Tucker, D.G., 'Hydro-electricity for public supply in Britain, 1881–1894,' *Industrial Archaeology R.* 1 (1976–7), 126–63.

22. Thomas, D.St.J. *The country railway.* Newton Abbot; David & Charles; 1976. Pp 160.

23. Lyes, D.C. *The leather glove industry of Worcester in the nineteenth century.* Worcester City Museum; 1976. Pp 88.

24. Robinson, G.M. *Late Victorian agriculture in the Vale of Evesham.* Oxford; School of Geography; 1976. Pp 32.

25. Schädlich, K., 'Politische und ökonomische Aspekte der britisch-deutschen Handelsrivalität am Ende des 19. Jahrhunderts,' *Jahrbuch für Geschichte* 15 (1977), 67–84.

26. Dunham, R.K.; Hobbs, R.J., 'Burtree pasture lead mine, Weardale,' *Industrial Archaeology R.* 1 (1976–7), 2–17.

27. Griffin, C.P., 'Some comments on capital formation in the British coalmining industry during the Industrial Revolution,' ibid. 81–3.

28. Daunton, M.J. *Coal metropolis: Cardiff 1870–1914.* Leicester UP; 1977. Pp xi, 260.

29. Adrian, L., 'The nineteenth-century Gazette Corn Returns for East Anglian corn markets,' *J. of Historical Geography* 3 (1977), 217–36.

30. Hopkins, E., 'The decline of the family work unit in Black Country nailing,' *International R. of Social History* 22 (1977), 184–97.

31. Parkins, J.A., 'The Lincolnshire contraband tobacco trade after the Napoleonic wars,' *J. of Transport History* new ser. 4 (1977), 86–101.

32. Cuca, R., 'Industrial change and the progress of labor in the English cotton industry,' *International R. of Social History* 22 (1977), 241–55.

33. Howkins, A., 'Structural conflict and the farmworker: Norfolk 1900–1920,' *J. of Peasant Studies* 4 (1977), 217–29.

34. Young, J.A. *An outline of postal services in Bournemouth, 1839–1899.* Dorset County Council, Education Committee; [1977]. Pp 17.

35. Barber, R. *Iron and after: boom time, depression and survival in a West Cumbrian town, Cleaton Moor, 1840–1960.* York University; 1976. Pp 71.

36. Jenkins, S.C.; Quayle, H.I. *The Oxford, Worcester & Wolverhampton Railway: a history of the 'Cotswold line' and its branches from the 1840s to the present day.* Blanford; Oakwood Press; 1977. Pp 128.

37. Taylor, J., 'John Rennie's reconstruction of Sheerness dockyard,' *Industrial Archaeology R.* 1 (1977), 255—64.
38. Griffin, C.P., 'Three generations of miners' housing at Moira, Leicestershire, 1811—1934,' ibid. 276—82.
39. Cannadine, D., 'The landowner as millionaire: the finances of the dukes of Devonshire, c. 1800—c. 1926,' *Agricultural History R.* 25 (1977), 77—97.
40. Daunton, M., 'The Cardiff Coal Trimmers' Union, 1888—1914,' *Maritime History* 5 (1977), 51—67.
41. Colyer, R., 'The land agent in nineteenth-century Wales,' *Welsh History R.* 8 (1977), 401—25.
42. Cannadine, D., 'Aristocratic indebtedness in the nineteenth century: the case re-opened,' *Economic History R.* 2nd ser. 30 (1977), 624—50.
43. Rubinstein, W.D., 'The Victorian middle classes: wealth, occupation and geography,' ibid. 602—23.
44. Porter, R.E., 'The marketing of agricultural produce in Cheshire during the 19th century,' *T. of the Historic Soc. of Lancashire and Cheshire* (1977 for 1976), 139—55.
45. George, A.D., 'Industrial archaeology in Bolton and district,' *Industrial Archaeology* 11—12 (1977), 8—20.
46. Hassan, J.A., 'The gas market and the coal industry in the Lothians in the nineteenth century,' ibid. 49—73.
47. Harte, N.B., 'The growth and decay of a hosiery firm in the nineteenth century,' *Textile History* 8 (1977), 7—55.
48. Summerson, J., 'The Victorian rebuilding of the City of London,' *London J.* 3 (1977), 163—85.
49. Fremdling, R., 'Railroads and German economic growth: a leading sector analysis with a comparison to the United States and Great Britain,' *J. of Economic History* 37 (1977), 583—604.
50. Cowie, L.W., 'The Brighton chain pier,' *History Today* 27 (1977), 593—9.
51. Stone, I., 'British direct and portfolio investment in Latin America before 1914,' *J. of Economic History* 37 (1977), 690—722.
52. Turner, J.H. *The London Brighton and South Coast Railway. 1: Origins and formation.* London; Batsford; 1977. Pp xv, 287.
53. Treasure, J.A.P. *The history of British advertising agencies, 1875—1939.* Edinburgh; Scottish Academic Press; 1977. Pp 20.
54. Stones, F. *The British ferrous wire industry, 1882—1962.* Sheffield; Northend; 1977. Pp xv, 418.
55. Rossington, T. *The story of Treeton colliery: one hundred years of coal mining, 1875—1975.* Rotherham Libraries; 1976. Pp 60.
56. Preston, J.M. *Industrial Medway: an historical survey.* Rochester; the author; 1977. Pp ix, 218.
57. Samuel, R. (ed.). *Miners, quarrymen and saltworkers.* London; Routledge; 1977. Pp xvi, 363.
58. Samuel, R., 'Mineral workers,' Hf57, 1—98.

59. Jones, M., 'Y chwarelwyr: the slate quarries of North Wales,' Hf57, 99—136.

60. Didsbury, B., 'Cheshire saltworkers,' Hf57, 137—204.

61. Douglass, D., 'The Durham pitman,' Hf57, 205—96.

62. Douglass, D., 'Pit talk in County Durham,' Hf57, 297—349.

63. Collison Black, R.D. (ed.). *Papers and Correspondence of William Stanley Jevons.* Vol. 3: Correspondence, 1863—1872; vol. 4: Correspondence, 1873—1878; vol. 5: Correspondence, 1879—1882; vol. 6: Lectures on political economy, 1875—1876. London; Macmillan; 1977. Pp xxi, 257; xxv, 306; xix, 202, xi, 140.

64. Heath, J.H., 'Boats and boatbuilders of the East Midlands in the nineteenth century,' *Transport History* 6—7 (1977), 75—80.

65. Howell, D.W. *Land and people in nineteenth-century Wales.* London; Routledge; 1977.

66. Moore, J.R., 'Halifax Corporation tramways: part II,' *T. of the Halifax Antiquarian Soc.* (1977 for 1975), 31—54.

67. Barke, M., 'Two industrialists in 19th century Brighouse,' ibid. 93—6.

68. Lowerson, J.R., 'Enclosure and farm holding in Brackley, 1829—51,' *Northamptonshire Past and Present* 6 (1978), 33—48.

69. Donnelly, F.K., 'The value of labour in 1819,' *B. of the Soc. for the Study of Labour History* 35 (1977), 33—4.

70. Spencer, K.M., 'Railways and the turnpikes in Preston, 1830—50,' *Transport History* 6—7 (1977), 45—53.

71. Bick, D.E. *The old metal mines of mid-Wales; [4]: West Montgomeryshire.* Newent; The Pound House; 1977. Pp 64.

72. Duckham, B.F., 'The Oaks disaster, 1886,' Bc1, 66—91.

73. Fraser, W.H., 'The Glasgow cotton spinners 1837,' Bc2, 80—97.

74. Treble, J.H., 'The performance of the Standard Life Assurance Company in the ordinary life market,' Bc2, 124—40.

75. Hume, J.R., 'Shipbuilding machine tools,' Bc2, 158—80.

76. Weit, R.B., 'The patent still distillers and the role of competition,' Bc9, 129—44.

77. Rule, J., 'The home market and the sea fisheries of Devon and Cornwall in the nineteenth century,' Bc10, 123—39.

78. Ward, J.T., 'West Riding landowners and mining in the nineteenth century,' Bc1, 45—65.

79. Baxter, B. and D. (ed.). *British locomotive catalogue, 1825—1923.* Vol. 1: General summary, index of locomotive-owning companies. Buxton; Moorland Publishing Co.; 1977. Pp 88.

80. Barker, T.C. *The glassmakers: Pilkington — the rise of an international company, 1826—1976.* London; Weidenfeld & Nicolson; 1977. Pp xxxi, 557.

81. Thomas, J. *The Skye railway.* Newton Abbot; David & Charles; 1977. Pp 168.

(g) Social Structure and Population

1. Vorspan, R., 'Vagrancy and the new poor law in late-Victorian and Edwardian England,' *English Historical R.* 92 (1977), 59—81.
2. Thomas, H., 'The industrialization of a Glamorgan parish,' *National Library of Wales J.* 19 (1976), 345—61.
3. Fines, J. (ed.). *Life at sea: a nineteenth century voyage to New Zealand: the diary of John Grayson.* Old Woking; Unwin Bros.; 1976. Pp xviii, 50.
4. Parssinen, T.M.; Prothero, I.J. (ed.), 'The London tailors' strike of 1834 and the collapse of the Grand National Consolidated Trades' Union: a police spy report,' *International R. of Social History* 22 (1977), 65—107.
5. Newman, A., 'Provincial Jewry in Victorian Britain: a report,' *T. of the Jewish Historical Soc. of England* 25 (1977 for 1973—5), 222—9.
6. Jones, D.J.V., ' "A dead loss to the community": the criminal vagrant in mid-nineteenth-century Wales,' *Welsh History R.* 8 (1977), 312—44.
7. Mingay, G.E. *Rural life in Victorian England.* London; Heinemann; 1977. Pp 212.
8. Harvey, C. *Ha'penny help: a record of social improvement in Victorian Scotland.* Milngavie; Heatherbank Press; 1976. Pp viii, 197.
9. Ebery, M.; Preston, B. *Domestic service in late Victorian and Edwardian England, 1871—1914.* Reading; Univ. Department of Geography; 1976. Pp 117.
10. Crossick, G. (ed.). *The lower middle class in Britain, 1870—1914.* London; Croom Helm; 1977. Pp 213.
11. Langdon, G. *The year of the map: portrait of a Wiltshire town in 1841.* Tisbury; Compton Russell; 1976. Pp 119.
12. Keating, P. (ed.). *Into unknown England, 1866—1913: selections from the social explorers.* London; Fontana; 1976. Pp 320.
13. Spiers, M. *Victoria Park, Manchester: a nineteenth-century suburb in its social and administrative context.* Manchester UP (for Chetham Soc.); 1976. Pp xiv, 104.
14. Springhall, J. *Youth, empire and society: British youth movements, 1883—1940.* London; Croom Helm; 1977. Pp 163.
15. Hartley, M.; Ingilby, J. *Life and tradition in west Yorkshire.* London; Dent; 1976. Pp 160.
16. Denman, M.J., 'Sources for urban history: 12: Documents and urban growth, Southampton 1878—1914,' *Local Historian* 12 (1977), 353—9.
17. Dennis, R.J., 'Distance and social interaction in a Victorian city,' *J. of Historical Geography* 3 (1977), 237—50.
18. McCord, N.; Rowe, D.J., 'Industrialisation and urban growth in north-east England,' *International R. of Social History* 22 (1977), 30—64.

19. Searby, P., 'Paternalism, disturbance and parliamentary reform: society and politics in Coventry, 1819—32,' ibid. 198—25.
20. Prochaska, F.K., 'Charity bazaars in nineteenth-century England,' *J. of British Studies* 16/2 (1977), 62—84.
21. McLaren, A., 'Abortion in England, 1890—1914,' *Victorian Studies* 20 (1977), 379—400.
22. Moore, M., 'Social work and social welfare: the organization of philanthropic resources in Britain, 1900—1914,' *J. of British Studies* 16/2 (1977), 85—104.
23. Pooley, C.G., 'The residential segregation of migrant communities in mid-Victorian Liverpool,' *T. of the Institute of British Geographers* new ser. 2 (1977), 364—82.
24. Dennis, R.J., 'Intercensal mobility in a Victorian city,' ibid. 349—63.
25. Shaw, M., 'The ecology of social change: Wolverhampton 1851—71,' ibid. 332—48.
26. Anderson, M. (et al.), 'The national sample from the 1851 census,' *Urban History Yearbook* (1977), 55—9.
27. Lowe, W.J., 'The Lancashire Irish and the Catholic Church, 1846—71: the social dimension,' *Irish Historical Studies* 20 (1976), 129—55.
28. Reid, C., 'Temperance, teetotalism and local culture,' *Northern History* 13 (1977), 248—64.
29. Read, D., 'Work and play in the Victorian north [review article],' ibid. 282—7.
30. Wohl, A.S. *The Victorian family.* London, Croom Helm; 1977. Pp 224.
31. Meacham, S. *A life apart: the English working class.* London; Thames & Hudson; 1977. Pp 272.
32. Huggett, F.E. *Life below stairs: domestic servants in England from Victorian times.* London; Murray; 1977. Pp 186.
33. Ratcliffe, B.M.; Challoner, W.H. (trs. & ed.). *A French sociologist looks at Britain: Gustave d'Eichthal and British Society in 1828.* Manchester UP; 1977. Pp vi, 169.
34. Colloms, B. *Victorian country parsons.* London; Constable; 1977. Pp 288.
35. Lowerson, J. (ed.). *Cliftonville, Hove: a Victorian suburb.* Brighton; University of Sussex; 1977. Pp 25.
36. L'Espérance, J., 'Doctors and women in nineteenth century society: sexuality and roll,' Hk12, 105—27.
37. Inkster, I., 'Marginal men: aspects of the social role of the medical community in Sheffield 1790—1850,' Bk12, 128—63.
38. Waddington, I., 'General practitioners and consultants in early nineteenth-century England: the sociology of an intra-professional conflict,' Hk12, 164—88.
39. Stott, M.E.M., 'In service [i.e. domestic],' *T. of the Halifax Antiquarian Soc.* (1977 for 1975), 21—4.

40. Constable, D. *Household structure in three English market towns, 1851—1871.* Reading; The University; 1977. Pp iii, 63.
41. Hartman, M.S. *Victorian murderesses: a true history of thirteen respectable French and English women accused of unspeakable crimes.* London; Robson Books; 1977. Pp x, 318.
42. Macfarlane, J., 'Denaby Main: a south Yorkshire mining village,' Bc1, 109—44.
43. Simpson, M.A., 'The west end of Glasgow 1830—1914,' Bc5, 44—85.
44. Thompson, F.M.L., 'Hampstead 1830—1914,' Bc5, 86—113.
45. Lloyd, T.H., 'Royal Leamington Spa,' Bc5, 114—52.
46. Edwards, K.C., 'The park estate, Nottingham,' Bc5, 153—69.
47. Tarn, J.W., 'Sheffield,' Bc5, 170—91.
48. Slater, T., 'Estate ownership and nineteenth century suburban development [in Cirencester] ,' Bc8, 145—57.
49. Slater, T., 'The Cirencester Improved Dwellings Company 1880—1914,' Bc8, 171—97.
50. Wall, R., 'Reconstitution and census: Colytonians in parish register and enumerator's book,' Bc10, 73—90.
51. Mitchison, R. *British population change since 1860.* London; Macmillan; 1977. Pp 99.

(h) Social Policy

1. Davies, A.C., 'The old poor law in an industrializing parish: Aberdare, 1818—36,' *Welsh History R.* 8 (1977), 285—311.
2. MacDonagh, O. *Early Victorian government, 1830—1970.* London; Weidenfeld & Nicolson; 1977. Pp xi, 242.
3. Woodroffe, K., 'The Royal Commission on the Poor Laws, 1905—9,' *International R. of Social History* 22 (1977), 137—64.
4. Alexander, J.L., 'Lord John Russell and the origins of the Committee of Council on Education,' *Historical J.* 20 (1977), 395—415.
5. Searby, P., 'The relief of the poor in Coventry, 1830—1863,' ibid. 345—61.
6. Baird, J.D., ' "Divorce and Matrimonial Causes": an aspect of "Hard Times",' *Victorian Studies* 20 (1977), 401—12.
7. Wohl, A.S. *The eternal slum: housing and social policy in Victorian London.* London; Arnold; 1977. Pp xxv, 386.
8. Donajgrodzki, A.P. (ed.). *Social control in nineteenth century Britain.* London; Croom Helm; 1977. Pp 258.
9. Philips, D. *Crime and authority in Victorian England; the Black Country.* London; Croom Helm; 1977. Pp 321.
10. Pasmore, A. *Verderers of the New Forest: a history of the New Forest, 1877—1977.* [Beaulieu] ; Pioneer Publications; [1976] . Pp viii, 298.
11. D'Arcy, F., 'The Malthusian League and the resistance to birth

control propaganda in late Victorian Britain,' *Population Studies* 31 (1977), 429—28.

(i) Education

1. Paz, D.G., 'Working-class education and the state, 1839—1849: the sources of government policy,' *J. of British Studies* 16 (1976), 129—52.
2. Gordon, P., 'Commitments and development in the elementary school curriculum 1870—1907,' *History of Education* 6 (1977), 43—52.
3. Burstyn, J.N., 'Women's education in England during the nineteenth century: a review of the literature, 1970—1976,' ibid. 11—19.
4. Adnett, N.J., 'The eclipse of the British classical political economy: the case of education,' *B. of Economic Research* 29 (1977), 22—36.
5. Blackie, J. *Bradfield, 1850—1975* [school history]. Bradfield; St Andrew's College; 1976. Pp xii, 255.
6. Unwin, P. *The Royal Naval School, 1840—1975*. Haslemere; The School; 1976. Pp 122.
7. Burrows, J. *University adult education in London: a century of achievement*. University of London; 1976. Pp x, 122.
8. Roper, H. *Administering the elementary education acts, 1870—1885*. University of Leeds; 1976. Pp 50.
9. Balls, F.E., 'The endowment of education in the nineteenth century: the case of the Bedford Harpur Trust,' *History of Education* 6 (1977), 103—13.
10. Pugh, D.R., 'A note on school board elections: some north-western contests in the nineties,' ibid. 115—20.
11. Palmer, R.J., 'The influence of F.W. Sanderson on the development of science and engineering at Dulwich College, 1885—1892,' ibid. 121—30.
12. Davies, B.L. *Hugh Owen, 1804—1881*. Cardiff; University of Wales Press; 1977. Pp 98.
13. Sherborne, J.W. *University College, Bristol, 1876—1909*. Bristol Branch of the Historical Association; 1977. Pp 26.
14. Gowing, M., 'Science, technology and education: England in 1870,' *Notes and Records of the Royal Soc. of London* 32 (1977), 71—90.
15. Fraser, G.M. (ed.). *The world of the public school*. London; Weidenfeld & Nicolson; 1977. Pp 210.
16. Price, D.T.W. *A history of Saint David's College Lampeter; vol. 1: to 1898*. Cardiff; University of Wales Press; 1977. Pp xv, 222.
17. McCann, P. (ed.). *Popular education and socialization in the nineteenth century*. London; Methuen; 1977. Pp xii, 276.

18. Dent, H.C. *The training of teachers in England and Wales, 1800–1975*. London; Hodder & Stoughton; 1977. Pp 163.
19. Silver, H.; Teague, S.J. (ed.). *Chelsea College, a history*. London; The College; 1977. Pp 96.
20. Jones, D.K. *The making of the education system, 1851–81*. London; Routledge; 1977. Pp 88.
21. Davies, W., 'The Welsh Department and the Board of Education and the establishment of a Carmarthenshire intermediate school,' *National Library of Wales J.* 20 (1977), 131–50.
22. Russell-Gebbett, J.P. *Henslow of Hitcham: botanist, educationalist and clergyman*. Lavenham; T. Dalton; 1977. Pp 139.
23. Bennett, P. *A very desolate position: the story of the birth and establishment of a mid-Victorian public school* [Rossall]. [Fleetwood]; Rossall Archives; 1977. Pp 146.
24. Haddon, C. *Great days and jolly days: the story of girls' school songs*. London; Hodder & Stoughton; 1977. Pp 126.

(j) Naval and Military

1. 'Admiral Ballard's memoirs, part VI: Up the Irrawaddy to Mandalay,' *Mariner's Mirror* 63 (1977), 25–31.
2. Lester, R.I., 'Construction and purchase of Confederate cruisers in Great Britain during the American Civil War,' ibid. 71–92.
3. Smith, V.T.C., 'The later nineteenth-century land defences of Chatham,' *Post-Medieval Archaeology* 10 (1976), 104–17.
4. Rose, J. *The perfect gentleman: the remarkable life of Dr James Miranda Barry, the woman who served as an officer in the British army from 1813 to 1859*. London; Hutchinson; 1977. Pp 160.
5. Harries-Jenkins, G. *The army in Victorian society*. London; Routledge; 1977. Pp xi, 320.
6. Baxter, C.F., 'The duke of Somerset and the creation of the British ironclad Navy, 1859–66,' *Mariner's Mirror* 63 (1977), 279–84.
7. Temple Godman, R. *The fields of war: a young cavalryman's Crimea campaign*. (ed. P. Warner). London; Murray; 1977. Pp viii, 215.
8. Hopkins, H. *The strange death of Private White: a Victorian scandal that made history*. London; Weidenfeld & Nicolson; 1977. Pp 273.
9. Strachan, H.F.A., 'The origins of the 1855 uniform changes – an example of pre-Crimean reform,' *J. of the Soc. for Army Historical Research* 55 (1977), 85–117.
10. Brown, D.K., 'The first steam battleships,' *Mariner's Mirror* 63 (1977), 327–33.
11. Patterson, A.T., 'A midshipman in the Boxer rebellion,' ibid. 351–8.

12. Wilson, K.M., 'The War Office, Churchill and the Belgian option,' *B. of the Institute of Historical Research* 50 (1977), 218—28.

13. Carter-Campbell, D.N. (ed.)., 'Glasgow to the relief of Ladysmith, 23rd October, 1899—2nd March, 1900,' *J. of the Soc. for Army Historical Research* 55 (1977), 138—52.

14. Winton, J. *Hurrah for the life of a sailor!: life on the lower-deck of the Victorian Navy.* London; Joseph; 1977. Pp 320.

15. Ranft, B. (ed.). *Technical change and British naval policy, 1860—1939.* London; Hodder & Stoughton; 1977. Pp xii, 178.

16. Ranft, B., 'The protection of British seaborne trade and the development of systematic planning for war, 1860—1906,' Hj15, 1—22.

17. Cowpe, A., 'The Royal Navy and the Whitehead torpedo,' Hj15, 23—36.

18. Lyon, H., 'The relations between the Admiralty and private industry in the development of warships,' Hj15, 37—64.

19. Towle, P., 'The evaluation of the experience of the Russo-Japanese war,' Hj15, 65—79.

20. Wells, A., 'Naval intelligence and decision-making in an era of technical change,' Hj15, 123—46.

21. Simpson, C. *The ship that hunted itself.* London; Weidenfeld & Nicolson; 1977. Pp 207.

22. Hough, R. *First Sea Lord: an authorized biography of Admiral Lord Fisher* (2nd ed.). London; Severn House; 1977. Pp 392.

23. Emery, F. *The red soldier: letters from the Zulu war, 1879.* London; Hodder & Stoughton; 1977. Pp 288.

24. Skelley, A.R. *The Victorian army at home: the recruitment and terms and conditions of the British regular, 1859—1899.* London; Croom Helm; 1977. Pp 366.

25. Judd, D. *The Boer war.* London; Hart-David MacGibbon; 1977. Pp 190.

26. Inglesant, D. (ed.). *The prisoner of Voronesh: the diary of Serjeant George Newman, 23rd Regiment of Foot, the Royal Welch Fusiliers, taken prisoner at Inkerman.* Old Woking; Unwin Bros.; 1977. Pp xiii, 261.

(k) Science and Medicine

1. Wall, R., 'Miscellany: infant mortality in the 1890's,' *Local Population Studies* 17 (1976), 48—50.

2. Corbishley, M.J., 'The Vicarage, Great Maplestead, Essex: sewage disposal between 1859 and 1910,' *Post-Medieval Archaeology* 10 (1976), 150—5.

3. Spring, R.J., 'A note on Thomas Graham, surgeon, author of botanical lectures delivered at the Royal Polytechnic Institution, London,' *Annals of Science* 34 (1977), 43—7.

4. Pearson, A. *Robert Hunt (1807—1887).* [St Austell] ; Federation of Old Cornwall Societies; 1976. Pp 123.

5. Laita, L.M., 'The influence of Boole's search for a universal method in analysis or the creation of his logic,' *Annals of Science* 34 (1977), 163—76.

6. Brooke, J.H., 'Natural theology and the plurality of the worlds: observations on the Brewster-Whewell debate,' ibid. 221—86.

7. Farrar, W.V.; Farrar, K.; Scott, E.L., 'The Henrys of Manchester, part 6: William Charles Henry; the maquesiafactory,' *Ambix* 24 (1977), 1—26.

8. Thompson, M.W. *General Pitt-Rivers: evolution and archaeology in the nineteenth century.* Bradford-on-Avon; Moonraker Press; 1977. Pp 164.

9. Moon, H.P. *Henry Walter Bates FRS, 1825—1892; explorer, scientist and Darwinian.* Leicester; Leicestershire Museums etc; 1976. Pp 99.

10. Russell, C.A. [et al.] . *Chemists by profession: the origins and rise of the Royal Institute of Chemistry.* Milton Keynes; Open UP; 1977. Pp x, 342.

11. Hodgkin, A.L. [et al.] . *The pursuit of nature: informal essays on the history of physiology.* Cambridge UP; 1977. Pp 180.

12. Woodward, J.; Richard, D. (ed.). *Health care and popular medicine in nineteenth century England: essays in the social history of medicine.* London; Croom Helm; 1977. Pp 195.

13. Woodward, J.; Richards, D., 'Towards a social history of medicine,' Hk12, 15—55.

14. McLaren, A., 'The early birth control movement: an example of medical self-help,' Hk12, 89—104.

15. Blackman, J., 'Popular theories of generation: the evolution of *Aristotle's Works.* The study of an anachronism,' Hk12, 56—88.

16. Hayward, R.A. *Sir William Fairbairn.* [Manchester] ; North Western Museum of Science and Industry; [1977] . Pp 20.

17. Fisher, R.B. *Joseph Lister, 1827—1912.* London; Macdonald & Jane's; 1977. Pp 351.

18. Emmerson, G.S. *John Scott Russell: a great Victorian engineer and naval architect.* London; Murray; 1977. Pp x, 342.

19. Colp, R. *To be an invalid: the illness of Charles Darwin.* Chicago/London; University of Chicago Press; 1977. Pp xiii, 285.

20. Allan, M. *Darwin and his flowers: the key to natural selection.* London; Faber; 1977. Pp 318.

21. Tyler, C. *Digging by steam: a history of steam cultivation by means of the application of steam power to the fork, mattock and similar implements.* Watford; Model and Allied Publications; 1977. Pp 173.

22. Gunther, A.E. *The life of William Carmichael M'Intosh, M.D., F.R.S., of St Andrews, 1838—1931, a pioneer in marine biology.* Edinburgh; Scottish Academic Press; 1977. Pp 214.

23. Williams, E.G. *The Chester Society of Natural Science founded by Charles Kingsley in 1871 later becoming the Chester Society of*

Natural Science, Literature and Art: its origin and development over one hundred years. [Chester; the author; 1977]. Pp iii, 88.

(*l*) *Intellectual and Cultural*

1. Hendrix, R., 'Popular humor and The Black Dwarf,' *J. of British Studies* 16 (1976), 108—28.
2. Owens, L.T. *J.H. Mason, 1875—1951, scholar printer.* London; Muller; 1976. Pp xvi, 192.
3. Lamb, G. *Victorian magic.* London; Routledge; 1976. Pp xii, 136.
4. Fiddes, V.; Rowan, A. (ed.). *David Bryce, 1803—1876: an exhibition to mark the centenary of Scotland's great Victorian architect.* Edinburgh; The University; 1976. Pp 132.
5. Frick, S., 'Joseph Sturge and the Crimean war; 2: The founding of the *Morning Star*,' *J. of the Friends' Historical Soc.* 53 (1975), 335—58.
6. Waites, B., 'The language and imagery of "class" in early twentieth-century literature (c. 1900—1925),' *Literature and History* 4 (1976), 30—55.
7. Helfand, M.S., 'T.H. Huxley's "Evolution and Ethics": the politics of evolution and the evolution of politics,' *Victorian Studies* 20 (1977), 159—77.
8. Vernon, S., 'Trouble up at t'mill: the rise and decline of the factory play in the 1830s and 1840s,' ibid. 117—39.
9. Reid, M., 'Camille Pissarro: three paintings of London of 1871. What do they represent?,' *Burlington Magazine* 119 (1977), 253—61.
10. Robinson, J.M., 'Sir Frederick Trench and London improvements,' *History Today* 27 (1977), 324—31.
11. Hockey, F., 'Stolen manuscripts: the case of George Hillier and the British Museum,' *Archives* 13 (1977), 20—8.
12. Fox, C., 'The development of social reportage in English periodical illustration during the 1840s and early 1850s,' *Past and Present* 74 (1977), 90—111.
13. Budd, S. *Varieties of unbelief: atheists and agnostics in English society, 1850—1960.* London; Heinemann; 1977. Pp viii, 307.
14. Wood, C. *Victorian panorama: paintings of Victorian life.* London; Faber; 1976. Pp 260.
15. Warren, G. *A stitch in time: Victorian and Edwardian needlecraft.* Newton Abbot; David & Charles; 1976. Pp 144.
16. Williamson, A. *Artists and writers in revolt: the Pre-Raphaelites.* Newton Abbot; David & Charles; 1976. Pp 208.
17. Manford, W.A. *A history of the Library Association, 1877—1977.* London; Library Association; 1977. Pp xii, 360.
18. Kelly, T. *A history of public libraries in Great Britain 1845—1975* (revd. ed.) London; Library Association; 1977.

19. James, L. (ed.). *Print and the people, 1819–1851*. London; Allen Lane; 1976. Pp 368.

20. Lemere, H.B.; Cooper, N. *The opulent eye: late Victorian and Edwardian taste in interior design*. London; Architectural Press; 1976. Pp 258.

21. Hayter, W. *Spooner: a biography*. London; W.H. Allen; 1977. Pp 191.

22. Rothenstein, J. *Modern English painters* (2 vols.; revd. ed.). London; Macdonald and Jane; 1976. Pp 268; 349.

23. Fawcett, J. (ed.). *Seven Victorian architects: William Burn, Philip and Philip Charles Hardwick, Sydney Smirke, J.L. Pearson, G.F. Bodley, Alfred Waterhouse, Edwin Lutyens*. London; Thames & Hudson; 1976. Pp 160.

24. Needham, P. (ed.). *William Morris and the art of the book*. London; Oxford UP; 1976. Pp 140.

25. Needham, P., 'William Morris: book collector,' Hl24, 21–47.

26. Dunlap, J., 'William Morris: calligrapher,' Hl24, 48–70.

27. Dreyfus, J., 'William Morris: typographer,' Hl24, 71–96.

28. Mander, R.; Mitcheson, J. *Lost theatres of London* (revd ed.). London; New English Library; 1976. Pp 240.

29. Wills, G. *Victorian glass*. London; Bell; 1976. Pp xi, 96.

30. Hardie, W.R. *Scottish painting, 1837–1939*. London; Studio Vista; 1976. Pp 112.

31. Inkster, I., 'A phase in middle class culture: phrenology in Sheffield, 1824–1850,' *T. of the Hunter Arch. Soc.* 10 (1977), 273–9.

32. McClean, R. *Joseph Cundall, a Victorian publisher: notes on his life and a check-list of his books*. Pinner; Private Libraries Association; 1976. Pp viii, 96.

33. Colls, R. *The collier's rant: song and culture in the industrial village*. London; Croom Helm; 1977. Pp 216.

34. Willis, K., 'The introduction and critical reception of Marxist thought in Britain, 1850–1900,' *Historical J.* 20 (1977), 417–59.

35. Collini, S., 'Liberalism and the legacy of Mill,' ibid. 237–54.

36. Kelly, T. *Books for the people: an illustrated history of the British public library*. London; Deutsch; 1977. Pp 271.

37. Cocks, Sir B. *Mid-Victorian masterpiece: the story of an institution unable to put its own house in order* [i.e. Houses of Parliament]. London; Hutchinson; 1977. Pp 208.

38. Towle, P., 'The debate on wartime censorship in Britain 1902–14,' *War and Society* (ed. B. Bond and I. Roy; London; Croom Helm), 1 (1976), 103–16.

39. Gooch, J., 'Attitudes to war in late Victorian and Edwardian England,' ibid. 88–102.

40. Maas, J. *The Prince of Wales's wedding: the story of a picture*. London; Cameron and Tayleur; 1977. Pp 100.

41. Zepos, P.J., 'Jeremy Bentham and the Greek independence,' *P. of the British Academy* 62 (1977 for 1976), 293—308.
42. Hendrick, G., 'Henry Salt, the late Victorian socialists, and Thoreau,' *New England Q.* 50 (1977), 409—22.
43. Thomas, D.O. *The honest mind: the thought and work of Richard Price.* Oxford; Clarendon; 1977. Pp xvi, 366.
44. Surtees, V. *A Beckford inheritance: the Lady Lincoln scandal.* Salisbury; Michael Russell Ltd; 1977. Pp viii, 147.
45. Service, A. *Edwardian Architecture: a handbook to building design in Britain, 1890—1914.* London; Thames & Hudson; 1977. Pp 216.
46. Schneewind, J.B. *Sidgwick's ethics and Victorian moral philosophy.* Oxford; Clarendon; 1977. Pp xvi, 465.
47. Penny, N. *Church monuments in romantic England.* New Haven/ London; Yale UP; 1977. Pp xi, 236.
48. Olle, J.G. *Ernest A. Savage: librarian extraordinary.* London; Library Association; 1977. Pp xiii, 225.
49. Moore, D.L. *Ada, countess of Lovelace, Byron's legitimate daughter.* London; Murray; 1977. Pp 397.
50. Masters, A. *Rosa Lewis: an exceptional Edwardian.* London; Weidenfeld & Nicolson; 1977. Pp xi, 210.
51. Kamm, J. *John Stuart Mill in Love.* London; Gordon & Cremonesi; 1977. Pp 253.
52. Howarth, T. *Charles Rennie Mackintosh and the modern movement.* (2nd ed.). London; Routledge; 1977. Pp li, 335.
53. Hopkins, H.E. *Charles Simeon of Cambridge.* London; Hodder & Stoughton; 1977. Pp 240.
54. Hall, T.H.; Muir, P.H. *Some printers and publishers of conjuring books and other ephemera, 1800—1850.* Leeds; Elmete Press; 1976. Pp x, 97.
55. Dobbs, B. and J. *Dante Gabriel Rossetti: an alien Victorian.* London; Macdonald & Jane's; 1977. Pp ix, 257.
56. Culme, J. *Nineteenth-century silver.* London; Hamlyn; 1977. Pp 232.
57. Cork, R. *Vorticism and abstract art in the first machine age* (2 vols.). London; Gordon Fraser Gallery; 1976. Pp xxiv, 321; xxiii, [to] 592.
58. Clayton, H. *Cathedral city: a look at Victorian Lichfield.* Lichfield; the author; 1977. Pp 171.
59. Chappell, P. *Dr S.S. Wesley, 1810—1876: portrait of a Victorian musician.* Great Wakering; Mayhew-McCrimmon; 1977. Pp x, 210.
60. Brantlinger, P. *The spirit of reform: British literature and politics, 1832—1867.* Cambridge, Mass./London; Harvard UP; 1977. Pp x, 293.
61. Bolsterli, M.J. *The early community at Bedford Park: 'corporate happiness' in the first garden suburb.* London; Routledge; 1977. Pp xii, 136.

62. Ball, A.W. *The public libraries of Greater London: a pictorial history, 1856–1914*. London; Library Association; 1977. Pp 108.
63. Adamson, S.H. *Seaside piers*. London; Batsford; 1977. Pp 116.
64. Lowerson, J.; Myerscough, J. *Time to spare in Victorian Britain*. Hassocks; Harvester Press; 1977. Pp 151.
65. Rees, B. *The Victorian Lady*. London; Gordon & Cremonesi; 1977. Pp 164.
66. Middlemas, K. *The pursuit of pleasure*. London; Gordon & Cremonesi; 1977.
67. Liscombe, R.W., 'Canova, Aberdeen and the Pitt monument,' *Burlington Magazine* 119 (1977), 700–5.
68. Jennings, B., 'The Reverend W.F. Powell and the restoration of Cirencester parish church,' Bc8, 158–67.
69. Verey, D., 'The architect and architecture of Watermoor House [Cirencester],' Bc8, 168–70.
70. Rees, J., 'The thesis of the two Mills,' *Political Studies* 25 (1977), 369–82.
71. Compton, P. *Victorian vortex: pleasures and peccadilloes of an age*. London; Hale; 1977. Pp 255.
72. Hendrick, G.; Ponton, J.F. *Henry Salt: a humanitarian reformer and man of letters*. Urbana/London; University of Illinois Press; 1977. Pp 228.
73. MacKenzie, N. and J. *The first Fabians*. London; Weidenfeld & Nicolson; 1977. Pp 446.
74. Parks, S. *John Dunton and the English book trade: a study of his career with a checklist of his publications*. New York/London; Garland Publishing; 1976. Pp ix, 452.

I. BRITAIN SINCE 1914

See also: Aa2, b31; Gh5; Hc1, f10, 19, 33, 35, 36, 54, 55, 80, g14, 51, i5–7, 18, l61, 13, 17, 18, 30

(a) General

1. Harte, N.B., 'Trends in publications on the economic and social history of Great Britain and Ireland, 1925–74,' *Economic History R.* 2nd ser. 30 (1977), 20–41.
2. Goldie, G.W. *Facing the nation: television and politics, 1936–1976*. London; Bodley Head; 1977. Pp 368.
3. Spiers, J.; Sexsmith, A.; Everitt, A. *The Left in Britain: a checklist and guide* [to the Harvester Primary Social Sources Microfilm Collection]. Hassocks; Harvester Press; 1976. Pp 168.
4. Pryce-Jones, D. *Unity Mitford, a quest*. London; Weidenfeld & Nicolson; 1976. Pp 276.

5. Checkland, S.G. *The upas tree: Glasgow, 1875–1975: a study in growth and contraction.* University of Glasgow Press; 1976. Pp xi, 124.
6. Birtill, G. *The war and after.* Chorley; Guardian Press; 1976. Pp 95.
7. Lever, J. *Home sweet home: housing designed by the London County Council and Greater London Council architects 1888–1975.* London; Academy Editions; 1976. Pp 111.
8. Pitcher, H.J. *When Miss Emmie was in Russia: English governesses before, during and after the October revolution.* London; Murray; 1977. Pp xiii, 246.
9. Seaborne, M.; Lowe, R. *The English school: its architecture and organization. Vol. 2: 1870–1970.* London; Routledge; 1977. Pp xix, 240.
10. Starmer-Smith, N. *The Barbarians: the official history of the Barbarian Football Club.* London; Macdonald & Jane's; 1977. Pp 240.
11. Kinsey, G. *Aviation: flight over the eastern counties since 1937.* Lavenham; T. Dalton; 1977. Pp 268.
12. Jenkins, A. *The forties.* London; Heinemann; 1977. Pp 232.
13. Fitzgerald, P. *The Knox brothers.* London; Macmillan; 1977. Pp 294.
14. Exwood, M. *John Logie Baird: 50 years of television.* London; Institute of Electronic and Radio Engineers; 1976. Pp 31.
15. Donaldson, F. *King George VI and Queen Elizabeth.* London; Weidenfeld & Nicolson; 1977. Pp 127.
16. Harris, J. *William Beveridge: a biography.* Oxford; Clarendon; 1977. Pp viii, 488.
17. Hall, R. *Marie Stopes: a biography.* London; Deutsch; 1977. Pp 351.
18. Lees-Milne, J. *Prophesying peace* [autobiography]. London; Chatto & Windus; 1977. Pp 256.
19. Ryder, J.; Silver, H. *Modern English society* (2nd ed.). London; Methuen; 1977. Pp xvii, 390.
20. Bartlett, C.J. *A history of postwar Britain, 1945–1974.* London; Longman; 1977. Pp viii, 360.
21. Eastwood, G.G. *Harold Laski.* London; Mowbrays; 1977. Pp x, 173.
22. Nicolson, N. *Mary Curzon.* London; Weidenfeld & Nicolson; 1977. Pp xii, 228.

(b) *Politics*

1. Gorodetsky, G., 'The Soviet Union and Britain's general strike of May 1926,' *Cahiers du mond russe et soviétique* 17 (1976), 287–310.
2. Goldston, R.S., 'Patronage in British government,' *Parliamentary Affairs* 30 (1977), 80–96.

3. Childs, D., 'The British Communist Party and the war, 1939—41: old slogans revived,' *J. of Contemporary History* 12 (1977), 237—53.

4. Marquand, D. *Ramsay MacDonald.* London; Cape; 1977. Pp xvi, 903.

5. Robbins, K. *The abolition of war: the 'Peace Movement' in Britain, 1914—1919.* Cardiff; University of Wales Press; 1976. Pp 255.

6. Briggs, A.; Saville, J. (ed.). *Essays in labour history, 1918—1939.* London; Croom Helm; 1977. Pp 292.

7. Thompson, R.W. *Churchill and Morton: the quest for insight in the correspondence of Major Sir Desmond Morton and the author.* London; Hodder & Stoughton; 1976. Pp 223.

8. Cole, G.D.H. (with preface by Dame Margaret Cole), 'The Striker Stricken: an operetta,' Ib6, 57—101.

9. Cole, M., 'The Society for Socialist Enquiry and Propaganda,' Ib6, 190—203.

10. Seya, P., 'Factionalism within the Labour Party: the Socialist League 1932—37,' Ib6, 204—31.

11. Saville, J., 'May Day, 1937,' Ib6, 232—84.

12. Macintyre, S., 'British Labour, Marxism, and working class apathy in the nineteen twenties,' *Historical J.* 20 (1977), 479—96.

13. James, R.R. *The British revolution: British politics, 1880—1939. Vol. 2: From Asquith to Chamberlain, 1914—1939.* London; Hamilton; 1977. Pp xii, 363.

14. Bentley, M. *The liberal mind, 1914—1929.* Cambridge UP; 1977. Pp viii, 279.

15. Boyle, A. *The riddle of Erskine Childers.* London; Hutchinson; 1977. Pp 351.

16. Muller, W.D. *The kept men: the first century of trade union representation in the House of Commons, 1874—1975.* Hassocks; Harvester Press; 1977. Pp xx, 283.

17. Bentley, M., 'Liberal politics and the Grey conspiracy of 1921,' *Historical J.* 20 (1977), 461—78.

18. Middleton, J. (ed.). *Women in the Labour Movement: the British experience.* London; Croom Helm; 1977. Pp 221.

19. Denby, M., 'Women in parliament and government,' Ib18, 175—90.

20. McDonald, O., 'Women in the Labour Party today,' Ib18, 144—60.

21. Walker, M., 'Labour women and internationalism,' Ib18, 84—93.

22. Rendel, M., 'The contribution of the women's Labour League to the winning of the franchise,' Ib18, 57—83.

23. Middleton, L., 'Women on Labour politics,' Ib18, 22—37.

24. Mackintosh, J.P. (ed.). *British prime ministers in the twentieth century; vol. 1: Balfour to Chamberlain.* London; Weidenfeld & Nicolson; 1977. Pp 282.

25. Fraser, P., 'Arthur James Balfour,' Ib24, 23—42.

26. Harris, J.E.; Hazlehurst, C., 'Henry Campbell-Bannerman,' Ib24, 43–77.
27. Hazlehurst, C., 'Herbert Henry Asquith,' Ib24, 78–117.
28. Morgan, K.O., 'David Lloyd George,' Ib24, 118–55.
29. Lloyd, T., 'James Ramsay MacDonald,' Ib24, 156–87.
30. Campbell, J., 'Stanley Baldwin,' Ib24, 188–218.
31. Beattie, A., 'Neville Chamberlain,' Ib24, 219–71.
32. Nugent, A.; King, R. (ed.). *The British Right: conservative and right wing politics in Britain.* Farnborough; Saxon House; 1977. Pp 231.
33. King, R., 'Support for fascism and the radical right: some explanations,' Ib32, 192–221.
34. Nugent, N., 'The political parties of the extreme right,' Ib32, 165–91.
35. Nugent, N., 'The ideas of the British Union of Fascists,' Ib32, 133–64.
36. Phillips, K., 'The nature of Powellism,' Ib32, 99–129.
37. Wilson, M., 'Grass-roots conservatism: motions to the party conference,' Ib32, 64–98.
38. Wilson, M.; Phillips, K., 'The Conservative Party from Macmillan to Thatcher,' Ib32, 29–63.
39. Bennett, R., 'The conservative tradition of thought: a right wing phenomenon,' Ib32, 11–25.
40. Bennett, R.; King, R.; Nugent, N., 'The concept of "the Right",' Ib32, 3–10.
41. Gilbert, M. *Winston S. Churchill, vol. 4: 1917–1922 – Companion documents.* London; Heinemann; 1977.
42. Cross, J.A. *Sir Samuel Hoare, a political biography.* London; Cape; 1977. Pp xv, 414.
43. Fisher, N. *The tory leaders: their struggle for power.* London; Weidenfeld & Nicolson; 1977. Pp ix, 209.
44. David, E. (ed.). *Inside Asquith's cabinet: from the diaries of Charles Hobhouse.* London; Murray; 1977. Pp x, 295.
45. Kibblewhite, L.; Rigby, A. *Aberdeen in the general strike.* Aberdeen People's Press; 1977. Pp 33.
46. Lash, J.P. *Roosevelt and Churchill, 1939–1941: the partnership that saved the west.* London; Deutsch; 1977. Pp 528.
47. Miller, W.L. *Electoral dynamics in Britain since 1918.* London; Macmillan; 1977. Pp 242.
48. Thomis, M.I., 'Conscription and consent: British Labour and the resignation threat of January 1916,' *Australian J. of Politics and History* 23 (1977), 10–18.
49. Williams, C.H., 'Non-violence and the development of the Welsh Language Society, 1962–c. 1974,' *Welsh History R.* 8 (1977), 426–55.
50. Young, N. *An infantile disorder? Crisis and decline of the New Left.* London; Routledge; 1977. Pp xxii, 490.

51. Walker, M. *The National Front.* London; Fontana; 1977. Pp 224.
52. Thompson, J.A., 'Lord Cecil and the pacifists in the League of Nations Union,' *Historical J.* 20 (1977), 949–59.
53. Ackroyd, C.; Margolis, K.; Rosenhead, J.; Shallice, T. *The technology of political control.* Harmondsworth; Penguin; 1977. Pp 320.
54. Schoen, D.E. *Enoch Powell and the Powellites.* London; Macmillan; 1977. Pp xviii, 317.
55. Pentney, J., 'Worms that turned: the inter-party mobility of British parliamentary candidates since 1945,' *Parliamentary Affairs* 30 (1977), 363–72.
56. Norton, P., 'Private legislation and the influence of the backbench M.P.,' ibid. 356–62.
57. Rowbotham, S. *A new world for women: Stella Browne, socialist feminist.* London; Pluto Press; 1977. Pp 128.
58. Newberry, J.V., 'Anti-war suffragists,' *History* 62 (1977), 411–25.
59. Burridge, T.D., 'A postscript to Potsdam: the Churchill-Laski electoral clash,' *J. of Contemporary History* 12 (1977), 725–39.
60. Renshaw, P., 'Anti-Labour politics in Britain, 1918–27,' ibid. 693–706.
61. Nairn, T. *The break-up of Britain: crisis and neo-nationalism.* London; NLB; 1977. Pp 368.
62. Pimlott, B. *Labour and the Left in the 1930s.* Cambridge UP; 1977. Pp xi, 259.
63. Cyr, A. *Liberal Party politics in Britain.* London; Calder; 1977. Pp 318.
64. Challinor, R. *The origins of British bolshevism.* London; Croom Helm; 1977. Pp 291.
65. Gilmour, I. *Inside right: a study of conservatism.* London; Hutchinson; 1977. Pp 294.
66. Shlaim, A.; Jones, P.; Sainsbury, K. *Britiah foreign secretaries since 1945.* Pp 267.
67. Lemieux, P.H., 'Political issues and liberal support in the February 1974 British general election,' *Political Studies* 25 (1977), 323–42.
68. Alt, J.; Crewe, I.; Särlvik, B., 'Angels in plastic: the Liberal surge in 1974,' ibid. 343–68.
69. Howard, C., 'MacDonald, Henderson, and the outbreak of war, 1914,' *Historical J.* 20 (1977), 841–70.
70. Close, D.H., 'The collapse of resistance to democracy: conservatism, adult suffrage, and second chamber reform, 1911–28,' ibid. 871–91.

(c) Constitution, Administration and Law

1. Bell, C.R.V. *A history of East Sussex Council, 1889–1974.* London; Phillimore; 1976. Pp 119.

2. Silkin, A., 'The "Agreement to Differ" of 1975 and its effect on ministerial responsibility,' *Political Q.* 48 (1977), 65—77.

3. Fair, J.D., 'The political aspects of women's suffrage during the first world war,' *Albion* 8 (1976), 274—95.

4. Howard, P. *The British monarchy in the twentieth century.* London; Hamilton; 1977. Pp 208.

5. Dickman, H.J. *Haverfordwest Rural District Council: history of the Council, 1894—1974.* [Haverfordwest; the author; 1976]. Pp 136.

6. Napier, B., 'Judicial attitudes towards the employment relationship — some recent developments,' *Industrial Law J.* 6 (1977), 1—18.

7. Turner, J.A., 'The formation of Lloyd George's "Garden Suburb": "Fabian-like Milner penetration?",' *Historical J.* 20 (1977), 165—84.

8. Frangopulo, N.J. *Tradition in action: the historical evolution of the Greater Manchester County.* Wakefield; EP Publishing; 1977. Pp xiv, 306.

9. Craig, F.W.S. (ed.). *British parliamentary election results, 1918—1949* (revd ed.). London; Macmillan; 1977. Pp xviii, 785.

10. Griffith, J. *The politics of the judiciary.* Manchester UP; 1977. Pp 224.

11. Lee, J.M., ' "Forward thinking" and war: the Colonial Office during the 1940s,' *J. of Imperial and Commonwealth History* 6 (1977), 64—79.

12. Jones, B. *Etholiadau seneddol yng Nghymru [parliamentary election results in Wales], 1900—1975.* Talybont; Y Lolfa; 1977. Pp 191.

13. Boadle, D.G., 'The formation of the Foreign Office Economic Relations Section, 1930—1937,' *Historical J.* 20 (1977), 919—36.

14. Mackintosh, J.P. *The government and politics of Britain* (4th ed.). London; Hutchinson; 1977. Pp 244.

(d) External Affairs

1. Woodward, L.; Lambert, M.E. *British foreign policy in the Second World War;* vol. 5. London; HMSO; 1976. Pp xvii, 542.

2. Beaver, P. *Yes! we have some: the story of Fyffes.* Stevenage; Publications for Companies; 1976. Pp x, 133.

3. Fox, J.P., 'The Jewish factor in British war crimes policy in 1942,' *English Historical R.* 92 (1977), 82—106.

4. Young, H.F., 'The misunderstanding of August 1, 1914,' *J. of Modern History* 48 (1976), 644—5.

5. Shai, A. *Origins of the war in the east: Britain, China and Japan, 1937—39.* London; Croom Helm; 1976. Pp 267.

6. Morris, L.P., 'British secret missions in Turkestan, 1918—19,' *J. of Contemporary History* 12 (1977), 363—79.

7. Trommer, A., 'MacDonald in Geneva in March 1933: a study in Britain's European policy,' *Scandinavian J. of History* 1 (1976), 293–312.

8. Haraszti, E.H., 'Three documents concerning Great Britain's policy in east-central Europe in the period after the Munich agreement,' *Acta Historica Academiae Scientiarum Hungaricae* 22 (1976), 139–75.

9. Leys, N. (ed.). *By Kenya possessed: the correspondence of Norman Leys and J.H. Oldham, 1918–1926.* Chicago/London; University of Chicago Press; 1976. Pp x, 382.

10. Gruner, W., ' "British Interest" in der Zwischenkriegszeit: Aspekte britischer Europa-Politik 1918–1938,' *Gleichgewicht – Revision – Restauration: Die Aussenpolitik der ersten Tschechoslowakischen Republik im Europasystem der Pariser Vorortverträge,* (ed. K. Bosl; Munich; Oldenburg; 1976), 85–151.

11. Zhivkova, L. *Anglo-Turkish relations, 1933–1939* [translated from the Bulgarian]. London; Secker & Warburg; 1976. Pp xv, 132.

12. Gorodetsky. G. *The precarious truce: Anglo-Soviet relations 1924–27.* Cambridge UP; 1977. Pp xiii, 289.

13. De Zayas, A.M. *Nemesis at Potsdam: the Anglo-Americans and the expulsion of the Germans: background, execution, consequences.* London; Routledge; 1977. Pp xxvii, 268.

14. Sluglett, P. *Britain in Iraq, 1914–1932.* London; Ithaca Press; 1976. Pp 360.

15. Medlicott, W.N.; Dakin, D.; Lambert, M.E. (ed.). *Documents on British Foreign Policy, 1919–1939; vol. 15: October 3, 1935–February 29, 1936* [The Italo-Ethiopian War and German affairs]. London; HMSO; 1976. Pp lxiv, 791.

16. The same (ed.). *Documents on British Foreign Policy 1919–1939, 1st series; vol. 20: March 1921–December 1922.* London; HMSO; 1976. Pp lxx, 970.

17. Reynolds, P.A.; Hughes, E.J. (ed.). *The historian as diplomat: Charles Kingsley Webster and the United Nations, 1939–1946.* London; Martin Robertson; 1976. Pp 198.

18. Wheeler-Bennett, Sir John. *Friends, enemies and sovereigns.* London; Macmillan; 1976. Pp 176.

19. Leventhal, F.M., 'Towards revision and reconciliation: H.N. Brailsford and Germany, 1914–1939,' Ib6, 163–89.

20. Lavrov, S.V., 'The struggle in the political circles of Great Britain around the Anglo-Soviet negotiations of 1920–1921 (in the light of new materials),' *Voprosy Istorii* 1977 (6), 59–80; English summary on p. 221.

21. Wylie, D., 'Confrontation over Kenya: the Colonial Office and its critics, 1918–1940,' *J. of African History* 18 (1977), 427–47.

22. Lammers, D., 'Nevil Shute and the decline of the "Imperial Idea" in literature,' *J. of British Studies* 16/2 (1977), 121–42.

23. Mansergh, N. (ed.). *The transfer of power, 1942–7, vol. 7: The Cabinet Mission, 23 March–29 June 1946.* London; HMSO; 1977. Pp lxxxiii; 1130.

24. *Selected documents relating to problems of security and cooperation in Europe, 1954–77.* London; HMSO; 1977. Pp x, 362.

25. Rock, W.R. *British appeasement in the 1930s.* London; Arnold; 1977. Pp viii, 111.

26. Lowe, P. *Great Britain and the origins of the Pacific war: a study of British policy in East Asia, 1937–1941.* Oxford; Clarendon; 1977. Pp xii, 318.

27. Flory, H., 'The Arcos raid and the rupture of Anglo-Soviet relations, 1927,' *J. of Contemporary History* 12 (1977), 707–23.

28. Andrew, C.M., 'The British secret service and Anglo-Soviet relations; part I: from the trade negotiations to the Zinoviev Letter,' *Historical J.* 20 (1977), 673–706.

29. Cohen, M.J., 'American influence on British policy in the Middle East during World War Two: first attempts at coordinating Allied policy on Palestine,' *American Jewish Historical Q.* 67 (1977), 50–70.

30. Tinker, H., 'Pressure, persuasion, decision: factors in the partition of the Punjab, August 1947,' *J. of Asian Studies* 36 (1977), 695–704.

31. Hauser, O., 'The year 1937: the decisive turning-point in British-German relations,' La3, 132–46.

32. Lowe, C.J., 'Italy and the Balkans, 1914–1915,' Hd15, 411–22.

33. Ekstein, M., 'Russia, Constantinople and the Straits,' Id15, 423–35.

34. Kent, M., 'Asiatic Turkey, 1914–1916,' Hd15, 436–51.

35. Nish, I.H., 'Japan and China, 1914–1916,' Hd15, 452–65.

36. Mason, C.M., 'Anglo-American relations: mediation and "permanent peace",' Hd15, 466–87.

37. Marsden, A., 'The blockade,' Hd15, 488–515.

38. Steiner, Z., 'The Foreign Office and the war,' Hd15, 516–31.

39. Robbins, K.G., 'Foreign policy, government structure and public opinion,' Hd15, 532–46.

40. Tibawi, A.L. *Anglo-Arab relations and the question of Palestine, 1914–1921.* London; Luzac; 1977. Pp xxvii, 523.

41. Spears, Sir E. *Fulfilment of a mission: the Spears mission to Syria and Lebanon, 1941–1944.* London; Cooper; 1977. Pp xi, 311.

42. Jain, J.P. *China in world politics: a study of Sino-British relations, 1949–1975.* London; Martin Robertson; 1977. Pp xii, 373.

(e) Religion

1. Zimmerman, J.D., 'A chapter in English Church reform: the Enabling Act of 1919,' *Historical Magazine of the Protestant Episcopal Church* 16 (1977), 215–25.

2. Scott, C. *Dick Sheppard: a biography*. London; Hodder & Stoughton; 1977. Pp 253.

3. Hewitt, G. *The problems of success: a history of the Church Missionary Society*. Vol. 2: Asia; Overseas partners. London; SCM Press; 1977. Pp xii, 424.

4. Duce, R. *Castle Gate Church on the twentieth century*. [Nottingham]; the church; 1966. Pp ii, 134.

5. Walker, D., 'Disestablishment and independence,' Bc4, 164—87.

6. Mews, S., 'Neo-orthodoxy, liberalism and war: Karl Barth, P.T. Forsyth and John Oman, 1914—19,' Bc6, 361—75.

7. Dunstan, A.; Peart-Binns, J.S. *Cornish bishop* [i.e. J.W. Husskin]. London; Epworth Press; 1977. Pp 174.

8. Dillistone, F.W. *C.H. Dodd: interpreter of the New Testament*. London; Hodder & Stoughton; 1977. Pp 255.

(f) Economic Affairs

1. Bell, S.H. *The first half of the century: a history of the Paint Research Association, 1926—76*. Teddington; Paint Research Association; 1976. Pp 30.

2. DeNovo, J.A., 'The Culbertson economic mission and Anglo-American tensions in the Middle East, 1944—1945,' *J. of American History* 63 (1977), 913—36.

3. Mayhew, K., 'The degree of unionization 1948—68,' with a reply by B. Burkitt and D. Bowers, *B. of Economic Research* 86 (1977), 51—6.

4. Griffin, A.R. and C.P., 'The non-political trade union movement,' Ib6, 133—62.

5. Garside, W.R., 'Juvenile unemployment and public policy between the wars,' *Economic History R.* 2nd ser. 30 (1977), 322—39.

6. Bean, R., 'Liverpool shipping employers and the anti-communist activities of J.M. Hughes, 1920—1925,' *Soc. for the study of Labour History* 34 (1977), 22—6.

7. Goffee, R.E., 'The butty system and the Kent coalfield,' ibid. 41—55.

8. *Food quality and safety: a century of progress*. (Proceedings of the symposium celebrating the centenary of the Sale of Food and Drugs Act 1875). London; HMSO; 1976. Pp vi, 243.

9. Rendle, B.J. *Fifty years of timber research: a short history of the Forest Products Research Laboratory, Princes Risborough*. London; HMSO; 1976. Pp xii, 117.

10. Neale, W.G. *The tides of war and the port of Bristol, 1914—1918*. Bristol; Port Authority; 1976. Pp xiii, 315.

11. Howdon, S.; Winch, D. *The Economic Advisory Council, 1930—1939: a study in economic advice during depression and recovery*. Cambridge UP; 1977. Pp viii, 424.

12. Prais, S.J. *The evolution of giant firms in Britain: a study of the*

growth of concentration in manufacturing industry in Britain, 1909–70. Cambridge UP; 1976. Pp xviii, 321.

13. Lovell, J., 'Trades Union Council Special Industrial Committee, Jan.–Apr. 1926,' Ib6, 36–56.
14. Wilkinson, F., 'Collective bargaining in the steel industry in the 1920's,' Ib6, 102–32.
15. Philo, G.; Hewitt, J., 'Trade unions and the media,' *Industrial Relations J.* 7 (1976), 4–19.
16. Watts, H.D., 'Market areas and spatial rationalization: the British brewing industry after 1945,' *Tijdschrift voor Economische en Sociale Geografie* 68 (1977), 224–40.
17. Church, R., 'Myths, men and motor cars: a review article,' *J. of Transport History* new ser. 4 (1977), 102–12.
18. Polard, S. *The British economic miracle.* London; Economics Association; 1976. Pp 19.
19. Stevenson, J.; Cook, C. *The slump.* London; Cape; 1977. Pp 352.
20. Richardson, W. *The CWS in war and peace, 1939–1976.* Manchester; Co-operative Wholesale Society Ltd; 1977. Pp xiii, 399.
21. Niall, I. *To speed the plough: mechanisation comes to the farm.* London; Heinemann; 1977. Pp 231.
22. Keatley, W.S. *The Fertiliser Manufacturers Association: the second fifty years 1925–1975.* [London; The Association; 1977]. Pp 72.
23. Johnston, J.P. *A hundred years eating: food, drink and the daily diet in Britain since the late nineteenth century.* Dublin; Gill & Macmillan; 1977. Pp xii, 148.
24. Hoole, K. *The East Coast main line since 1925.* London; I. Allan; 1977. Pp 128.
25. Hayman, R. *The Institute of Fuel: the first 50 years.* London; The Institute; 1977. Pp 112.
26. Berkovitch, I. *Coal on the switchback: the coal industry since nationalisation.* London; Allen & Unwin; 1977. Pp 237.
27. Moran, M. *The politics of industrial relations: the origins, life and death of the 1970 Industrial Relations Act.* London; Macmillan; 1977. Pp 192.
28. Jones, G.G., 'The British government and the oil companies, 1912–1924: the search for an oil policy,' *Historical J.* 20 (1977), 647–72.
29. Newby, H. *The deferential worker: a study of farm workers in East Anglia.* London; Allen Lane; 1977. Pp 462.
30. Rubin, G.R., 'The origins of Industrial Tribunals: munitions tribunals during the first world war,' *Industrial Law J.* 6 (1977), 149–64.
31. Richardson, K. *The British motor industry, 1896–1939.* London; Macmillan; 1977. Pp 258.
32. White, G., 'Scottish traders to Baffin Island, 1910–1930,' *Maritime History* 5 (1977), 34–50.

33. Noyes, A., 'The industrial economy of North Staffordshire in the second world war,' *North Staffordshire J. of Field Studies* 16 (1976), 73—86.
34. Godwin, A., 'Early years in the trade unions,' Ib18, 94—112.
35. McCarthy, M., 'Women in trade unions today,' Ib18, 161—74.
36. Gaffin, J., 'Women and cooperation,' Ib18, 113—43.
37. Pocock, R.F. *Nuclear power: its development in the United Kingdom.* Old Woking; Unwin Bros.; 1977. Pp 272.
38. Ward-Jackson, C.H. *The 'Cellophane' story: origins of a British industrial group.* [Bridgwater]; British Cellophane Ltd.; 1977. Pp x, 144.

(g) Social Structure and Population

1. Peel, J. *The lives of the fellows of the Royal College of Obstetricians and Gynaecologists, 1929—1969.* London; Heinemann Medical; 1976. Pp xviii, 390.
2. Marwick, A. *The home front: the British and the Second World War.* London; Thames & Hudson; 1976. Pp 192.
3. Stevenson, J. *Social conditions in Britain between the wars.* Harmondsworth; Penguin; 1977. Pp 295.
4. Weiner, S.L., 'The competition for certainty: the polls and the press in Britain,' *Political Science Q.* 91 (1976—7), 673—96.
5. Winter, J.M., 'The impact of the first world war on civilian health in Britain,' *Economic History R.* 2nd ser. 30 (1977), 487—507.
6. Bulmer, M. *Mining and social change.* London; Croom Helm; 1977. Pp 318.
7. Marr, W.L., 'The United Kingdom's international migration in the inter-war period: theoretical considerations and empirical testing,' *Population Studies* 31 (1977), 571—9.
8. Winter, J.M., 'Britain's "lost generation" of the first world war,' ibid. 449—66.

(h) Social Policy

1. Deacon, A. *In search of the scrounger: the administration of unemployment insurance in Britain, 1920—1931.* London; Bell; 1976. Pp 110.
2. Gosden, P.H.J.H. *Education in the Second World War: a study in policy and administration.* London; Methuen; 1976. Pp x, 527.
3. Deacon, A., 'Concession and coercion: the politics of unemployment insurance in the 1920's,' Ib6, 9—35.
4. Jones, C. *Immigration and social policy in Britain.* London; Tavistock Publications; 1977. Pp ix, 291.
5. Elliott, B.J., 'The League of Nations Union and history teaching in England: a study in benevolent bias,' *History of Education* 6 (1977), 131—41.

6. Coman, P. *Catholics and the welfare state.* London; Longman; 1977. Pp ix, 118.
7. Bradburn, E. *Margaret McMillan: framework and expansion of nursery education.* Redhill; Denholm House Press; 1976. Pp 192.
8. Wilson, E. *Women and the welfare state.* London; Tavistock Publications; 1977. Pp 208.
9. Ferguson, S., 'Labour women and the social services,' Ib18, 38—56.
10. Sutherland, G., 'The magic of measurement: mental testing and English education 1900—40,' *T. of the Royal Historical Soc.* 5th ser. 27 (1977), 155—72.

(i) Naval and Military

1. Smith, M., 'The Royal Air Force, air power and British foreign policy, 1932—37,' *J. of Contemporary History* 12 (1976), 153—74.
2. Grant, R. *The 51st Highland Division at war.* London; Allen; 1977. Pp 160.
3. James, A.E.T. *The Royal Air Force: the past 30 years.* London; Macdonald & Jane's; 1976. Pp 230.
4. Hardy, H. *The minesweepers' victory.* [Weybridge] ; Keydex; 1976. Pp 345.
5. Smith, E.D. *East of Katmandu: the story of the 7th Duke of Edinburgh's Own Gurkha Rifles*; vol. 2: 1948—1973. London; Cooper; 1976. Pp xx, 212.
6. Hyde, H.M. *British air policy between the wars, 1918—1939.* London; Heinemann; 1976. Pp xx, 539.
7. Connell, G.G. *Fighting destroyer: the story of HMS 'Petard'.* London; Kimber; 1976. Pp 271.
8. Bowyer, C. *Beaufighter at war.* London; Allan; 1976. Pp 160.
9. Longmate, N. *Air raid: the bombing of Coventry, 1940.* London; Hutchinson; 1976. Pp 302.
10. Snyder, G.S. *The 'Royal Oak' disaster.* London; Kimber; 1976. Pp 240.
11. Harker, R.W. *Rolls-Royce from the wings: military aviation, 1925—71.* Oxford; Oxford Illustrated Press; 1976. Pp viii, 168.
12. Musgrove, G. *Pathfinder force: a history of 8 Group.* London; Macdonald & Jane's; 1976. Pp x, 302.
13. Tomlinson, M. *The most dangerous moment* [Japanese attacks in the Indian Ocean] . London; Kimber; 1976. Pp 205.
14. Beesley, P. *Very special intelligence: the story of the Admiralty's Operational Intelligence Centre, 1939—1945.* London; Hamilton; 1977. Pp xv, 271.
15. Barker, R. *The blockade busters.* London; Chatto & Windus; 1976. Pp 224.
16. Lewin, R. *Slim, the standardbearer: a biography of Field-Marshall the Viscount Slim.* London; Cooper; 1976. Pp xv, 350.

17. Wingfield, A.J. *The Bolton Artillery: a history, 1860–1975*. Bolton; B.V.A.A.; 1976. Pp 78.

18. Quartararo, R., 'Imperial defence in the Mediterranean on the eve of the Ethiopian crisis (July–October 1935),' *Historical J.* 20 (1977), 185–220.

19. Marwick, A. *Women at war, 1914–1918*. London; Croom Helm; 1977. Pp 176.

20. Till, G., 'Letters from the first world war,' *Mariner's Mirror* 63 (1977), 285–92.

21. Buckley, S., 'The failure to resolve the problem of venereal disease among the troops of Britain during World War I,' *War and Society* (ed. B. Bond and I. Roy; London; Croom Helm); 2 (1977), 65–85.

22. Bialer, U., 'The danger of bombardment from the air and the making of British air disarmament policy 1932–4,' ibid. 1 (1976), 202–15.

23. Vinden, F.H., 'The introduction of War Office Selection Boards in the British Army: a personal recollection,' ibid. 2 (1977), 119–28.

24. Wells, A.R., 'Staff training and the Royal Navy 1918–1939,' ibid. 2 (1977), 86–106.

25. Price, A. *Blitz on Britain: the bomber attacks on the United Kingdom, 1939–1945*. London; I. Allan; 1977. Pp 192.

26. Forty, G. *Desert Rats at war. 2: Europe*. London; Allan; 1977. Pp 160.

27. Hunt, B.; Preston, A. (ed.). *War aims and strategic policy in the Great War, 1914–1918*. London; Croom Helm; 1977. Pp 131.

28. Gooch, J., 'Soldiers, strategy and war aims in Britain 1914–18,' Ii27, 21–40.

29. Slack, C.M. *Grandfather's adventures in the Great War, 1914–1918*. Ilfracombe; Stockwell; 1977. Pp 284.

30. Shay, R.P. *British rearmament in the thirties: politics and profits*. Princeton UP; 1977. Pp xiii, 315.

31. Price, A. *Spitfire: a documentary history*. London; Macdonald & Jane's; 1977. Pp 159.

32. Peis, G. *The mirror of deception: how Britain turned the Nazi spy machine against itself*. London; Weidenfeld & Nicolson; 1977. Pp 190.

33. Parkinson, R. *Dawn on our darkness: the summer of 1940*. London; Granada; 1977. Pp ix, 296.

34. Parkinson, R. *The Auk: Auchinleck, victor at Alamein*. London; Hart-David MacGibbon; 1977. Pp 272.

35. Pack, S.W.C. *Operation 'Husky': the Allied invasion of Sicily*. Newton Abbot; David & Charles; 1977. Pp 186.

36. Nicol, G. *Uncle George: Field-Marshal Lord Milne of Salonica and Rubislaw*. London; Reedminster Publications; 1976. Pp 341.

37. Middlebrook, M.; Mahoney, P. *Battleship: the loss of the 'Prince*

of Wales' and the 'Repulse'. London; Allen Lane; 1977. Pp x, 366.

38. Beckwith, E.G.C. (ed.). *The Mansel diaries: the diaries of Captain John Mansel, prisoner of war, and camp forger, in Germany 1940–45.* Blockley; the editor; 1977. Pp xi, 156.

39. Hartcup, G. *Code name Mulberry: the planning, building and operation of the Normandy harbours.* Newton Abbot; David & Charles; 1977. Pp 160.

40. Faulk, H. *Group captives: the re-education of German prisoners of war in Britain, 1945–1948.* London; Chatto & Windus; 1977. Pp 233.

41. Cruickshank, C.G. *The fourth arm: psychological warfare 1938–1945.* London; Davis-Poynter; 1977. Pp 200.

42. Baylis, J. *British defence policy in a changing world.* London; Croom Helm; 1977. Pp 220.

43. Bond, B. *Liddell Hart: a study of his military thought.* London; Cassell; 1977. Pp x, 289.

44. Blaxland, G. *The plain cook and the great showman: the First and Eighth Armies in North Africa.* London; Kimber; 1977. Pp 303.

45. Barker, A.J. *Dunkirk: the great escape.* London; Dent; 1977. Pp 240.

46. Barclay, G.St J. *Their finest hour.* London; Weidenfeld & Nicolson; 1977. Pp ix, 192.

47. Allen, L. *Singapore, 1941–1942.* London; Davis-Poynter; 1977. Pp 343.

48. Trythall, A.J. *'Boney' Fuller: the intellectual general, 1878–1966.* London; Cassell; 1977. Pp xiii, 314.

49. Stewart, D. *T.E. Lawrence.* London; Hamilton; 1977. Pp xii, 352.

50. Till, G., 'Airpower and the battleship in the 1920's,' Hj15, 108–23.

51. Henry, D., 'British submarine policy 1918–1939,' Hj15, 80–107.

52. Williamson, D.G., 'Cologne and the British, 1918–1926,' *History Today* 27 (1977), 695–702.

53. Debo, R.K., 'Mésentente glaciale: Great Britain, France and the question of intervention in the Baltic, 1918,' *Canadian J. of History* 12 (1977), 65–86.

54. Hyde, H.M. *Solitary in the ranks: Lawrence of Arabia as airman and private soldier.* London; Constable; 1977. Pp 288.

55. Smith, P.C. *The great ships pass: British battleships at war, 1939–1945.* London; Kimber; 1977. Pp xiii, 544.

56. Terraine, J. *The road to Passchendaele: the Flanders offensive of 1917: a study in inevitability.* London; Cooper; 1977. Pp xxiv, 365.

57. Costello, J.; Hughes, T. *The Battle of the Atlantic.* London; Collins; 1977. Pp 314.

58. Gould, R.W. *Locations of British cavalry, infantry and machine gun units, 1914–1924.* [London]; Heraldene Ltd; 1977. Pp 48.

59. Cassar, G.H. *Kitchener: architect of victory.* London; Kimber; 1977. Pp 573.
60. Gaston, P. *Thirty-eighth parallel: the British in Korea.* Glasgow; Hamilton & Co; 1976. Pp xii, 164.

(j) *Intellectual and Cultural*

1. Archer, I. *The Jags: the centenary history of Patrick Thistle Football Club.* Glasgow: Molendinar Press; 1976. Pp 95.
2. Reynolds, E. *Northampton Repertory Theatre.* [Northampton; The Theatre] ; 1976. Pp 20.
3. Bowker, B.M. *England rugby: a history of the national side, 1871–1976.* London; Cassell; 1976. Pp xiv, 199.
4. Newman, A. *The United Synagogue, 1870–1970.* London; Routledge; 1977. Pp xv, 239.
5. Gottlieb, F., 'Leonard Woolf's attitudes to his Jewish background and to Judaism,' *T. of the Jewish Historical Soc. of England* 25 (1977 for 1973/5), 25–37.
6. Hauser, O., 'A.J.P. Taylor,' *J. of Modern History* 49 (1977), 34–9.
7. Boyer, J.W., 'A.J.P. Taylor and the art of modern history,' ibid. 40–72.
8. Watt, D.C., 'Some aspects of A.J.P. Taylor's work as diplomatic historian,' ibid. 19–33.
9. Taylor, A.J.P., 'Accident prone, or what happened next,' ibid. 1–18.
10. Kerr, R.; Liddell, A. *Story of the Girl Guides* (2 vols.). London; Girl Guides Association; 1976. Pp 223; 120.
11. Minihan, J. *The nationalization of culture: the development of state subsidies to the arts in Great Britain.* London; Hamilton; 1977. Pp xii, 276.
12. Morris, R.J.B. *Parliament and the public libraries.* London; Mansell Information Publishing; 1977.
13. Barnes, J. *The beginnings of the cinema in England.* Newton Abbot; David & Charles; 1976. Pp 240.
14. Morris, J.A. *Writers and politics in modern Britain (1880–1950).* London; Hodder & Stoughton; 1977. Pp vii, 109.
15. Cantor, L.M.; Matthews, G.F. *Loughborough from college to university: a history of higher-education at Loughborough, 1909–1966.* Loughborough University; 1977. Pp iii, 199.
16. Hewison, R. *Under siege: literary life in London, 1939–1945.* London; Weidenfeld & Nicolson; 1977. Pp x, 219.
17. Green, M. *Children of the sun: a narrative of 'decadence' in England after 1918* (revd. ed.). London; Constable; 1977. Pp 552.
18. Gould, J. *Modern houses in Britain, 1919–1939.* London; Soc. of Architectural Historians; 1977. Pp 65.
19. White, C.L. *The women's periodical press in Britain, 1946–1976.* London; HMSO; 1977. Pp 85.

20. Stead, P. *Coleg Harlech: the first fifty years.* Cardiff; University of Wales Press; 1977. Pp xv, 135.
21. Waring, D., 'Conservation of historic buildings in Cirencester,' Bc8, 198–200.
22. Banham, M.; Hillier, B. (ed.). *A tonic for the nation: the Festival of Britain 1951.* London; Thames & Hudson; 1977. Pp 200.
23. *Coleg Technegol Rhydaman, 1927–1977 = Ammanford Technical College, 1927–1977.* The College; [1977]. Pp 85.

J. MEDIEVAL WALES

(a) General

1. Moore, D., 'Cambrian antiquity — precursors of prehistorians,' *Welsh Antiquity: essays mainly on prehistoric topics presented to H.N. Savory*, ed. G.C. Boon and J.M. Lewis (Cardiff, 1976), 193–221.
2. Lewis, W.J. *Hanes darluniadol Dyfed [An illustrated history of Dyfed]*; vol. 1: *Sir Aberteifi [Cardiganshire].* (New ed.). Dyfed County Council; 1976. Pp 90.
3. Walker, D. *The Norman conquerors.* Swansea; C. Davies; 1977. Pp 109.
4. Miles, J. *Princes and people of Wales* (2nd ed.). Risca; Starling Press; 1977. Pp 192.

(b) Politics

1. Lowe, D.E., 'The council of the prince of Wales and the decline of the Herbert family during the second reign of Edward IV (1471–1483),' *B. of the Board of Celtic Studies* 27 (1977), 278–97.
2. Taylor, A.J., 'A fragment of a *dona* account of 1284,' ibid. 253–62.

(c) Constitution, Administration and Law

1. Huws, D., 'Leges Howelda at Canterbury,' *National Library of Wales J.* 19 (1976), 340–3.

(d) External Affairs

(e) Religion

1. Lewis, J.M., 'Early Christian monuments in Dyfed, west of Taf,' *Welsh Antiquity: essays mainly on prehistoric topics presented*

to *H.N. Savory*, ed. *G.C. Boon and J.M. Lewis* (Cardiff, 1976), 177—92.

2. Victory, S. *The Celtic Church in Wales.* London; SPCK; 1977. Pp xii, 146.

3. Richter, M. *Giraldus Cambrensis: the growth of the Welsh nation* (revd. ed.). Aberystwyth; National Library of Wales; 1976. Pp x, 148.

4. Cule, J., 'Some early hospitals in Wales and the border,' *National Library of Wales J.* 20 (1977), 97—130.

5. Butler, L.A.S.; Evans, D.H.; Barker, G.W.W., 'Valle Crucis abbey: an excavation in 1970,' *Archaeologia Cambrensis* 125 (1977 for 1976), 80—126.

6. Fenn, R.W.D., 'The age of the saints,' Bc4, 1—23.

7. Walker, D., 'The Welsh Church in the middle ages,' Bc4, 24—53.

8. Cowley, F.G. *The monastic order in South Wales, 1066—1349.* Cardiff; University of Wales Press; 1977. Pp xiii, 317.

(f) Economic Affairs

1. Smith, L.B., '*Tir prid*: deeds of gage in late-medieval Wales,' *B. of the Board of Celtic Studies* 27 (1977), 263—77.

(g) Social Structure and Population

1. Bartrum, P.C., 'Further notes on the Welsh genealogical manuscripts,' *T. of the Honourable Soc. of Cymmrodorion* (1976), 102—18.

2. Reeves, A.C., 'The custumal of Rumney Manor,' *B. of the Board of Celtic Studies* 27 (1977), 298—302.

3. Butler, L.A.S., 'Continuity of settlement in Wales in the central middle ages,' Ca24, 61—6.

(h) Naval and Military

1. Knight, J., 'The medieval castles in Monmouthshire,' *Gwent Local History* 42 (1977), 40—7.

(i) Intellectual and Cultural

1. Roberts, B.F., 'Fersiwn dingestow of Brut y Brenhinned,' *B. of the Board of Celtic Studies* 27 (1977), 331—61.

2. Radford, C.A.R., 'The mediterranean sources of sculpture in stone among the insular Celts and the survival into the full middle ages,' Ca24, 113—23.

(j) Topography

1. Booth, J. *Antique maps of Wales.* Montacute; Montacute Bookshop; 1977. Pp xiii, 132.

K. SCOTLAND BEFORE THE UNION

(a) General

1. Nicolaisen, W.F.H. *Scottish place-names: their study and signifi-fance.* London; Batsford; 1976. Pp xxviii, 210.
2. Marshall, R.K. *Mary of Guise.* London; Collins; 1977. Pp 288.
3. Crawford, B.E., 'The earldom of Caithness and the kingdom of Scotland,' *Northern Scotland* 2 (1976–7), 97–117.
4. Dickinson, W.C. *Scotland from the earliest times to 1603.* 3rd ed. revd. by A.A.M. Duncan. Oxford; Clarendon; 1977. Pp xi, 442.
5. Fraser, A. *The Royal Burgh of Inveraray.* Edinburgh; St Andrews Press; 1977. Pp 224.
6. Fraser, D. *Edinburgh in olden times.* Montrose; Standard Press; 1976. Pp 156.
7. Davidson, F. and J. *An inventory of the seventeenth century tombstones of Angus.* Arbroath; the authors; 1977. Pp xxviii, [93 leaves].
8. Mackay, R.L. *The history of the Clan Mackay: its origin, history and dispersal.* [Wolverhampton]; the author; [1977]. Pp 30.
9. Starforth, D.M.H. *A short history of the Clan MacDougall.* [Edinburgh; Scottish Business Education Council; 1977. Pp 50.
10. Walker, B. *Clay buildings in north east Scotland.* [Dundee; Scottish Vernacular Buildings Working Group; 1977]. Pp 67.

(b) Politics

1. Barrow, G.W.S. *Robert Bruce and the community of the realm of Scotland* (2nd ed.). Edinburgh UP; 1976. Pp xx, 502.
2. Simpson, G.C., 'The Declaration of Arbroath revitalised,' *Scottish Historical R.* 56 (1977), 11–33.
3. Daiches, D. *Scotland and the Union.* London; Murray; 1977. Pp viii, 212.
4. Murray, P.J., 'The excommunication of Edinburgh Town Council in 1558,' *Innes R.* 27 (1976), 24–34.
5. Stevenson, D. *Revolution and Counter-Revolution in Scotland, 1644–1651.* London; Royal Historical Soc.; 1977. Pp xi, 283.
6. Devine, T.M., 'The Cromwellian union and the Scottish burghs: the case of Aberdeen and Glasgow 1652–60,' Bc2, 1–16.

(c) Constitution, Administration and Law

1. Duncan, A.A.M. (ed.). *Formulary E: Scottish letters and brieves, 1286–1424.* Glasgow; University of Glasgow; 1976. Pp 52.
2. Boyle, A., 'Matrilineal succession in the Pictish monarchy,' *Scottish Historical R.* 56 (1977), 1–10.

3. Donaldson, G., 'The legal profession in Scottish society in the sixteenth and seventeenth centuries,' *Juridical R.* new ser. 21 (1976), 1—19.

(d) External Affairs

1. Ferguson, W. *Scotland's relations with England: a survey to 1707.* Edinburgh; Donald; 1977. Pp vii, 319.

(e) Religion

1. Boyle, A., 'Some saints' lives in the breviary of Aberdeen,' *Analecta Bollandiana* 94 (1976), 95—106.
2. Greaves, R.L., 'The social awareness of John Knox: the problems of poverty and educational reform,' *Renaissance and Reformation* 12 (1976), 36—48.
3. Burns, C. (ed.). *Calendar of papal letters to Scotland of Clement VII of Avignon, 1378—1394.* Edinburgh; Scottish History Soc.; 1976. Pp lxii, 240.
4. McGurk, F. (ed.). *Calendar of papal letters to Scotland of Benedict XIII of Avignon, 1394—1419.* Edinburgh; Scottish History Soc.; 1976. Pp xxv, 456.
5. King, P., 'Coupar Angus and Cîteaux,' *Innes R.* 27 (1976), 49—69.
6. McLennan, B., 'The Reformation and the burgh of Aberdeen,' *Northern Scotland* 2 (1976—7), 119—44.
7. Sheldon-Williams, I.P., 'Eriugena and Cîteaux,' *Studia Monastica* 19 (1977), 75—92.
8. Di Folco, J., 'Discipline and welfare in the mid-seventeenth century Scots parish,' *Records Scottish Church History Soc.* 19 (1977), 169—83.
9. Mackay, P.H.R., 'The reception given to the Five Articles of Perth,' ibid. 185—201.
10. Cameron, J.K., 'The Renaissance tradition in the reformed Church of Scotland,' Bc6, 251—69.

(f) Economic Affairs

1. Tonkin, J.W., 'Two Hanseatic houses in the Shetlands,' *Hansische Geschichtsblätter* 94 (1976), 81—2.
2. Lindsay, J.M., 'The iron industry in the Highlands: charcoal blast furnaces,' *Scottish Historical R.* 56 (1977), 49—63.
3. Coull, J.R., 'Fisheries in Scotland in the 16th, 17th and 18th centuries: the evidence in Macfarlane's geographical collections,' *Scottish Geographical Magazine* 93 (1977), 5—14.
4. Madden, C., 'The feuing of Ettrick Forest,' *Innes R.* 27 (1976), 70—84.

(g) Social Structure and Population

1. Shaw, F.J., 'Landownership in the Western Isles in the seventeenth century,' *Scottish Historical R.* 56 (1977), 34–48.
2. Whittington, G., 'Placenames and the settlement pattern of dark-age Scotland,' *P. of the Soc. of Antiquaries of Scotland* 106 (1977 for 1974/5), 99–110.
3. Brooks, N.P.; Whittington, G., 'Planning and growth in the medieval Scottish burgh: the example of St Andrews,' *T. of the Institute of British Geographers* new ser. 2 (1977), 278–95.
4. Morrison, A., 'The question of Celtic survival or continuity in some elements of rural settlement in the Scottish Highlands,' Ca24, 67–76.
5. Macdonald, A.D.S., 'Old Norse "paper" names in north and east Scotland,' Ca24, 107–11.
6. Morrison, A. *The MacLeods: the genealogy of a clan*. Section 5: the MacLeods of Gairloch, Assynt, Geanies, Flanders, Cambuscurry, Cadboll, Sallachy, Handa, Coigeach and Eddrachillis. Edinburgh; Associated Clan MacLeod Societies; [1977]. Pp 121 & 51.

(h) Naval and Military

1. Stevenson, D., 'The myth of the founding of the Scots Guard in 1642,' *Scottish Historical R.* 56 (1977), 114–18.
2. Macdonald, A.D.S.; Laing, L.R., 'Excavations at Lochmaben Castle, Dumfriesshire,' *P. of the Soc. of Antiquaries of Scotland* 106 (1977 for 1974/5), 124–57.
3. Macinnes, J., 'West Highland sea power in the middle ages,' *T. of the Gaelic Soc. of Inverness* 48 (1976), 518–56.
4. Prestwich, M.C., 'The English campaign in Scotland in 1296 and the surrender of John Balliol: some supporting evidence,' *B. of the Institute of Historical Research* 49 (1976), 135–8.

(i) Intellectual and Cultural

1. Graham, A., 'The development of Scottish antiquarian records, 1600–1800,' *P. of the Soc. of Antiquaries of Scotland* 106 (1977 for 1974/5), 183–90.
2. Steer, K.A.; Bannerman, J.W.M. *Late medieval monumental sculpture in the west Highlands*. Edinburgh; Royal Commission on the Ancient and Historical Monuments of Scotland; 1977. Pp xxvi, 230.
3. Hay, G. *Architecture of Scotland* (2nd ed.). Stocksfield; Oriel Press; 1977. Pp 96.
4. Craig, W.S. *History of the Royal College of Physicians of Edinburgh*. Oxford; Blackwell Scientific; 1976. Pp xxix, 1127.

5. Durkan, J.; Kirk, K. *The University of Glasgow, 1451–1577.* University of Glasgow Press; 1977. Pp xiv, 498.
6. Watt, D.E.R. *A biographical dictionary of Scottish graduates to A.D. 1410.* Oxford; Clarendon; 1977. Pp xliii, 607.

L. IRELAND TO ca. 1640

(a) General

1. Edwards, R.D. *Ireland in the age of the Tudors: the destruction of Hiberno-Norman civilization.* London; Croom Helm; 1977. Pp 222.
2. Shannon Archaeological and Historical Society. *The other Clare: between unknown and well known: stages in the history of South Clare.* [Shannon; The Society; 1977]. Pp 34.
3. Hayes-McCoy, G.A. (ed.). *Historical Studies X:* papers read before the eleventh Irish Conference of Historians. Indreabhán, Galway; Cló Chois Fharraige; 1976 [i.e. 1977]. Pp 203.
4. O Corráin, D., 'A handlist of publications on early Irish history,' La3, 172–203.
5. Almqvist, B.; Greene, D. (ed.). *Proceedings of the Seventh Viking Congress, Dublin, 15–21 August 1973.* London; Viking Soc. for Northern Research; 1976. Pp 160.
6. Barrington, T.J. *Discovering Kerry: its history, heritage and topography.* Dublin; Blackwater Press; 1976. Pp 336.

(b) Politics

1. Furlong, N. *Dermot, king of Leinster and the foreigners.* Tralee; Anvil Books; 1973. Pp 211.

(c) Constitution, Administration and Law

1. Mac Niocaill, G., 'Aspects of Irish law in the late thirteenth century,' La3, 25–42.

(d) External Affairs

1. Dolley, M. *Some Irish dimensions to Manx history.* Belfast; The Queen's University; 1976. Pp 23.
2. McTurk, R.W., 'Ragnarr Lodbrook in the Irish Annals,' La5, 93–123.

(e) Religion

1. Bradshaw, B., 'The Edwardian Reformation in Ireland, 1547–52,' *Archivium Hibernicum* 34 (1976–7), 83–99.

2. Flanagan, M.T., 'Hiberno-papal relations in the later twelfth century,' ibid. 55—70.
3. Hughes, K.; Hamlin, A. *The modern traveller to the early Irish Church.* London; SPCK; 1977. Pp x, 131.
4. Logan, F.D., 'The visitation of the archbishop of Cashel to Waterford and Limerick, 1374—5,' *Archivium Hibernicum* 34 (1976—7), 50—4.
5. Simms, K., 'The concordat between the primate John Mey and Henry O'Neill,' ibid. 71—82.
6. O'Dwyer, B.W., 'The crisis in the Cistercian monasteries in Ireland in the early thirteenth century (II),' *Analecta Cisterciensia* 32 (1976), 3—112.

(f) Economic Affairs

1. Carson, R.A.G.; O'Kelly, C., 'A catalogue of the Roman coins from Newgrange, Co. Meath, and notes on the coins and related finds,' *P. of the Royal Irish Academy* C 77 (1977), 35—55.
2. De Paor, L., 'The Viking towns of Ireland,' La5, 29—37.
3. Graham-Campbell, J.A., 'The Viking-age silver hoards of Ireland,' La5, 39—74.
4. O Ríordáin, B., 'The High Street excavations [Dublin],' La5, 135—40.
5. Bateson, J.D., 'Four post-medieval coin hoards from Ulster,' *Ulster J. of Archaeology* 3rd ser. 39 (1976), 56—61.
6. Briggs, C.S.; Graham-Campbell, J.A., 'A lost hoard of Viking-age silver from Magheralagan, County Down,' ibid. 20—4.
7. Butlin, R.A. (ed.). *The development of the Irish town.* London; Croom Helm; 1977. Pp 144.
8. Proudfoot, V.B., 'Economy and settlement in rural Ireland,' Ca24, 83—106.

(g) Social Structure and Population

1. Barry, T.B. *The medieval moated sites of south-eastern Ireland: counties Carlow, Kilkenny, Tipperary and Wexford.* Oxford; British Arch. Reports; 1977. Pp 247.

(h) Naval and Military

1. Hayes-McCoy, G.A. *Sixteenth century Irish swords in the National Museum of Ireland.* Dublin; Stationery Office; [1977]. Pp 63.

(i) Intellectual and Cultural

1. Greene, D., 'The influence of Scandinavian on Irish,' La5, 75—82.
2. Henson, R.P.C., 'The D-text of Patrick's *Confession*: original or reduction?,' *P. of the Royal Irish Academy* C 77 (1977), 251—6.

3. Hughes, K. *The early Celtic idea of history and the modern historian* [inaugural lecture] . Cambridge UP; 1977. Pp 24.
4. Kissane, D.N., '*Uita Metrica Sanctae Brigidae*: a critical edition with introduction, commentary and indexes,' *P. of the Royal Irish Academy* C 77 (1977), 57–192.
5. Oftedal, M., 'Scandinavian place-names in Ireland,' La5, 125–33.
6. Stalley, R., 'Corcomroe abbey: some observations on its architectural history,' *J. of the Royal Soc. of Antiquaries of Ireland* 105 (1977 for 1975), 21–46.
7. Breffny, B.de. *Castles of Ireland.* Photographs by G. Mott. London; Thames & Hudson; 1977. Pp 208.

M. IRELAND SINCE c. 1640

See also: Ib15

(a) General

1. Cowie, D. *Ireland: the land and the people.* New York; Barnes; 1976. Pp 248.
2. O'Farrell, P., 'Emigrant attitudes and behaviour as a source for Irish history,' La3, 109–31.
3. O'Connell, M.R. (ed.). *The correspondence of Daniel O'Connell, vols. 5 (1833–1836) and 6 (1837–1840).* Dublin; The Blackwater Press; 1977. Pp viii, 424; viii, 413.

(b) Politics

1. Powell, J.S., 'Henry Grattan: enlightenment in Ireland,' *History Today* 27 (1977), 159–66.
2. Carlton, C. (ed.). *Bigotry and blood: documents on the Ulster troubles.* Chicago; Nelson-Hall; 1977. Pp xxii, 160.
3. O'Beirne-Ranelagh, J., 'The I.R.B. from the Treaty to 1924,' *Irish Historical Studies* 20 (1976), 26–39.
4. O'Day, A. *The English face of Irish nationalism: Parnellite involvement in British politics, 1880–86.* Dublin; Gill & Macmillan; 1977. Pp x, 210.
5. Rumpf, E.; Hepburn, A.C. *Nationalism and socialism in twentieth-century Ireland.* Liverpool UP; 1977. Pp xvii, 275.
6. Gallagher, M. *Electoral support for Irish political parties.* London; Sage Publications; 1976. Pp 75.
7. Farrell, M. *Northern Ireland, the Orange state.* London; Pluto Press; 1976. Pp 406.
8. O Brion, L. *Revolutionary underground: the story of the Irish*

Republican Brotherhood. Dublin; Gill & Macmillan; 1976. Pp x, 245.

9. Davis, R. *Arthur Griffith.* Dundalk; Dundalgan Press for Irish Hist. Association; 1976. Pp 48.

10. Riach, D.C., 'Daniel O'Connell and American anti-slavery,' *Irish Historical Studies* 20 (1976), 3–25.

11. Lyons, F.S.L. *Charles Stewart Parnell.* London; Collins; 1977. Pp 704.

12. Coughlan, R.J. *Napper Tandy.* Dublin; Anvil Books; 1976. Pp xii, 276.

13. Edwards, Ruth D. *Patrick Pearse, the triumph of failure.* London; Gollancz; 1976. Pp xvii, 384.

14. Hoppen, K.T., 'Landslords, society and electoral politics in mid-nineteenth century Ireland,' *Past and Present* 75 (1977), 62–93.

15. Hoppen, K.T., 'Politics, the law and the nature of the Irish electorate, 1832–1850,' *English Historical R.* 92 (1977), 746–78.

16. McCarthy, M., 'The impact of Larkinism on the Irish working class,' *B. of the Soc. for the Study of Labour History* 35 (1977), 12–16.

17. Morgan, A., 'James Connolly of Belfast, 1910–14,' ibid. 9–11.

18. Patterson, H., 'The new unionism and Belfast,' ibid. 7–9.

19. Dangerfield, G. *The damnable question: a study in Anglo-Irish relations.* London; Constable; 1977. Pp xvi, 400.

20. Powell, J.S., 'Dividing Ireland, 1912–1914,' *History Today* 27 (1977), 658–66.

21. Levenson, S. *Maud Gonne.* London; Cassell; 1977. Pp xi, 436.

22. MacDonagh, O. *Ireland: the Union and its aftermath* (revd. ed.). London; Allen & Unwin; 1977. Pp 176.

23. McHugh, R. (ed.). *Dublin 1916: an illustrated anthology.* London; Arlington Books; 1976. Pp xxiii, 399.

24. Stewart, A.T.Q. *The narrow ground: aspects of Ulster, 1609–1969.* London; Faber; 1977. Pp 208.

25. Millar, J., 'Thomas Sheridan (1646–1712) and his "Narrative",' *Irish Historical Studies* 20 (1976), 105–28.

26. Vaughan, W.E., 'Landlord and tenant relations in Ireland between the famine and the land war, 1850–1878,' Bc9, 216–26.

27. O'Neill, T.P., 'In search of a political path: Irish republicanism, 1922–1927,' La3, 147–71.

28. Malcolmsen, A., 'The politics of "natural right": the Abercorn family and Strabane borough, 1692–1800,' La3, 43–90.

29. Miller, J., 'The earl of Tyrconnel and James II's Irish policy, 1685–1688,' *Historical J.* 20 (1977), 803–23.

(c) *Constitution, Administration and Law*

1. Sainty, J.C., 'The secretariat of the chief governors of Ireland, 1690–1800,'*P. of the Royal Irish Academy* 77/C/1 (1977), 1–33.

2. Gallagher, M., 'The presidency of the Republic of Ireland: implications of the "Donegan affair",' *Parliamentary Affairs* 30 (1977), 373—84.
3. Gribbon, H.D., 'The Irish Linen Board,' Bc9, 77—87.

(d) External Affairs

(e) Religion

1. Campbell, P.J., 'Andrew Campbell, bishop of Kilmore, 1753—1769,' *J. of the County Louth Arch. and Historical Soc.* 18 (1977 for 1976), 296—7.
2. Walsh, M., 'Andrew Campbell, bishop of Kilmore, 1753—1769: student days in Spain,' ibid. 298—303.
3. Tierney, M. *Croke of Cashel: the life of Archbishop Thomas William Croke, 1823—1902.* Dublin; Gill & Macmillan; 1976. Pp xvi, 293.
4. Helmick, R.C., 'Church structure and violence in Northern Ireland,' *The Month* 138 (1977), 273—6.
5. Brennan, S.J. *A brief history of Aghalee parish to commemorate the three hundredth anniversary of the consecration of Aghalee parish church, 1st May 1677—1st May 1977.* Newcastle, Co. Down; Mourne Observer Press; 1977. Pp 30.
6. Fenning, H., 'The Irish Dominican province (1761—1765) with some notes on its missionaries in Scotland (1765—1773),' *Archivum Fratrum Praedicatorum* 47 (1977), 387—438.

(f) Economic Affairs

1. Burke, P.M.A., 'The Irish grain trade, 1839—48,' *Irish Historical Studies* 20 (1976), 156—69.
2. McCutcheon, A. *Wheel and spindle: aspects of Irish industrial history.* Belfast; Blackstaff Press; 1977. Pp viii, 83.
3. Bolger, P. *The Irish co-operative movement: its history and development.* Dublin; Institute of Public Administration; 1977. Pp xiv, 434.
4. Lockhart, D.G., 'The linen industry and the advertising of towns and villages in Ireland, 1700—1750,' *Textile History* 8 (1977), 163—6.
5. Lockhart, D.G., 'Dunmanway, Co. Cork, 1746—9 [select documents],' *Irish Historical Studies* 20 (1976), 170—5.
6. Lovell., 'The Irish and the London dockers,' *B. of the Soc. for the Study of Labour History* 35 (1977), 16—18.
7. Agricultural Research Institute of Northern Ireland. *Jubilee report, 1926—1977.* Hillsborough; [The Institute; 1976]. Pp 86.
8. Crawford, W.H., 'The influence of the landlord in eighteenth century Ulster,' Bc9, 193—203.

9. Cullen, L.M., 'Merchant communities overseas, the Navigation Acts, and Irish and Scottish responses,' Bc9, 165—76.
10. Dickson, D., 'Aspects of the rise and decline of the Irish cotton industry,' Bc9, 100—15.
11. Murray, K.A.; McNeil, D.B. *The Great Southern and Western Railway*. Dublin; Irish Railway Record Soc.; 1976. Pp 206.

(g) Social Structure and Population

1. Clarke, R.S.J. *Gravestone inscriptions, vol. 16: County Down, barony of Ards*. Belfast; Ulster Historical Foundation; 1976. Pp x, 181.
2. Montgomery-Massingberd, H. (ed.). *Burke's introduction to Irish ancestry*. London; Burke's Peerage; 1976. Pp viii, 64.
3. Walsh, M., 'The Hadsors and some other Louth exiles in France and Spain,' *J. of the County Lough Arch. and Historical Soc.* 18 (1977 for 1976), 263—71.
4. Macourt, M.P.A., 'Non-subscribing presbyterians and the Irish census in the 19th century: an example of confusion for statisticians,' *T. of the Unitarian Historical Soc.* 16 (1977), 113—5.
5. Carleton, T., 'Aspects of local history in Malone, Belfast,' *Ulster J. of Archaeology* 3rd ser. 39 (1977), 62—7.
6. O Gràda, C., 'Some aspects of nineteenth century Irish emigration,' Bc9, 65—73.
7. Carney, F.J., 'Aspects of pre-famine Irish household size: composition and differentials,' Bc9, 32—46.
8. Smythe-Wood, P. (ed.). *Index to Clonfert and Kilmacduagh wills*. [Ballycastle; the editor] ; 1977. Pp 19.
9. O'Sullivan, P.; Godwin, N. (ed.). *A world of stone* [with reprint of an 1893 report on the District of Aran Islands]. Dublin; O'Brien Press; [1977]. Pp 248.

(h) Naval and Military

1. O Snodaigh, P., 'Notes on the volunteers, militia, yeomanry and orangemen of County Louth,' *J. of the County Louth Arch. and Historical Soc.* 18 (1977 for 1976), 279—93.

(i) Intellectual and Cultural

1. Pittion, J.-P., ' "A Literary Journal" (Dublin, 1744—9): reflections on the role of French culture in eighteenth-century Ireland,' *Hermathena* 121 (1976), 129—41.
2. Brett, C.E.B. *Roger Mulholland: architect, of Belfast, 1740—1818*. [Belfast] ; Ulster Architectural Heritage Soc.; 1976. Pp 20.
3. Maher, H. *Galway authors: a contribution towards a biographical*

and bibliographical index, with an essay on the history of literature in Galway. Galway County Libraries; 1976. Pp vi, 116.

4. Stanford, W.B. *Ireland and the classical tradition.* Dublin; Allen Figgis; 1976. Pp x, 261.

5. Gailey, A., 'The bonfire in north Irish tradition,' *Folklore* 88 (1977), 3—38.

6. Malins, E.; the Knight of Glin. *Lost demesnes: Irish landscape gardening, 1660—1845.* London; Barrie & Jenkins; 1976. Pp xvi, 208.

7. Sheehy, J. *J.J. McCarthy and the Gothic revival in Ireland.* [Belfast] ; Ulster Architectural Heritage Soc.; 1977. Pp 71.

8. Clarke, D. *Dublin.* London; Batsford; 1977. Pp x, 182.

9. Richmond, J. *James Henry of Dublin: physician, versifier, pamphleteer, wanderer and classical scholar.* Blackrock; the author; 1976. Pp 64.

10. Hayes-McCoy, G.A., 'Sir Walter Scott and Ireland,' La3, 91—108.

11. Calwell, H.G. *Andrew Malcolm of Belfast, 1818—1856: physician and historian.* Belfast; Brough Cox & Dunn Ltd; 1977. Pp xvii, 138.

12. Mac Suibhne, P. *Paul Cullen and his contemporaries: with their letters from 1820 to 1902, vol. 5.* Naas; Leinster Leader Ltd; 1977. Pp 354.

13. Lanigan, K.M.; Tyler, G. (ed.). *Kilkenny: its architecture and history.* [Kilkenny] ; An Taisce, Kilkenny Association; 1977. Pp 108.

AUTHOR INDEX

Abernathy, G.R., Fk3
Acaster, E.J.T., Gf41
Ackroyd, C., Ib53
Adams, E., Gi26
Adams, I.H., Ab10
Adams, S.L., Fb35
Adamson, S.H., Hl63
Addy, J., Ge17
Addyman, P., Df16
Adnett, N.J., Hi4
Adrian, L., Hf29
Ahier, P., Bb55
Aked, C.K., Ab6
Alcock, L., Db2
Alcock, N.W., Ej20; Fh4
Aldsworth, F., Bb94
Alexander, J., Ha4
Alexander, J.L., Hh4
Alford, J.A., Ec16
Allan, M., Hk20
Allen, J., Ek13
Allen, L., Ii47
Allen, W.S., Fj2
Allison, A.F., Aa45
Allison, K.J., Bb41
Allsopp, B., Bb105
Almqvist, B., La5
Alvey, R.C., Ej28, k22
Alt, J., Ib68
Anand, V.S., Hb40
Andersen, J., Ej32
Anderson, A.B., Fe61
Anderson, M., Hg26
Anderson, R.G.W., Ab5
Andrew, C.M., Id28
Andrews, A., Ga6
Anstey, R., Gf24, 25, 32
Archer, C.A., Ab48
Archer, I., Ij1
Archibald, M.M., Ef26
Armitage, P.L., Ej5
Arngart, O., Ei25

Arnold, C.J., Ff23
Aronson, T., Hb41
Ashley, M., Fi19
Ashworth, W.S., Bb55
Aspinall, B., Hf11
Aston, Margaret, Ee48
Aston, Michael, Ba36
Aston, T.H., Ei6
Atkins, P.J., Gf14
Atthill, R., Bb26
Auckland, R.G., Aa29
Aveling, J.C.H., Ba13
Aylmer, G.E., Bb122
Ayto, J., Ei61

Backus, I., Fe5
Baird, J.D., Hh6
Baker, D., Bc6; Ee12
Baker, D.S., Ge1
Baker, J.H., Fc31, 34
Baker-Jones, D.L., Ge18
Balfour Paul, J., Bd7
Ball, A.W., Hl62
Ball, M., Bb23
Balls, F.E., Hi9
Banham, M., Ij22
Bannerman, J.W.M., Ki2
Barbary, J., Fi6
Barber, G., Ei21
Barber, R., Hf35
Barclay, G.St J., Ii44
Bard, N.P., Fb21, g6
Barke, M., Hf67
Barker, A.J., Ii45
Barker, E.E., Db8
Barker, G.W.W., Je5
Barker, J., Fg28
Barker, R., Ii15
Barker, T.C., Hf80
Barkley, J.M., He35
Barlow, F., Da1, 3
Barnes, J., Ij13

121

Constable, D., Hg40
Conway, E., Aa24
Cook, C., Ab31, 41; If19
Cook, S.G., Fc17
Cookson, J.E., Hb10
Cooper, J., Gh6
Cooper, J.K.D., Ej8
Cooper, J.P., Ba50
Cooper, N., Hl20
Cooper, R., Bb29
Copley, G.J., Fa20
Corbishley, M.J., Hk2
Cordeaux, E.H., Aa21
Cork, R., Hl57
Cornwall, J., Fb29, g25
Cornwall, J.C.K., Eg14
Corran, H.S., Bb124
Costello, J., Ii57
Cotton, A.N.B., Fb12
Coughlin, R.J., Mb12
Coull, J.R., Kf3
Cowan, E.J., Fi14
Cowie, D., Ma1
Cowie, L.W., Ga14; Hf50
Cowley, F.G., J38
Cowling, T.G., Fk41
Cowpe, A., Hj17
Cox, B., Df5
Cox, B.G., Bb52
Cox, J.S., He30
Crafts, N.F.R., Gf35, g7
Craig, F.W.S., Ab15; Hb60; Ic9
Craig, M.A., Eb4
Craig, W.S., Ki4
Cramp, R., Df13
Crampton, R.J., Hd28
Craster, J.M., Gh5
Craton, M., Ba14
Crawford, B.E., Ka3
Crawford, P., Fa18
Crawford, W.H., Mf8
Crawley, C.W., Bb14
Creaton, H.J., Aa56
Cregier, D.M., Hb27
Cressy, D., Fg12
Crewe, I., Ib68
Cromwell, V., Hb59

Crook, D., Eg9, k16
Crook, E.J., Ee34
Crosby, T.L., Hb17, 58
Cross, A., Ga4
Cross, J.A., Ib42
Cross, M.C., Fe9, 53
Crossick, G., Hg10
Cruickshank, C.G., Ii41
Crum, M., Fk27
Crummy, P., Fa2
Cuca, J.R., Hf32
Cule, J., Je4
Cullen, L.M., Ba66, c9; Mf9
Culme, J., Hl56
Cunliffe, B., Ek34
Cunningham, P., Aa42
Cunningham, T.M., Hf4
Curtis, T.C., Fc39
Cuttino, G.P., Ec6
Cyr, A., Ib63

Daiches, D., Bb50; Kb3
Dakin, D., Id15, 16
Dales, R.C., Ei40
Dangerfield, G., Mb19
Darby, H.C., Eg4, k12
Darcy, C.P., Gi36
D'Arcy, F., Hh11
Daunton, M.J., Hf28, 40
David, A.C.F., Gh10, i13
David, E., Ib44
Davidson, F., Ka7
Davies, A.C., Hh1
Davies, B.L., Hi12
Davies, E.T., Ge26
Davies, K.C., Ab49
Davies, K.G., Gb8
Davies, R.G., Eb2, e11
Davies, R.W., Cb2
Davies, W., Db4
Davies, W., Hi21
Davis, J., Fc12
Davis, R., Mb9
Davis, R.W., Hb22
Dawson, G.J., Cb4
Deab, W., Fc11
Deacon, A., Ih1, 3

125

Edwards, O.D., Gb9
Edwards, P.S., Fb32
Edwards, Robert D., La1
Edwards, Ruth D., Mb13
Edwards, W.J., Ba4; Gg2
Eedle, M.de G., Bb85
Ekstein, M.G., Hd33, 38; Id33
Elliott, B., Fe24
Elliott, B.J., Ih5
Elliott, M., Gb12
Ellis, P.B., Fa30
Ellison, S.K., Aa23
Elton, G.R., Aa46, c15, 18; Fa9, c18
Elvey, E.A., Ec1
Emery, F., Hj23
Emery, F.V., Fk28
Emmerson, G.S., Hk18
Emmison, F.G., Bc3; Fe64
Engerman, S.L., Gf30
Epstein, J., Hb8
Erickson, C., Ee6
Ethridge, K., Ba67
Evans, B., Ef28
Evans, D.H., Je5
Evans, G.R., Ei43, 44, 45
Everitt, Alan, Ek1
Everitt, Alastair, Ia3
Evetts-Secker, J., Fe21
Exwood, M., Ia14

Fadden, K., Ej24
Faik, J.D., Ic3
Fairclough, G., Ek22
Faller, L.B., Gc1
Faraday, M., Eg31
Farley, M.F., Hd3
Farmer, D.L., Ef10
Farrant, J.H., Aa44; Gf46
Farrant, S., Ab39
Farrar, K., Hk7
Farrar, W.V., Hk7
Farrell, M., Mb7
Farwell, B., Hd12
Faulk, H., Ii40
Faull, M.L., Ca25; Df6
Fawcett, J., Hl23

Fearon, J.H., Gf9
Feather, J., Fj14
Feilitzen, O.von, Df8
Feldback, O., Gh23
Fenn, R.W.D., Je6
Fenning, H., Me6
Ferguson, S., Ih9
Ferguson, W., Kd1
Fernie, E.C., Ej9, 13
Fiddes, V., Hl4
Field, C.D., Aa38
Field, P.J.C., Ee21
Findlater, R., Ba1
Fines, J., Hg3
Finucane, R.C., Ee49
Firth, G., Gf45
Fisher, H.E.S., Ba54
Fisher, J.H., Ei59
Fisher, N., Ib43
Fisher, R.B., Hk17
Fisher, R.M., Fa6, e73, k37
Fitzgerald, P., Ia13
Flanagan, M.T., Le2
Fletcher, A., Fe70
Fletcher, J.M., Ei17
Flinn, M.W., Gg6
Florance, A., Ha24
Flory, H., Id27
Foner, E., Gi25
Forbes, D., Gf12
Forde-Johnston, J., Ba58
Foreman, H., Ge23
Foreville, R., Ee16
Forey, A.J., Ed8
Forrest, G., Aa52
Forster, A.M.C., Fe40
Forty, S., Ii26
Foster, B., Ei32
Foster, D., Hb52
Foster, E.R., Fc28
Foster, S., Fe35
Fowkes, D.V., Fh13
Fowler, K.A., Ed2
Fowler, P.J., Ca3
Fox, C., Hl12
Fox, J.P., Id3
Frangopulo, N.J., Ic8

133

Author Index

Macinnes, J., Kh3
Macintyre, S., Ib12
McJimsey, R.D., Fd4
Mackay, J.A., Bb47
Mackay, P.H.R., Ke9
Mackay, R.L., Ka8
McKenzie, D.F., Fk6
MacKenzie, J., Hk73
MacKenzie, N., Hl73
McKinley, R.A., Bb111
Mackintosh, J.P., Ba17; Ib24, c14
McKitterick, D.J., Gi6
Maclagan, I., Bb9
McLaren, A., Hg21, k14
McLaren, C.A., Ae50
McLaverty, J., Gi41
McLean, R., Hl32
McLennan, B., Ke6
McLeod, K., Ba22
McMullen, N., Fg11
MacMurrough, Dermot, Ld7
Macnaghten, A., Ga10
McNeil, D.B., Mf11
Mac Niocaill, G., Lc1
Macourt, M.P.A., Mg4
Mac Suibhne, P., Mi12
McTurk, R.W., Ld2
McWhirr, A., Bc8; Ca27
Madden, C., Kf4
Madden, L., Ab58
Maddison, F., Ei12
Madox, R., Fa33
Maher, H., Mi3
Mahoney, P., Ii37
Malcolmson, A., Nb28
Malcolmson, R.W., Gc6
Malet, H., Gf51
Mallalieu, H.L., Hb16
Mander, R., Hl28
Manley, F., Fe28
Manning, R.B., Fe72, g13
Mansergh, N., Id23
Marc'hardour, G., Fa4
Margolis, K., Ib53
Marmoy, C.F.A., Bb116
Marquand, D., Ib4
Marr, W.L., Ig7

Marriott, P.J., Ha11
Marrow, J., Ab59
Marsden, A., Id37
Marshall, D., Gi29
Marshall, P.J., Gf16
Marshall, R.K., Ka2
Marshall-Cornwall, J., Fd2
Martin, B.W., He4
Martin, C.J.M., Fi17
Martin, J., Ei36
Martin, J.M., Gg4
Martin, R.A., Gf5
Martins, S.W., Gf52
Martz, L.L., Fe28, 45
Marwick, A., Ig2, i19
Mason, C.M., Id36
Mason, E., Eb3
Mason, F., Gc4
Massa, D., Fk7
Masters, A., Gj4; Hl50
Mate, M., Ef19
Mather, F.C., Ge15
Matthew, H.C.G., Hb71
Matthews, G.F., Ij15
Matthews, W.G., Bb102
Maxted, I., Gi42
May, P., Fg8
May, W.E., Gb11
Mayes, P., Df4
Mayhew, K., If3
Mayhew, N.J., Ef17, 22, 24
Meacham, S., Hg31
Mead, V.K., Ef14
Medlicott, W.N., Id15, 16
Mercer, D., Bb48
Merry, D.H., Aa21
Metcalf, D.M., Dd3, f15; Ef18
Metcalf, P., Bb84
Metlitzki, D., Ei33
Mewes, K., Hd47
Mews, S., Ie6
Meyer, M.A., Dc1
Middlebrook, M., Ii37
Middlemas, K., Hl66
Middleton, L., Ib18, 23
Miles, D., Eg19
Miles, H., Ek30

134

Miles, J., Ja4
Miles, T., Ek30
Miles, T.J., Ek32
Millar, G.J., Fi1
Millar, J., Mb25
Miller, C.H., Fe29
Miller, J., Mb29
Miller, S.T., Gf17
Miller, W.L., Ib47
Mills, A.D., Bb71
Milne, M., Hb39
Milward, P., Fe74
Milward, R.J., Fa11
Minchinton, W.E., Bb91, c10; Gf27
Mingay, G.E., Ba7, 30; Hg7
Minihan, J., Ij11
Mitchell, D., Hb55
Mitchell, R., Bb100
Mitchell, S.J.D., Bb6
Mitchenson, T., Hl28
Mitchison, R., Hg51
Money, E., Gi27
Money, J., Ga11
Monier-Williams, R., Bb87
Montgomery-Massingberd, H., Mg2
Moon, H.P., Hk9
Moon, P., Id23
Moore, D., Ja1
Moore, D.C., Hb15
Moore, D.L., Hl49
Moore, J.R., Hf66
Moore, J.S., Bb21
Moore, M.J., Hg22
Moran, J., Ei10
Moran, M., If27
Morfey, W.M., Bb12
Morgan, A., Mb17
Morgan, K.O., Ib28
Morgan, P., Bb79
Morley, B.M., Eh10; Fi15
Morrill, J.S., Fb14, c5
Morris, J., Ea3
Morris, J.A., Ij14
Morris, L.P., Id6
Morris, R.J.B., Ij12
Morrison, A., Kg4, 6

Morrison, J.J., Ac6
Morton, A.L., Fb5
Moss, D.E., Fa22
Moss, D.J., Gf6
Moss, M.S., Hf20
Mossner, E.C., Gi48
Mothersill, J., Ea3
Mott, G., Li7
Moyes, A., If33
Moyes, R.H., Fa2
Muir, P.H., Hl54
Muller, W.D., Ib16
Mulligan, L., Fj4
Munby, A.N.L., Ab30
Munby, L.M., Bb108
Munford, A.P., Bb65
Munford, W.A., Hl17
Munsche, P.B., Gc7
Munson, J.E.B., Hb45
Murphy, M.J., Gi43
Murray, K.A., Mf11
Murray, P.J., Kb4
Musgrove, G., Ii12
Myers, M., Gb18
Myerscough, J., Hl64

Nairn, T., Ib61
Napier, B., Ic6
Nash, M., Gi44
Nasir, S.J., Ba57
Neal, L.D., Gf18
Neale, W.G., If10
Needham, P., Hl24, 25
Nelson, J.L., Db11
Nelson, J.M., Gi45
Nelson, P., Hc4
Nenner, H., Fc9
Neuburg, V.E., Ab36
Neumann, G., Ed3
Neville, R.G., Bc1; Hc12
Newberry, J.V., Ib58
Newbould, D.C., Hb11
Newby, H., If29
Newman, A., Hg5; Ij4
Newman, J.E., Eg7
Newman, J.H., He31
Newman, P.R., Fe23

Simpson, D.H., Fg9
Simpson, F.G., Ca14
Simpson, G.G., Kb2
Simpson, M.A., Bc5; Hg43
Sims, J.M., Aa39
Sinclair Williams, C.L., Eg28
Singleton, F.J., Gf55
Skelley, A.R., Hj24
Skempton, A.W., Gf20
Skinner, A.S., Gi31
Slack, C.M., Ii29
Slack, P., Fa5
Slater, T., Df19; Hg48
Slater, T.R., Ba43
Sluglett, P., Id14
Smith, A.G.R., Fc14
Smith, C., Ca9
Smith, D., Ef29
Smith, D.J., Bb57
Smith, D.M., Ee24
Smith, E.D., Ii5
Smith, E.O., Fj5
Smith, L.B., Jf1
Smith, M., Ii1
Smith, P.C., Ii55
Smith, R.A.H., Aa28
Smith, V.T.C., Hj3
Smith, W.E.L., Ee23
Smith, W.J., Gf56
Smout, T.C., Ba66, c9; Gf67
Smyth, A.P., Da9
Smythe-Wood, P., Mg8
Snow, V.F., Fc40
Snyder, G.S., Ii10
Snyder, H.L., Fb22, k8
Sorrell, A., Cb1
Soubeille, G., Fk17
Soulsby, I.N., Eg6
Sparrow, C., Df15
Spaul, J.E.H., Bb86
Spears, Sir E., Id41
Speck, W.A., Ga12, b6
Spence, R.T., Fc20
Spencer, H., Ee37
Spencer, K.M., Hf70
Spiers, J., Ia3
Spiers, M., Hg13

Spring, E., Hc7
Spring, R.J., Hk3
Springhall, J., Hg14
Spufford, M., Fh9
Spufford, P., Ab37, c16
Squibb, G.D., Bd11
Staines, D., Ei1
Stalley, R., Li6
Stanford, W.B., Mi4
Starforth, D.M.H., Ka9
Starmer-Smith, N., Ia10
Stead, P., Ij20
Steane, J.M., Ek31
Steeds, D., Hd40
Steel, D.J., Aa47
Steele, E.D., He26
Steele, I.K., Gf21
Steer, F.W., Aa36
Steer, K.A., Ki2
Steinberg, J., Hd25
Steiner, Z., Hd17, 38; Id38
Steintrager, J., Gi30
Stell, G.F., Ge4
Stenton, M., Ab7
Stephen, M.A., Aa50
Stephens, J.N., De1
Stephens, M.D., Gi7
Stephens, R., Bc3
Stephens, W.B., Ac5
Stern, K., Ei55
Stevens, J., Ej23
Stevenson, D., Kb5, h1
Stevenson, J., Hb56; If19, g3
Stewart, A.T.Q., Mb24
Stewart, D., Ii49
Stewart, I., Ef16
Stieg, M.F., Fb24
Stoate, T.L., Fh5
Stockdale, E., Bb125
Stone, I., Hf51
Stone, L., Fg4, h7
Stones, F., Hf54
Stoob, H., Ed7
Storey, R., Ab48, 51, 52
Storey, R.L., Ac3
Stott, M.E.M., Hg39
Stow, G.B., Eb15, i31

Strachan, H.F.A., Hj9
Streeten, A.D.F., Eh14
Streitberger, W.R., Fc30
Strohm, P., Ei8
Strong, R., Fk21
Stroud, B., Gi49
Stubbings, F., Gi21
Stubbs, J.O., Hc3
Studd, J.R., Eb5
Sullivan, F.B., Gh29
Summerson, J., Hf48
Summerton, N.W., Hd5
Sundstrom, R.A., Fe15
Surtees, V., Hl44
Sutermeister, H., Df9
Sutherland, G., Ih10
Sutherland, J., Hb50
Sutherland, N.M., Fe42
Swales, R.J.W., Fb30, c22
Swanson, R.N., Fb16
Sweet, D.W., Hd24, 26, 27
Sylvester, R.S., Fa4, j3
Szittya, P.R., Ee7

Tallis, J.A., Ab23
Tamke, S.S., He8
Tarn, J.N., Hg47
Taswell, W., Fa23
Tatton-Brown, T., Ej12
Taylor, A., Ca1
Taylor, A.J., Ef27; Jb2
Taylor, A.J.P., Ij9
Taylor, J., Hf37
Taylor, P., Ek27
Taylor, R., Ab26
Taylor, S., Ba18
Teague, St.J., Hi19
Temmel, M.R., Hb1
Temperley, N., Gi50
Temple Godman, R., Hj7
Terraine, J., Ii56
Teversham, T.F., Ha19
Thatcher, B.M., He32
Thirsk, J., Fh8
Tholfsen, T.R., Hb13
Thomas, C., Ca2
Thomas, D., Ba70; Fg3

Thomas, D.A., Hl43
Thomas, D.J., Hf22
Thomas, E.G., Gh19
Thomas, H., Hg2
Thomas, J., Hf81
Thomas, J.G., Bb79
Thomas, K.V., Fg10
Thomas, M., Gb1
Thomis, M.I., Gb15, f22; Hb26; Ib48
Thompson, C.R., Fk30
Thompson, E.P., Ba49
Thompson, F.M.L., Hg44
Thompson, J.A., Ib52
Thompson, M., Ej17
Thompson, M.P., Fj8
Thompson, M.W., Hk8
Thompson, R., Fa1
Thompson, R.H., Ff11
Thompson, R.W., Ib7
Thomson, D., Ab57
Thomson, D.F.S., Ei14
Thomson, R.M., Ee30, i34
Thomson, W.R., Ee40
Thorne, H.D., Hf9
Thorne, R.G., Hf15
Thurburn, R.G., Gh20
Thurlow, W., Fi16
Tibawi, A.L., Id40
Tierney, M., Me3
Till, G., Ii20, 50
Tindall, G., Bb80
Tinker, H., Id30
Tinsley, H.M., Ek17
Tittler, R., Fb10, c4, f24
Tobias, R.C., Aa37
Tolmie, M., Fe1, 62
Tomlinson, M., Ii13
Tonkin, J.W., Kf1
Toole Stott, R., Aa33
Toon, P., Ac11
Torry, G., Bb77
Towle, P., Hj19, 138
Townsend, M., Gi51
Treasure, J., Hf53
Treble, J.H., Hf74
Trevor-Roper, H., Ha1

141

SUBJECT INDEX

Abbot, George (Archbishop of
Canterbury), Fe18
Abercorn family, Mb28
Aberdare (Wales), Hh1
Aberdeen, Ib45; Kb6, e6; bishop
of, *see* Elphinstone, Gordon;
breviary, Ke1; earl of, *see*
Gordon
Aberdeenshire, Bb115
Abergavenny, Lord, *see* Nevill
Aberystwyth, Hi12
Abington, John, Ff16
Abortion, Hg21
Abyssinia, Id15
Accounts, Ee5
Acton (Midd.), Ek27
Acton, Harold, Ij17
Acton, Lord, *see* Dalberg
Adam, Sir Charles, Gh15
Admiralty, Hj16, 18, 19
Advertising, Hf53
Advocates, Faculty of, Kc3
Aethelbald (King), Dd3
Africa, Cb2; He7; Id9; north, Ii44;
south, Hd12, 44; west, Gf26
Agadir, Hd29
Aghalee (Co. Down), Me5
Agricultural Research Institute of
Northern Ireland, Mf7
Agriculture, Aa7, 8, b32; Ba30,
48, 55; Ca11; Ef1, 2, g3; Ff3,
20; Gf1, 71; Hb58, 66, e11, f4,
8, 12, 24, 33, 44, 65, 68, g7,
11, k21; If21–3, 29; Ministry
of, If8
Agnosticism, Ge7; Hl13
Air: craft, Ia11, b3, 50; Force, Ii1,
3, 6, 11, 12; Ministry, Ii6; raid
precautions, Ii9
Alabaster, Ej2, 26
Alamein, battle of, Ii34
Albemarle, duke of, *see* Monck;

earls of, Eg25
Albert (Prince Consort), Hb43, 63
Aldbury (Herts.), Fc12
Aldhelm, De6
Aldred, bishop, De4
Alexander, bishop of Lincoln,
Eh12, j9
Alexander III (King of Scots), Ka3
Alexander, Boyd Francis, Ha4
Alexander romance, Ei32
Alfred, King, Df11
Allen, H.C., Hj11
Allen, Dr John, Hb20
Allinson, T.R., Hk1
Alms, Ef27
Alphonsi, Petrus, Ei28
Althorp, Lord, *see* Spencer
Amazon (river), Hk9
Ambassadors, Ba3
amber, Ef14
America, Gf27, i3; anti-slavery in,
Mb10; civil war, Hj2; colonial,
Fi2; loyalists, Gd1; revolution,
Ga6, b8, 9, 11, i25, 45; South,
Hd37, 46, f51; United States
of, Hd2, 37, 48–50, f11, 19,
49; Id5, 29, 36, f2, 12; War of
Independence, Ge1
Amersham (Bucks.), Bb38
Ammanford (Carm.), Ij23
Ampthill (Beds.), Ej24; Lord, *see*
Russell
anchoresses, Ee39
Ancient Deeds, Aa14
Andover (Hants.), Bb86; Fa3
Anglesey, Bb104
Anglo-Irish relations, Mb19, 22;
treaty, Mb3
Anglo: French relations, Hd13;
Irish relations, Mb19, 22; Irish
treaty, Mb3; Russian Joint
Advisory Council, Id12; Scottish

Football, Association, Ij1; Rugby, Ia10, j3

Fooz, Everlin de, Ee46

Foreign: Missions Scheme (Scotland), He6; Office, Hd17; Ic13, d1, 4, 14—16, 38; policy, Hb18, d15

Forest, Da2; Products Research Laboratory, If9

Forestry, Gf1; If9

Forsyth, P.T., Ie6

Fortifications, Ba58; Ca1, 5, 6, 12, 13, b4; Hj3; Lg1, i7

Fort Pitt, Gh6

Fox, Charles James, Gb7, 16; George, Fe61; Henry Richard Vassall, 3rd Lord Holland, Hb20

Frampton Cotterell (Glos.), Bb21

France, Ef30; Gf35; Hd13, 20, 32, g41, j10; Ii53; Mg3; trade with, Fd3

Freemasons, Ge8

friars, Ee6, 7, 8, 40, 41, i4, 5, 26, j25, k19—21

Frigates, Gh1

Frome (river), Ff4

Frontier, Roman, Ca7

Froude, John Anthony, Ac14

Fuel, Institute of, If25

Fuller, J.F.C., Ii48; Thomas, Fa8

Furness Vale, Ff10

Fyffes, Id2

Gaelic Athletic Association, Me3

gage, deeds of, Jf1

Gainsborough, Thomas, Gi24

Gainsford, Thomas, Fb35

Galway, Mi3

Gandhi, Mohandas Karamchand (Mahatma), Id23

gaol delivery, Ec11, 12

Gardiner, Stephen (bishop of Winchester), Fb14, e14

Gas, Hf46

Gaspée, Gb11

Gautier, Thomas, Fe3

Gaveston, Piers, Eb1

genealogy, Jg1; Mg1, 2; royal, Db12

Generation, theories of, Hk15

Geneva, Fe42; Id7

Gentry, Ba7, 24; Eb14, 20, e12, f9, 12, g7, 9, 10, 29, 30, i56, 57; Jb1

Geography, historical, Ab10; Jj1

Geology, Aa9; Fk40; Gj5; Hk4

George III (king), Ga6, d4; IV (king), Hb53; VI (king), Ia15, c4

George, William and Rebecca, Fg28

Gerald of Wales, *see* Giraldus Cambrensis

Germany, Hd25, 26, 29, 30, 32, 38, 47, 49, f25, 49; Id3, 4, 13, 15, 18, 19, 31, i40; Nazi, Ia4

Gibson, Edmund, Fk28

Giffard, Bonaventura, Fe34

Giraldus Cambrensis, Ei38; Je3

Girdlestone, Edward, He25

Girl Guides Association, Ij10

Gladstone, William Ewart, Hb1, 2

Glasgow, Bb50; Hf11, 73, g43; Ia5; Kb6; University of, *see* Universities

Glass, Ca13; Eh11, j10, k22; Hf80, 129

Glastonbury abbey (Som.), Ee45; Fe67

Gloucester, Ej6, k5; Ff11, h1, i12; Humphrey, duke of, Ec15

Gloucestershire, Bb13; Ca4; Eb14, g5; Fc21; Gc2

Godalming (Surrey), Ca9

Godmanchester (Hunts.), Eg16

Godwin, William, Gi33

Goldsmiths, Ff7

Gonne, Maud, Mb21

Goode, William, He1

Gordon, George, 4th earl of Huntly, Ke6; George Hamilton, 4th earl of Aberdeen, Hl67; William, bishop of Aberdeen, Ke6

155

Portugal), Gh13
Johnes, Thomas, Gf10
Johnson, Joseph, Gi15, 32;
    Samuel, Ga13
Jubilees, Ha2
judges, Ec7; Ic10

Katherine of Valois, Ec13
Kay-Shuttleworth, James, Hi1
Keble, John, He4
Kelmscott Press, Hl25, 27
Kelvedon (Essex), Fc37
Kemble, Fanny, Gi29
Kent, Ab55; Bb49, 51, 78; Ef12,
    g28; Fa20, 21, 25, c6, 12, e49,
    g2; If7
Kenya, Id21
Kerry (county), La6
Keswick (Cumb.), He7
Kett, Robert, Fb29, 31
Kettering (Northants.), Fg14; Gf5
Keynes, John Maynard, If11
Kibworth Harcourt (Leics.), Eg13
Kiffin, William, Fe46
Kildare Rebellion, Fb27
Kilgetty (Pemb.), Fk39
Kilkenny (county), Lg1; Mi13
Kilmore, bishop of, see Campbell
King, Edward, He22; Gregory,
    Fh10
King-lists, Db12
King's Bench, court of, Ec8; Fe22
Kingsley, Charles, Hk23
king's servants, Eb11, 12, 22, c3,
    6, f12, g9
kingship, see Monarchy
Kintyre, Ki2
Kirby Bellars (Leics.), priory, Ei2
Kirkby Moorside (Yorks.), Ej15
Kirkham (Lancs.), Gf55
Kirk party, Kb5; sessions, Ke8
Kitchener, Horatio Herbert, earl,
    Ii58
Kniveton family, Eg29
Knox, Dillwyn, Ia13; John, Ke2;
    Ronald, Ia13
Korea, Ii60

Korsakov, N.I., Ga4

Labour: force, Ba62; Hf69; (agri-
    cultural), Ef13, g3, 12; He11,
    f33; (industrial), Hg7; move-
    ment, Aa48; Ib23; Party, see
    Parties
Ladysmith (South Africa), Hj13
Lamb, William, 2nd viscount
    Melbourne, Hb11, 16
Lambarde, William, Fa26
Lambe, Thomas, Fe1
Lambert, John, Fa11
Lambley (Notts.), Ej28
Lampeter (university college),
    Hi16
Lanarkshire, Bd13
Lancashire, Aa6; Fe8, 51, 61, f8,
    10, g22, k1; Ge22, f53, 56,
    i36; Hb47, 52, f2, g27
Lancaster, Hf13; duchy of, Ef11
Land: agents, Hf41; clearances,
    Gf12; market, Ef12; Ff19;
    ownership, Ba49, 50, b88;
    Ef32; Hc7, f39, 42, 78, g48;
    Jf1; Kg1; Mb14, 26, f8; reform,
    Hb5; scape, Ba36, b41; Hf22;
    Mi6; tenure, Eg18
Lanfranc, archbishop of Canter-
    bury, Ee22
Langton, Stephen (archbishop of
    Canterbury), Ee17
Language, Irish, Li1; Norse, Li1
Larkin, James, Mb16
Laski, Harold, Ia21, b59
Laud, William (archbishop of
    Canterbury), Fe46
Law, Aa53; Ec16; Ic10; Anglo-
    Saxon, Db13; Canon, Ec1, 29;
    courts of, see courts; inter-
    national, Hd19; Irish, Lc1;
    reform of, Fa4; Hc7; Scan-
    dinavian, Db10; Scottish, Hc6;
    Kc1, 3; Welsh, Jc1, f1; written,
    Db13
Lawrence, T.E., Ha11; Ii49, 54
Lawyers, Ba25; Eg30; Fa21, e73;

159

Subject Index

St John family, Eg32
saints, *see* Hagiography
St Victor, Hugh of, Ei30
Sale of Food and Drugs Act (1875), If8
Salford (Lancs.), Aa24; Hb37, 67
Salisbury (Wilts.), Ej1; Fc5; bishop of, *see* Burnet, Jewel; earl of, *see* Cecil; John of, Eb13, i36; marquess of, *see* Cecil; his manuscripts, Aa16
Salt, Ek12; Hf57, 60
Salt, Henry, Hl42, 72
Sampson, Richard (bishop of Chichester), Fa6
Sancton (Yorks.), Df6
sanctuary, Ec15
Sanders, William, Hf5
Sanderson, F.W., Hi11
Sandon, viscount, *see* Ryder
Sandwich (Kent), Fa25
Sarajevo, Hd33, 38
Sareshel, Alfred of, Ei39
Satire, Gb5
Savage, Ernest A., Hl48
Sawston (Cambs.), Ha19
Saye and Sele, lord, *see* Fiennes
Scandinavia, Da9; Kg5
Scarborough (Yorks.), Ef5
Schmidt, Wolf Dietrich, Ii32
Schools, Bb2, 6, 12, 31, 36, 57, 102, 104; Ei49; Fg10, 14; Hi15, 23, 24; Ia9; Boards, Hc4, i10; charity, Ge23; grammar, Hi9
Science, Hi11, 14; *see* Chemistry, Geology, Mathematics, Medicine, Metallurgy, Physiology, Zoology
Scotland, Aa50, b13; Ba66, b90, c2, 9, d7; Fg18, i19; Gb9, e15, f1, 11, 63–71, g6, 7, i14, 22, 46; Hf9, 46, 74, g8, 14, 30; Ib61, f32; English wars with, Fi1; Royal Bank of, Ba41; south-east, He10; west, Hf20
Scots Guards, Kh1

Scott, R.F., Ha15; Sir Walter, Mi10
Scottish: National Movement, Aa30; National Portrait Gallery, Ab57
Scrope, Thomas, 10th Lord, Fc20
sculpture, Df10, 13; Ej9, 11, 31, 32, k26; Hl47; Ji2; *and see* Art
Seamen, Gf7
Sea power, Kh3
Sects, Fb5
Secularism, He26, l13
Seeley, John Robert, He9
Selborne, lord, *see* Palmer
Selden, John, Fh8
Seneca, Ei37
sermons, *see* Preaching
Service, domestic, Hg9, 32, 39; Secret, Id28
Settlements: medieval, Aa49; Bb32; Ca6; Jg3; Kg4; in forests, Da2; Jewish, Fe26; Norman, Ba23; Ja3, h1; prehistoric, Ba23; Roman, Ba23, Ca4, 6, 9, 11; Romano-British, Bb32; Ca3; Saxon, Ba23; Df9; Scottish, Kg2; Viking, Ba23
Seventh Hussars, Hj8
Sewage, Hk2
Sexuality, Fg24; Hg21; Ia18
Seymour, Edward, earl of Hertford and duke of Somerset, Fe4; Edward, Adolphus, 12th duke of Somerset, Hj6
Shaftesbury, earl of, *see* Cooper
Shakespeare, William, Fk19
Sheen (Surrey), Ek11
Sheep farming, Ef2, 11, j5; Ff3; markets, Fg5
Sheerness (Kent), Hf37
Sheffield (Yorks.), Bb102; Hg28, 37, 47, 131
Sheldon, Gilbert, Fe31
Sheppard, Dick, Ie2
sheriffs, Eg9; in Scotland, Gc10
Sherlock, William, Fj8
Sherwood forest (Notts.), Eg9